The Computer Game Design Course

The Computer Game Design Course

principles, practices and techniques for the aspiring game designer

Jim Thompson

Barnaby Berbank-Green

Nic Cusworth

Thames & Hudson

First published in the United Kingdom in 2007 by
Thames & Hudson Ltd, 181A High Holborn,
London WC1V 7QX

www.thamesandhudson.com

British Library Cataloguing-in-Publication Data
A catalogue record for this book is available from the British Library

ISBN-13: 978-0-500-28658-6
ISBN-10: 0-500-28658-2

Printed and bound in China

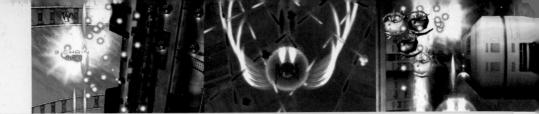

Contents

Introduction

What this book can do for you

The *Computer Game Design Course* was written with three main aims:

- To provide an insight into one of the biggest entertainment industries in the world. Globally, the computer game market is worth billions of dollars.

- To describe the stages involved in developing a game concept, using industry examples; also to introduce gaming terminology. This will provide the necessary basic knowledge to further an understanding of games and their development.

- To provide practical exercises that require some of the skills and techniques necessary to becoming a computer game designer.

Each chapter in this book will give you an introduction to a topic, and present you with the basic information needed to get started. When this is coupled with the associated practical and theoretical exercises in each chapter, you should begin to understand how to formulate your ideas and begin to think like a games developer. Some of the exercises are based on material used on games design courses in UK and US institutions at degree level. They are not a substitute for dedicated study or years of experience, however. The content of this book is intended to start you off on the long but exciting journey to becoming a professional in the games industry.

Keeping up with change

The games industry is a rapidly developing phenomenon; technological innovation sees continual change in the devices people use to play games. As the market develops, players become more sophisticated, and the types of game they play are ever-changing. As well as the mainstream games companies, thanks to the Internet there is plenty of activity on the fringe of game development, such as browser games, and user-developed modifications and additions to games. With so many possibilities, this is an exciting time to be involved in the industry.

A book like this could never hope to give utterly comprehensive coverage of such a dynamic subject. Rather like a guidebook, it provides you, the novice designer, with a good grounding and indications of how to develop and achieve your aspirations.

Every answer this book provides is also a signpost for your ongoing exploration.

Developing experience

How you approach this book is up to you. Some people like to methodically work through a book from start to finish, carefully digesting each piece. Others prefer to skim through the whole thing first and then go back to sections that interested them. Either way has its own merits. You could attempt all the exercises and get a feel for the bits that fascinate you and the bits you are less interested in. Having successfully completed an exercise you may wish to repeat it with a different subject and see if your second result improves on the first. When you have completed an exercise try to get a friend's opinion – see if they agree or disagree with your solution. Getting outside input is important, as others often mention things you would otherwise never have thought about. Asking relevant questions is one of the key skills of a designer – usually 'How can I make it better?'

By chatting with friends, you will begin to develop the skill of asking these questions yourself, and so finding out what you need to do to improve your knowledge, and your designs.

This book is organised into three sections: Design Theory, Design Process and Design Production.

Each section may contain information presented in three different forms: articles, case studies and exercises. Articles describe the relevant facts and theories. Case studies provide context for this information by showing practical examples. Exercises challenge you to put into practice the theories you have learnt about.

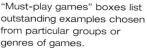

"Must-play games" boxes list outstanding examples chosen from particular groups or genres of games.

Design Theory

This section explores the roots of computer game design, starting with the fundamental principles of gaming and moving on to more specialised computer game genres and styles, and the ideas behind their development.

Panels provide checklists and summaries; intended to give a quick overview of a concept.

Lavish screenshots and game artwork illustrate examples of the key gaming topics explained in the text.

Design Process

This section introduces the specific design process involved in developing computer games. It covers the inception of concepts for character, environment, game mechanics and structure. Exercises encourage experimentation with the application of theories.

Arrowed boxes pick out specific details in screenshots, offering an insight into the intricate workings of a game.

Design Production

This section outlines the main features of the production process from beginning to end. Many people with different skills and expertise come together in developing a game. This section should provide you with a sense of what kind of role is right for you and the skills you will need to develop.

01: Design Theory

History

The beginning of gameplay

Mankind has been playing games since historical records began. One of the earliest known is an ancient Egyptian game called Senet, which archeological evidence dates to as early as 3500BC. The Royal Game of Ur was also played in ancient Egypt. Two game boards were found by Sir Leonard Woolley in the 1920s while he was investigating the ancient city of Ur. These have been dated to 2600BC.

◄ ▼ Simplicity
Go and chess both have deceptively simple components – black and white pieces on a squared board – but they are games of many complex strategies. Go is at least 4,000 years old and chess over 1,000 years old.

◄ Ancient games
Wall paintings show ancient Egyptians playing strategy games 3,000 years ago.

▼ Unchanging
Backgammon and mah-jongg have been played the same way for hundreds of years.

Ancient games are still relevant – they demonstrate that throughout history mankind has been developing recreational activities, or games, which have a set of commonly agreed ways to act in order to achieve an outcome, usually with a winner and a loser. The nature of gameplay was investigated by Johan Huizinga in his seminal work *Homo Ludens* ('man as player') in 1938. He defined play and the playing of games as follows:

'Play is a voluntary activity or occupation executed within certain fixed limits of time and place, according to rules freely accepted but absolutely binding, having its aim in itself and accompanied by a feeling of tension, joy, and the consciousness that it is "different" from "ordinary life".'

This root definition of gameplay encompasses whatever game is being played, from chess to the latest digital game.

▶ Game mechanics

What many people refer to as 'rules' are what game designers call 'game mechanics'. These are the roots of gameplay and form a system by which a game is progressed.

For example – rolling a die in Snakes and Ladders causes a random outcome and determines the length of a player's move, while in draughts leaping your piece over an opponent's removes it from play. Most games are made up of a series of related and complementary mechanics. Often, it is the mechanics which define a game, and they may be the main factor in a computer game's success. Here are some common examples of game mechanics:

Luck
This is random chance, an outcome that the player has no control over; often represented by a roll of a die or the draw of a card. This mechanic is often used for movement or conflict resolution within a game.

Strategy
This is almost the exact opposite of luck. A player's ability to plan turns and moves within a game determines the outcome.

Diplomacy
This refers to how players interact – do they collaborate and help each other? At what point should they stop helping and act selfishly?

Resource management
A mechanic in a game may give a player a certain amount of assets, which must be used carefully if he is to succeed.

A player who spends them too quickly may be unable to act later. Hoarding them too long might cause a player to miss his chance.

Territory control
Control of the gamespace is often important. A player should protect and develop the area he owns while seeking to deny his opponent the opportunity to do the same.

◀ Random outcome
Dice are used in games to generate a random outcome; to determine a player's move, for example.

◀ Figurative pieces
In contrast to the simple, stylised counters and tokens used in ancient board games, many modern games have figurative playing pieces. Their form may give an indication of their powers.

Goals and rewards
A crucial aspect of a game is that it has a definite goal, and reaching this usually allows an individual to win. Goals can include eliminating the other player(s) from the game, achieving an identified target (for example by amassing a number of points), winning a race, or collecting a certain type of token.

Achieving the goal – winning – can be its own reward. A player may have defeated his opponent through his superior game-playing skill or he may simply have been lucky with random factors.

Many modern games, digital and non-digital, do not rely on winning as the sole reward but are designed so that all of the players can derive some enjoyment from the process of playing the game. This is an important factor to remember. The players of your game will all want a challenging and enjoyable experience no matter what the outcome.

Universal characteristics
The examples on these pages show that playing games is an inherent and integrated aspect of many cultures. Many aspects of game playing connect with people's desire for entertainment, challenge and reward. It might seem odd for a book on digital games to start with a discussion of ancient board games but the understanding of gameplay, game mechanics and game rewards begins with the consideration of our game-playing heritage.

Non-digital games

Board games, card games and role-playing games

In spite of continuing technological advances, games that do not require a computer to play them – including traditional board games, card games and role-playing games – are just as popular today as they ever were. As an aspiring games designer, you should be familiar with these games as they can be an invaluable source of inspiration. Many of the characteristics and mechanics found in these games translate into computer games.

Board games

Games played on a specially designed board can cover a whole range of themes, from abstract examples, such as Chess and Go, to simulation-style games like Risk and Monopoly. Board games are often viewed as light-hearted family entertainment, and generally do not require a huge time investment. One of the main differences between board games (whatever their subject matter) is whether player

 Simulation
Monopoly and Risk are simplified simulations of real-life situations. As in life, players depend on a combination of strategy and luck to succeed.

success is based on luck or ability to think strategically. Games that depend heavily on luck (based around mechanics such as dice-rolling or card-drawing) leave the player little scope in their gameplay beyond accepting random chances. Examples include include Snakes and Ladders and Sorry. Games which rely more on a player's strategic ability, without any random occurrences, are often considered more satisfying, as it is your ability as a player which decides the outcome. Games such as Icehouse and Carcassonne have few random factors and rely chiefly on the player's skill.

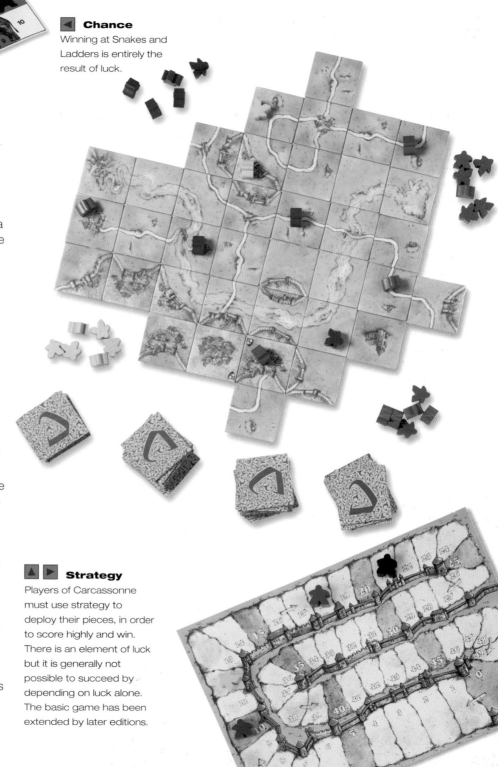

Chance
Winning at Snakes and Ladders is entirely the result of luck.

Many innovative, modern board games have emerged from Europe, and particularly Germany. Games such as The Settlers of Catan, Carcassonne and Citadels all share similar traits. They each have a simple set of rules combined with an ingenious game mechanic. These make them simple to learn, but leave a wide range of strategic options for the players. They have a relatively short length of play and are intended to generate social interaction among the players; they are certainly held in high regard amongst keen board-gamers as extremely enjoyable games.

Card games

Adding to the myriad of traditional card games, 1993 saw the introduction of a new card game called Magic: The Gathering, by Wizards of the Coast. This signified a completely new genre of game. Players collect cards which represent magical creatures, spells and fantastic items. Taking on the game role of a wizard they then 'duel' to see who the victor is. Though this game uses many familiar terms and conceits from fantasy role-playing it is a completely different style of game. An important marketing aspect of this game is that players must buy random cards to play it. In each new publication of Magic: The Gathering, Wizards of the Coast purposely make some cards rarer than others. This means that particular cards accrue a very high real-world value, due to their power in the game and their physical scarcity in the real world.

Magic: The Gathering spawned the term 'collectible card game' (CCG). Since the launch of Magic: The Gathering there have been many releases of CCGs, covering themes from horror to NFL; the enthusiasm for this style of game seems to endure.

Strategy
Players of Carcassonne must use strategy to deploy their pieces, in order to score highly and win. There is an element of luck but it is generally not possible to succeed by depending on luck alone. The basic game has been extended by later editions.

◄ **Game cards**

Players of Magic: the Gathering buy cards in sealed packets, ensuring a random selection.

Role-playing

Dungeons and Dragons was created by Gary Gygax and Dave Arneson. The game was first produced in 1974 and was the result of the development of the Chainmail rule system which was essentially a medieval miniatures war-game. Influenced by a wealth of fantasy literature, the writers took this medieval world and introduced elements of fantasy such as magic and monsters. The nature of the game was innovative too. As a player you took on the role of an adventurer, as did the people you were playing with. The game was organised by a Dungeon Master who controlled and delivered the story that was your adventure. Much of the game action took place in the players' imaginations as the Dungeon

Fighting power

The creature's power number shows how strong it is in battle. The players fight their 'duels' on a tabletop with their cards laid out in formation.

► **CCG elements**

Duel Masters is a collectible card game, or CCG, in the same vein as Magic: The Gathering and many other imitators which feature common elements.

Creature info

The creature's name and type is displayed at the top of the card. It costs six 'manas' to bring this particular being into battle.

Character stats

The text box gives details of the special rules and abilities associated with the character, for example, its attacking style. There may be additional information here that isn't strictly needed for gameplay, but adds interest.

Master described magical worlds and terrible foes to the players. The players' responses dictated what happened next in the game. As your character survived the perils presented to you in your quests, you gained experience and equipment in order to improve your skills and reach new levels of power. Dungeons and Dragons spawned a whole industry of role-playing games; nearly every genre is now represented by a role-playing game – science fiction, horror, Wild West, superhero. What is important about Dungeons and Dragons is that it gave rise to the game concept of role-playing; where you, the player, take on the persona of a character and experience the make-believe world set by the game designer through that character's eyes. The game mechanics and terminology developed for use in these early role-playing games are still influencing role-playing computer games today.

Must-play board/card games:

- Chess
- Go
- Risk
- Monopoly
- Icehouse
- Carcassonne
- Magic: The Gathering
- Duel Masters
- Dungeons and Dragons

Tabletop war games

This refers to those games usually played on a large playing surface (the tabletop!) with miniature figures. One of the first people to write rules for such activities was H. G. Wells, who wrote *Little Wars* in 1913. This is generally held to be the first war game and provided rules for battles concerning movement, combat and terrain. As with Dungeons and Dragons, rules for miniature battles have proliferated and it is now possible to battle in almost any historical period, real or imagined. Unlike role-playing games, tabletop war games concern themselves with large groups of figures that usually represent whole armies at war. Results of combat are resolved randomly with dice and players' consideration of massive-scale effects such as troop morale and terrain have a great deal of influence on the outcome of the game.

One of the most commercially successful war games is Games Workshop's Warhammer range. Warhammer is set in a pseudo-medieval fantasy world where armies clash for control of the land. Games Workshop also produces a science-fiction war game called Warhammer 40,000. This game sees similar races fighting in the distant future with a variety of high-tech weaponry. An important part of this hobby is the collection and painting of miniature figures. While this is not integral to playing the game it is obvious from the players' commitment and efforts that the intricate painting of the figures is considered a central attraction of the hobby. Besides Games Workshop there are many other miniatures companies with equally exciting, innovative and diverse rules systems and miniatures.

As with paper-and-pencil role-playing games, these tabletop games are the forerunners of the real-time strategy games now available on PCs. Concepts and mechanics from the physical versions of these games form the basis of many of the mechanics on-screen.

▲ **Tabletop to PC**
Warhammer 40,000: Dawn of War is an example of a tabletop war-game that has made the jump to being a real-time strategy game for the PC platform.

Shoot-'em-ups

Maximum destruction

Shoot-'em-ups are also known as shmups and, as the name suggests, involve shooting things up – a lot. A typical shmup has the player controlling a spaceship with a quick-firing weapon. Enemies attack the player's ship and the objective is usually to destroy them as quickly as possible.

The first shmup was Spacewar!, created in 1962. It ran on a DEC PDP-1 – an early computer system – and was created by Stephen 'Slug' Russell at MIT. This was not only the first shmup, it was also arguably the first ever computer game.

Space Invaders, released in 1978, was the game that really captured the public's imagination. It was undoubtedly the first mass-market computer game and it was also a shmup. Created by Toshihiro Nishikado, it had simple, intuitive controls – move left, move right, and shoot – a simple, pressing objective, and a clearly laid-out presentation. Space Invaders incorporated many unprecedented features as well as features combined for the first time: waves of enemies; bonuses for shooting more difficult-to-hit enemies; increasing difficulty; destructible shields; a high-score table; a three-lives system; and well thought-out audio design.

Commercial success

Space Invaders not only pushed the design of computer games forward, it also made hundreds of millions of dollars in arcades. At the time, arcades were the only places computer games could be played, costing players a small amount of money for each game. The incredible commercial success of Space Invaders suddenly marked computer games as a viable business opportunity, and new companies sprang up very quickly, attempting to copy its money-making formula. Space Invaders was also instrumental in launching the first home console system, the Atari 2600, as many people bought it simply so they could play Space Invaders at home.

Genre developments

Elements of Space Invaders were copied, refined, and mutated in the games that followed. This led to all sorts of innovations, many of which were made possible only by more powerful hardware becoming available. Galaxian (1979) introduced multi-coloured aliens which swooped down to attack the player. Defender (1980) introduced a horde of new ideas such as a playfield which wrapped around horizontally, incredible use of sound, smart bombs,

◀ **New features**
Space Invaders appears primitive by modern standards, but at the time of its release it combined many innovative features.

▶ **Innovations**
The scrolling playfield of Defender pushed the schmup genre forward. It was later updated in 3D for the PS2 (far right).

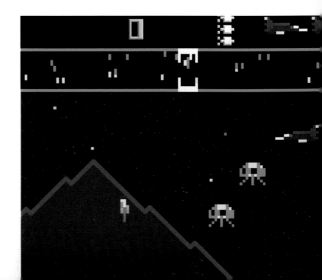

different alien types and humans to protect. Defender's control system was also unusual in that the joystick was used to move the player's ship up and down while a button thrust the ship in the direction it was facing, and another button switched the ship's direction. Three other buttons were used to shoot, hyperspace and fire smart bombs. Other innovations such as vertical scrolling, multiple weapons, and power-ups all progressed the schmup genre.

New twists

Much later, in 1987, R-Type arrived. R-Type was a horizontal scrolling shmup which brought level design into the mix of ideas. R-Type built on many of the advances of its predecessors, but provided an entirely different playing experience. Its designers set out patterns of enemies and terrain so that there was an optimal way to get through each level. The way through had to be learned by trial and error, though much of it could be found with quick thinking. This added a tremendous challenge to the game. The innovation was backed up by a wonderful art style and a great range of weapons, enemies and bosses.

Ikaruga was originally released in 2001, and was developed by Treasure Co. Ltd, well-known for creating very dense, well-crafted games with unique mechanics. Ikaruga was no exception in that it added an entirely new spin on the old shmup standards.

The player's ship in Ikaruga could flip between two polarities (black/white) and the enemies and their weapons fired in one of these two polarities. The player's ship could absorb energy by switching to the colour of the bullets and colliding with them, but different-coloured shots killed the player's ship instantly. The absorbed energy could be used to fire a more powerful weapon capable of destroying many of the enemies on the screen. Ikaruga also had a chaining system which accumulated points faster if more enemies of the same polarity were killed consecutively. Ikaruga was notable for how tough it was to beat. To hardcore shmup fans this became the game to beat.

Developer Kenta Cho deserves a mention as he has made some unique shmups, completely independently – with no external financing, help, or distribution. He has excited the indie games scene with freeware games such as TUMIKI Fighters and Gunroar. Kenta Cho is the designer, programmer and artist for all of his creations.

Must-play shmups:

- Asteroids (Atari)
- Galaxian (Namco)
- Scramble (Konami)
- Robotron 2084 (Williams Electronics)
- Xevious (Namco)
- Gradius (Konami)
- R-Type (Irem/Nintendo)
- Ikaruga (Treasure, G.rev)
- TUMIKI Fighters (ABA Games/Kenta Cho)
- Geometry Wars (Bizarre Creations)

◄ ▼ **Evolution**
Ikaruga is renowned for its stunning visuals and demanding action, requiring rapid reactions.

First-person shooter

Kill or be killed

Probably the most recognised genre of computer games, the first-person shooter (FPS) is so called because the view you are given is as if you were seeing through a character's eyes. The first game to cement FPS games as a distinct genre was id Software's Wolfenstein 3D. Wolfenstein appears crude by today's standards but it set in motion a massive area of gaming.

Hot on the heels of Wolfenstein was the famous Doom which has seen many sequels and has been adapted into a film. Doom pitched the player as an unnamed marine in the near future based upon Mars. An experiment in teleportation has gone wrong and now the hordes of hell and zombies stalk the player.

Doom had improved graphics and more complex maps but the kill-or-be-killed gameplay remained the same. One of the new features of Doom was that you could play against other human players over a computer network in specially made levels called arenas. This gave rise to what is now known as a deathmatch. When a player is killed in a multiplayer game he usually returns to the game (called 'respawning') after a short interval, while the player who dispatched the other player gets a score for his 'kill'. Doom enabled the players to create their own maps and levels (known as WAD files) through applications of level editors. Literally tens of thousands of user-made Doom maps were

 Graphic hit
By pushing early PCs to their graphic limits, Wolfenstein 3D became a smash hit.

Sophistication
Doom built on Wolfenstein's success, and as well as being more visually sophisticated, gave the player an exciting array of enemies and weaponry to dispatch them with.

constructed and made available over the Internet. This spawned what has now become known as 'modding' (or producing modifications for games). Many developers of FPS games now release the game-editing programs as a matter of course and it is seen as a good way of prolonging the life of a game by keeping up interest via user-generated material. Valve Software actively makes the best user-generated mods available through its web-based Steam portal.

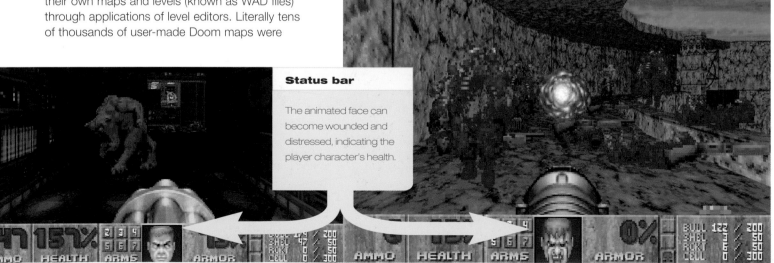

Status bar
The animated face can become wounded and distressed, indicating the player character's health.

Must-play FPS games:

- Doom (id Software)
- Quake (id Software)
- Half Life (Valve Software)
- Return to Castle Wolfenstein (id Software)
- Marathon (Bungie)
- GoldenEye 007 (Rareware)
- Battlefield 1942 (EA Games)
- Thief (Looking Glass Studios)
- Rainbow Six (Red Storm)
- Max Payne (Remedy)
- XIII (Ubisoft)

▶ Fully 3D

In Quake, characters and environments were both rendered in three dimensions. Enemies were complex 3D models with a certain amount of artificial intelligence. The gameplay was fast and furious, with a variety of moves available to the player. Play could be single- or multi-player.

▼ In-game data

Marathon provided a comprehensive in-game data panel, showing the weapon used and remaining ammunition. It also had a strong, distinct style, with some truly alien enemies.

Increasing complexity

Once the idea had been developed there followed a rush of FPS games to meet the demands of players. A notable development was Bungie's Marathon. It did not receive as much attention as other games because initially it was available only on Macintosh computers. But it was one of the first FPS games to have a complex story. You played a security officer sent to the colony ship UESC Marathon, orbiting a colony on the planet Tau Ceti IV, in response to a distress call. The game required you to defeat aliens and defend the colonists. The story unfolded through frequent use of computer terminals which told of events via the viewpoint of the ship's artificial intelligence (AI) computers. There were two sequels to Marathon and it also saw the release of a level editor and the incorporation of multiple-player games. Bungie went on to develop one of the Xbox's trademark games, Halo.

AMMUNITION
8 .44 CLIPS (x8)
3 MA-75B CLIPS (x52)
3 MA-75B GRENADES (x7)
1 SHOTGUN SHELLS (x2)

MA-75B ASSAULT RIFLE/ GRENADE LAUNCHER

15m

► Key first-person shooter games

The following details of FPS games and their developers provide an overview of some of the pivotal innovations in the field.

1 Halo: Combat Evolved
The player's damage-absorbing shield is shown by the blue bar at top right.

2 Half Life
Pulling the pin out of a grenade in order to blast through an obstacle.

GoldenEye 007 (Rareware)
One of the earliest FPS games on a console, the Nintendo 64. The widespread critical acclaim for this game means that it is still cited as one of the best FPS games to this day.

Star Wars Jedi Knight: Dark Forces 2 (Lucas Arts)
The beginning of film franchises being adapted to FPS games allowed players to experience other aspects of the Star Wars universe.

Thief (Looking Glass Studios)
The player played a thief in a world that was a cross between the Middle Ages and the Victorian era. This game is notable because the player had to sneak and be stealthy to succeed.

Rainbow Six (Red Storm Entertainment)
This modern SWAT/military game was based upon the popular Tom Clancy novels. It saw the inclusion of squad-based tactics with non-player character helpers and a mission-success requirement much like the 'real-world' scenarios it was meant to imitate.

Half Life (Valve Software)
This is one of the most famous FPS games, encompassing story, combat and adventure in one package. The sequels to this game continue to be extremely popular and the modding community surrounding this game is massive.

Max Payne (Remedy Entertainment)
The player takes on the role of a New York cop cast into a murky world of crime and deception. This game is of note because of its use of a game mechanic referred to as 'bullet time'. The player could elect to slow the action down enough to see the passage of a bullet, while making his actions and reactions in real time. This enabled the player to make complex acrobatic manoeuvres in combat, as seen in movies such as *The Matrix*. The game also occasionally switched the camera to a cinematic mode, panning around a victim to show their end in grisly cinematic style.

Deus Ex (Ion Storm)
This science-fiction game had a great deal of role-playing and story as well as action and adventure. Game critics praised this game highly and it is still held to be one of the benchmarks of the genre.

Halo: Combat Evolved (Bungie)
This was one of the landmark games for the Xbox and continues to be so with its sequels. The introduction of vehicle use and cinematic techniques make this game notable.

Battlefield 1942 (Digital Illusions CE)
This saw a large-scale rendition of World War 2 battles where the player could use nearly anything and drive, fly, or sail any vehicle. It could be played as a single-player game (versus the machine) or as a multi-player game where large numbers of people could perform different roles on opposing forces.

XIII (Ubisoft)
The unique feature of this game – a modern-day spy FPS game based on a cult Belgian comic – is that it is rendered in a comic or cel-shaded style, with the action often occurring in comic-style panels.

GAMEOGRAPHY

Title Max Payne
Developer Remedy
Entertainment
Key features
- Lavish, stylish visuals
- Cinematic movement
- Mayhem opportunities

A notable benchmark in the early history of FPS games is Quake, produced by id Software. This was the first first-person character game to be made in true 3D, with characters as well as environments being rendered in 3D. The basic game engine of Quake went on to be licensed to other companies to make their own games, which became successful in their own right. The popularity of Quake continues, with new versions of the game being released.

Influencing violence?

As FPS games became ever more realistic, a debate raged about whether these games caused people to be violent in real life. Public figures and psychologists claimed that playing these violent games desensitised people and made them more liable to engage in real acts of violence. Other prominent figures produced equally compelling evidence that these games did nothing of the sort. This is a highly complex argument which cannot be fully explored or resolved here. Of note, though, is the fact that games started to come with an age rating, similar to films, which indicated their content and themes.

The future

There is a long lineage of FPS games and this list barely begins to catalogue them. The FPS genre can certainly claim to be one of the most popular areas of gaming and shows no sign of letting up, with many different game mechanics and story settings being used and developed. The increased ability of modern gaming machines to provide better visuals and better NPC interaction through artificial intelligence routines means that this aspect of gaming is rapidly approaching a cinematic ideal.

Platform games

Hazardous gameworlds

The platform game is one of the most enduring and influential genres of computer games. From Donkey Kong to Sonic the Hedgehog, the scope and sophistication of the platform game genre has evolved with every hardware innovation.

Many games not actually considered to be platform games feature large sections of gameplay that borrow heavily from the traditions of the platform game genre. The term 'platform game' usually conjures up the image of a cute (often animal) 'mascot' character – think Sonic, Mario, or Yoshi – jumping around an eye-bleedingly vibrant environment, dodging an array of deadly obstacles.

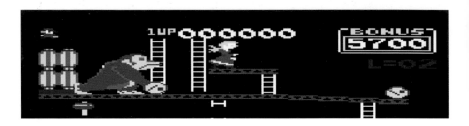

▲ Enemy ape
Donkey Kong was not always a hero; originally he was a giant ape who had kidnapped Mario's girlfriend, and rolled barrels to hinder her rescue.

▼ ▶ Icons
Though they are simple in form, Donkey Kong and Sonic the Hedgehog have become two of the most emblematic game icons ever.

The core elements that make up a platform game are: an engaging player character; a story involving the theft of something sacred to the player character by an evil dictator; a protracted quest to return the player character's universe to normality; and a world so fraught with danger it's a wonder it had any indigenous life in the first place.

This standard setup has become a cliché in platform games, which may explain the reason for the genre's decline in popularity in the last few years. However, the history of computer games would be incomplete without some of the pivotal titles from the platform game genre.

Basic concepts

Historically, the platform game has been the key genre that pushed computer game technology. While the first platform games used a static single screen that the player had to complete to progress (Donkey Kong, Manic Miner), they introduced the concept of

the 'jump' to gameplay. Activision's Pitfall extended this concept with multiple static screens linked together, creating the linear concept of progressing left to right (or right to left) through a level to complete a goal.

Super Mario Brothers added a scrolling environment, power-ups, and coin-collection. Sonic added speed and graphical sophistication, while Super Mario World and Yoshi's Island progressed platform game design by adding sophisticated environmental puzzle-solving.

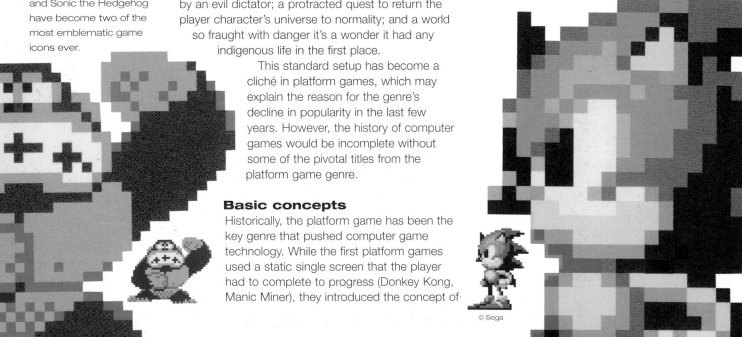

© Sega

© Sega

◄ **3D games**
Many platform games,
such as Sonic (far left),
made the transition to 3D.
New characters emerged,
such as Jak & Daxter (left).

Must-play platform games:

- Super Mario World (Nintendo)
- Sonic the Hedgehog (Sega)
- Yoshi's Island (Nintendo)
- Crash Bandicoot (Naughty Dog)
- Super Mario 64 (Nintendo)
- Jak and Daxter (Naughty Dog)
- Super Mario Sunshine (Nintendo)

Into the 3D world

With the move toward 3D and the launch of the Sony Playstation, Sega Saturn, and Nintendo 64, the race was on to translate the platform game genre into a fully 3D game experience.

Platform games in their purest form work best in 2D because the side-on perspective allows the player a wide, fixed view to assess the challenges ahead. In 3D the camera has a limited view and its position can rarely be predicted.

When Naughty Dog created Crash Bandicoot (launched in 1996), they solved this issue by creating what was effectively a 2D game, projected in 3D. In Crash Bandicoot the player is simply running 'into' the screen in the same way that Mario runs from left to right. The camera is fixed on a path, allowing the designers the luxury of knowing exactly what was visible on screen at any one time.

The simplicity and familiarity of this concept helped soften the impact of 3D platform gaming to an audience new to the world of polygons.

Sega took a different route with its first 3D platform game, Clockwork Knight. This game was essentially a 2D platform game, but the environments were made of polygons.

With the arrival of Mario 64 on the Nintendo 64 the genre was successfully re-visioned from a 2D world into a fully explorable 3D world. Progress came with the introduction of the analogue stick on the N64 controller. This allowed the player a high level of control that was missing in earlier offerings.

The platform genre has lately declined in popularity, but it was these games that sold consoles and made companies. People bought an NES for Super Mario Bros, a Genesis/Megadrive for Sonic, or a Super Nintendo for Super Mario World. Lessons learned from key platform game titles are even now incorporated into the all-encompassing 'action game'. Pure action such as Sony's God of War, Ubisoft's Prince of Persia, and Capcom's Devil May Cry™ owe a lot to a certain charismatic Italian plumber.

▼ ► **Changing Mario**
The development of Mario, both visually and in game sophistication, can be traced from his early days in arcade booths.

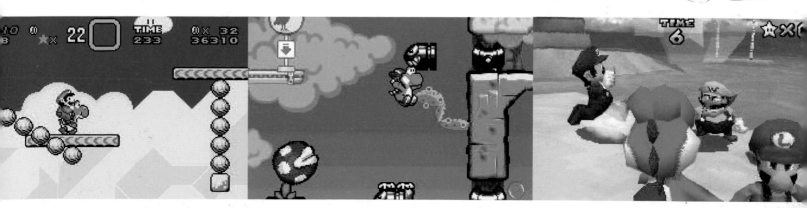

Strategy games

The gameworld in your hands

Strategy games usually place the player in command of a large number of characters and resources. To succeed, the player has to manage: the collection and consumption of resources; the development of the skills of the population, their acquisition of technology and their general disposition; the amount of control within the game, and to try to increase it; to resist the actions of the opponent AI or another player trying to do the same with their faction. Sometimes these games are turn-based but they usually happen concurrently, hence the name real-time strategy (RTS) games.

Emperor Caesar
The Romans Despotism
120 A.D. 10 Gold (-0 per turn)

Economics

An important factor in the success of a civilization is how prosperous it is. In Civilization, this information is presented as a simple balance sheet.

Customisation

Civilization allows much visual customisation at the outset, for example of characters, as shown here.

World view

An overview of part of a Civilization world shows settlements, with resource and opponent data in the menu bars.

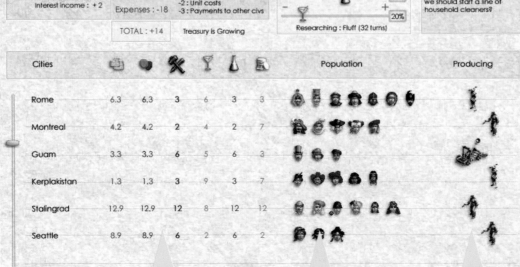

DOMESTIC ADVISOR

Income from cities : +25	Income : +32	-8 : Corruption
Income from other civs : + 5		-5 : Maintenance
Interest income : +2	Expenses : -18	-2 : Unit costs
		-3 : Payments to other civs
	TOTAL : +14	Treasury is Growing

gold allocation — 60%
— 20%
Researching : Fluff (32 turns)

Your sparkling Civilization is home to Mr. Clean. Perhaps we should start a line of household cleaners?

Cities							Population	Producing
Rome	6.3	6.3	3	6	3	3		
Montreal	4.2	4.2	2	4	2	7		
Guam	3.3	3.3	6	5	6	3		
Kerplakistan	1.3	1.3	3	9	3	7		
Stalingrad	12.9	12.9	12	8	12	12		
Seattle	8.9	8.9	6	2	6	2		

Managing resources

In a resource-management game such as Civilization, detailed data concerning resources and disposition is critical to the game.

Players can win Civilization in different ways. They may conquer rival civilizations, or win a cultural or technological victory. The comparitive status of these aspects can be assessed during the game.

◄ Familiar world
The Sims live in a world that reflects our own, with all the opportunities and pitfalls of modern life.

Strategy games can draw a direct lineage from tabletop games such as board games and war games with lead figures. But with computers to provide virtual playing pieces and opponents they have now become an established computer game genre. They fall into two broad camps—building games where the collection of resources and development of position is paramount, and military games which focus on single battles or engagements and depend less on development and more on strategy with the given material and men at hand.

► Growth strategy
Sim City requires the player to care for the inhabitants of a modern city, and to make it prosper and grow.

▼ Managing lives
A Sim is a one of the simulated humans in The Sims. The player manages the Sims' lives, to help them achieve success.

God's eye view

Strategy games provide the player with a 'god's eye view' – he can see the whole playing world and move around it or zoom into specific parts as he sees fit. The ability to move quickly around the map and identify troublespots is a vital part of the game.

Within the game the player will have people to be looked after, nurtured and developed in order to succeed. There will also be resources such as food, materials or strategic locations. Using the people under his command the player can harvest the food and exploit the resources to feed his people and provide them with the raw materials they need.

Technology tree

A common feature of RTS games is a series of stages of progression which the player will have to move through in a set order to get better equipment and skills for his people. This is commonly referred to as a technology (tech) tree. For example, a player of a historical game will have to pass through a level of bronze-working technology before he can start working with iron. Within some RTS games, tech trees ask the player to make choices, excluding possible paths of development. This forces the player to make the best of what the game provides them with, often referred to as an 'optimisation exercise'.

Fog of war

Opposing forces may come into contact and will inevitably try to assimilate or destroy their opponents. The side with the best technology or larger population usually wins. As a rule, the player cannot 'see' the section of the playfield where the opponents are until he has sent a player unit there. This mechanic is termed 'fog of war', after the real-world military phrase referring to the smoke-haze on a battlefield which can obscure views.

Civilization

Sid Meier's Civilization series of games (Firaxis Games) are probably among the best-known games in the strategy genre. Within these games players take on the management of a primitive people and attempt to raise their civilization up to the modern day by the careful acquisition of land, development of technology and the resistance or defeat of the in-game opponents.

Image © The Creative Assembly

► **Rome Total War**

Rome Total War is one of the most polished RTS games, which also attempts to put the player into historically accurate situations. Here you can see a highly detailed overview map as well as a resource window.

An interesting variation on this type of game is the Sim City series (EA Games, see previous page). In Sim City the player must control a modern city, developing it from a small town into a bustling metropolis. The player is forced to take on all the roles of a typical city governing body and keep the inhabitants of the city happy and productive by continually balancing consumption and production in the development of their city. Sim City gave rise to the hugely popular game The Sims (see previous page), by the same designer, Will Wright. In The Sims the player controls virtual individual people and attempts to make them happy and fruitful.

Military RTS games

There are many military RTS games which run from a historical past to an imagined future. Age of Empires (Microsoft) allows the player to take a primitive tribe from the Stone Age to the Iron Age. Age of Empires 3, a sequel, explores the new-world colonies of the Americas up to the end of the 19th century.

Another historical military RTS of note is the Total War series from Creative Assembly. These games attempt to recreate historically accurate battles and campaigns from ancient and medieval history. The player has the ability to command hundreds of troops at once but can also zoom right into the action to see individuals doing battle. These games are renowned for their accuracy in setting and visuals and have even been used by makers of historical documentary films to recreate scenes from ancient times.

ROME TOTAL WAR

Image © The Creative Assembly

1 Cities, garrisons and other features of tactical importance.
2 World map giving an overview of the global state of the game.
3 A local area map giving an overview of surrounding countryside and strategic points.
4 The faction commander as highlighted on the local area map.
5 The troops under the control of the faction commander.

 ► **Zooming in**

In Rome Total War, you can view armies from above, issue battle orders, then zoom in to witness the conflict first-hand.

Image © The Creative Assembly

Image © The Creative Assembly

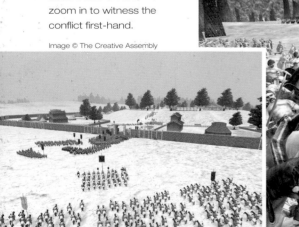

Warhammer 40,000
faithfully reproduced
Games Workshop
miniatures. Players can
even 'paint' their armies.

Fantasy war games

Blizzard Games are famous for their fantasy war
game WarCraft, and its science-fiction counterpart,
StarCraft. Both of these games were immensely
successful and well received by critics. They were
easy for players to learn and had extremely well
designed visuals. They are usually credited for
making the RTS genre more popular.

No list of RTS games would be complete without
mentioning the Command and Conquer series
(Westwood Studios, now EA Games). This was
another military RTS but set in the near future with
various 'what if?' scenarios. Command and Conquer
continues to be developed as a franchise with the
storyline moving incrementally into the future.

Also of interest is the development of RTS games
based on the highly successful tabletop games from
Games Workshop. Its Warhammer and Warhammer
40,000 games have both seen development into
digital games in a curious reversal of inspiration. Both
of these games benefit from years of market success
and provide the digital game developer with a rich
heritage of source material to draw from.

Enemies

In Warhammer 40,000, enemy
units conform to their typical
racial sterotypes in terms of
their behaviour. They provide
the player with a variety of
challenges. Some enemy
races are controlled and
methodical in their actions.
Others can be wild and
unpredictable, providing an
especially challenging
experience on the battlefield.

◀ ▶ **Mass combat**
The mass combat game
featured the diverse units
and foes present in the
Warhammer 40,000 world.

Weapons

In this futuristic scenario,
well-placed support
weapons defend the
player's territory.

Puzzle games

Good for the brain

Puzzle games are probably the most widely played types of computer games, as many pieces of electronic equipment come with some puzzle games included. Perhaps most notably, all computer operating-systems contain free puzzle games, such as Solitaire (with playing cards) or a shape puzzle. Puzzles are available on dedicated game machines, mobile phones, and even through your web browser, without the need to install special software.

Puzzle games reach a large audience, possibly due to the fact that there is a wealth of precedent of people setting brain teasers for each other. Puzzles such as tangrams, jigsaws and crosswords have a long history and are still popular today. Variations on established puzzle patterns emerge and find favour with the public, such as the Sudoku craze.

Puzzles are an easily accessible form of entertainment and usually for a single person. They are suitable for filling in bits of free time such as commuting or work breaks. With puzzles so established in society it is no wonder they have made the leap to a digital setting. Puzzle games take on different formats based upon the nature of the puzzle and can be categorised into several themes.

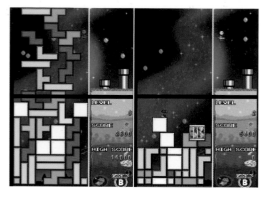

◀ Shape-fitting
Tetris is based on the shapes made by arranging four squares. As they fall from the top of the screen the player must orient them so that they fit neatly without any gaps, in order to make a completed layer of squares disappear.

Shape association puzzles

Arguably the most famous of the shape association type puzzle games is Tetris. Invented by Alexey Pajitnov in 1985 for an IBM PC, Tetris was a worldwide phenomenon spawning many copies and variations; most noteworthy was the extremely popular Nintendo GameBoy version.

Another similar game of this type is Puyo Puyo produced by Compile in 1991. This had a similar appearance and aim to Tetris but the mechanic of matching to get the rows to disappear was different.

Games such as Bejeweled and Zuma by Pop Cap Games built on the legacy of earlier shape association games, and are available on a wide number of platforms.

▲ Three in a row
In Bejeweled, the player must swap adjacent gems to line up three of the same type. The gems then disappear, and others fall down to take their place.

Building puzzles

An example of a building-type puzzle is Pipe Mania, developed by The Assembly Line in 1989. This game requires the player to construct a pipe from a random assortment of shorter pipes in order to allow liquid to flow from the start to the finish of the level. The popularity of this game can be seen by the number of variants and similar games produced over the years.

▶ Pipe-arranging
In Pipe Mania, the player is presented with a series of random pipe shapes, and must arrange them in such a way that they cross the screen.

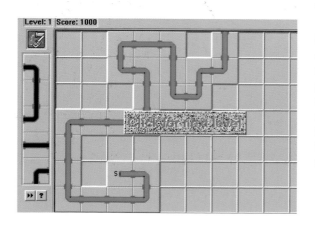

Level: 1 Score: 1000

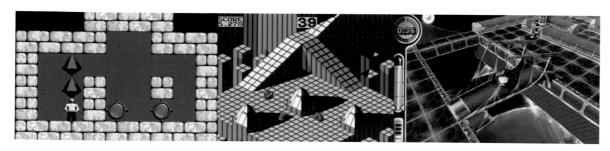

Maze games

Mazes and labyrinths are among the oldest forms of puzzles, including computer game puzzles. Sokoban, by Hiroyuki Imabayashi, was published in 1982. Sokoban is Japanese for 'warehouse keeper'. In this game the player must push boxes around a maze into their designated positions. It is easy for the player to make a wrong move and get a box stuck, and the more complex puzzles require a very definite order of moves.

An early variant of a maze game was Marble Madness by Atari in 1984. In this game, players had to roll a marble around a complex landscape without it becoming stuck or falling off a precipice, to complete a puzzle level.

On the PSP, a game with a similar theme is Archer Maclean's Mercury by Awesome Studios. The player has to negotiate a tilting maze again, but this time must guide a blob of mercury around the maze. In the game, the mercury can be split into separate drops and made to change colour, to activate colour-coded switches. The increased power of the PSP makes the simulation of the mercury very convincing, and the screen visuals extremely engaging.

Added complexity

The maze concept can be made more complex if the player has to move a character around a space, and interact with other characters. One of the most famous examples of this idea is Lemmings by DMA Design, published in 1991. Cartoon lemmings enter a door and walk until the player guides them to the exit. If the player allows the lemmings to wander they usually fall to their doom or blunder into a deadly trap. The player must quickly work out a series of actions to guide the lemmings to safety.

Traditional puzzles

Traditional puzzles and solitaire games inspire digital versions. Instantly recognisable is Solitaire which comes with all Windows operating systems. Other firm favourites include variants of mah-jongg solitaire, or Shanghai. This requires the player to match pairs of similar tiles in an ornate stack in order to remove them. As the tiles are removed the player can access tiles on lower levels.

An extension of a traditional puzzle which has found new life on a different platform is Dr Kawashima's Brain Training for the Nintendo DS. This has become a smash hit and presents the player with familiar number, word and association puzzles. The interactive capability of the Nintendo DS means that players can respond in a variety of ways. Interestingly the game claims that 'exercising' your brain for a few minutes a day can keep your mind young and alert – a rare case of a game claiming to be good for the player.

Mazes and logic

Sokoban (left) forces the player to visualise the outcome of his moves. A wrong move may mean that the game is impossible to complete. Ramps, bridges, and moving obstacles add complexity to a simple ball-and-maze game in Marble Madness (middle). Archer Maclean's Mercury (right) is a modern take on the ball-and-maze concept, with the added twist of guiding a liquid.

Health claims

Dr Kawashima's Brain Training not only tests your mind, but claims to keep your brain healthy, too.

Traditional

Shanghai is an example of a digital game based on a traditional solitaire game using mah-jongg tiles.

Game structure types

'Linear' v 'sandbox'

Game structure is the 'architecture' of the game – how it all fits together, how the levels are laid out and how higher objectives are staged. When you step back from the immediate experience of gameplay and begin to assess what you are doing within a game and what your goals are, you might become aware that games treat players in two distinct ways. Some games provide the action in a set sequence of events, with little or no variation every time you play it. Other games leave the player to his own devices and let him find his own way around.

▼ Narrative thread

Resident Evil™ is a game with a strong narrative thread. This affects the game in that the encounters during play tend to follow in an order which tells the story as well. To progress in the game the player has to complete the challenges presented.

A game which has a single path to follow in order to successfully complete it is often referred to as a 'linear' game. Linear games have explicit goals that the player must achieve in the near future to progress; these games are often level-based. 'Sandbox' games are those in which there seems to be much more freedom about when and how to achieve goals, which may be implied rather than explicit. Sandbox games allow the player to approach challenges in more or less any order. ('Sandbox' is a reference to childhood play, where the games children play in their sandboxes have no restraints, and the children can mix and match play elements.) Some sandbox-style games are truly open-ended and can never be completed, although these are likely to become quite repetitive. They are often based in large, open environments.

Debate

There is much debate in the game-playing community as to which structure is better – linear or sandbox. Some say that sandbox-style, open-ended games give the player the ultimate freedom to do as they will. The counter-argument is that linear, objective-based games give a more structured game and focus the player's actions and excitement on the relevant parts. Of course, there is no right or wrong answer to this argument. It depends on individual taste, and a structure that is appropriate for one game may be completely unsuitable for another.

Cinematic vision

Cinema is a useful analogy when considering linear games. When you watch a film you get the story and nothing else – there is little interaction. Your imagination may add a few items that your subconscious feels might be going on beyond what is on the screen, but in the main it is purely the film that you experience. From this, you get an enjoyable story, and are presented with the film director's point of view as to how a series of events happened. Many people have favourite film directors and seek out their work because they like the way the directors present a dramatic story. There is no need to generate an original version of events because the director creates a dramatic narrative. In a similar way, many people enjoy linear games with a clear and defined narrative sequence – they like the way the designers build the drama and present a sequence of events.

Advantages of linear style

As a designer of games there are questions to be answered, and some practical considerations to make, when deciding on the appropriate structure for your game. In terms of design there are good reasons to choose to make an objective-based linear game over an open-ended non-linear game. With an objective-based linear game the designer knows where the player will be so all the design, art and code effort can go into those areas. This means the game will have much higher production values. It will look better and there should be better paced and choreographed action.

Resident Evil 4™, for example, is very linear. Although players are able to wander freely around most places they have visited before, they cannot do much unless they follow the path they are supposed to follow. But because it is linear, the experience of playing is extremely rich, and there is a lot packed into small areas. If the game were turned into a free-roaming, mission-based, open-ended structure, the

Mix of styles

The Legend of Zelda: The Windwaker presents an interesting blend of linear and sandbox styles. The game is linear in that there are quests that must be completed in order. However, between these quests, the player is allowed to wander around and experience a rich and varied gameworld.

game would either be far more expensive and more difficult to make or it would have to compromise in either the quantity or quality of the experiences.

If the designer of the game has an established reputation, similar to a film director, then players may buy the game on the strength of the designer. This approach can result in a strong game with a dynamic and significant storyline.

 **Ever-changing**
Animal Crossing is
an example of a truly
open-ended game, and
has no defined ending,
yet it manages to remain
consistently interesting
through surprises,
community activities
and special events.

Which type of structure?

Not sure which structure
type a game conforms to?
Try breaking it down.

'Linear' means
everything happens in a
set sequence: level one –
level two – level three.

'Non-linear' means
there is no set sequence,
although there are usually
some restrictions: drive
to Los Santos – do a
mission – fly to San Fierro
– do a mission – drive
back to Los Santos – play
mini games.

New possibilities

Almost all of the early computer games had explicit
objectives and were linear in structure. The first highly
successful non-linear, open-ended computer game
was Elite.

Elite was impressive for many reasons: it was in
3D; you only had one life; you could save your game
in order to return to it later; it was from a first-person
viewpoint; it featured whole galaxies to explore; you
could upgrade your ship; you could choose how to
make money (trading, piracy, mining or a mixture);
and the universe seemed possessed of a life of its
own. Elite achieved all this and more by virtue of
having wonderfully elegant rules and a simple
structure. Every system visited consisted of just one

star, one planet and one orbiting space station.
When you arrived at the system you only really
had three choices: go to the star to scoop up fuel;
go into deep space to fight unending waves of ships
(for bounty or piracy); or go to the planet to trade,
upgrade and repair. The difference between the
systems was really just dependent on a text file
and some parameters that altered prices and
whether the police ships attacked you if you'd
broken some law.

There are many other wonderful rules in Elite
and so many of these ideas have been refined and
extended in later games such as the Grand Theft
Auto series, Animal Crossing and City of Heroes.

Interaction

Returning to the cinema metaphor, if you don't like watching another director's film, you may get the overwhelming urge to become involved in the action yourself and have the opportunity to do as you please, and interact with the situation and the other characters as the whim takes you. All you want is an outside agency to provide the setting, characters and props and then leave you to it. Preferring this point of view leads to the development of a sandbox game. The developers and designers create an environment and setting, populate it with characters and props, and then step back and leave you, the player, to your own devices.

Advantages of sandbox style

In an open-ended game the designers have to design everything, and decide where the gameworld ends. Even with modern processing power, sandbox games still need defined limits. However, when the limits have been decided on, the player is free to do what they will, attempt to complete the game or just have fun with the tools and equipment provided. There is a part of the human psyche that enjoys being an individual and asking 'what if?' Sandbox games provide an outlet for this urge to experiment and challenge the environment.

▼ Structure type?

1 Metroid Pinball takes its theme from a semi-linear adventure game, but was developed as a more traditional puzzle game.

2 Myst is arguably a puzzle game, but in later incarnations the story and potential role-playing angle have been explored.

3 Pro Evolution Soccer attempts to deliver a realistic (and fairly linear) soccer-playing experience.

4 Gotham Racing depicts high-performance car racing and works in a linear way, though the player can choose between fantasy settings for the races.

5 The Legend of Zelda: Twilight Princess offers a linear narrative to follow, but with opportunities to explore the varied delights of a richly detailed world.

▼ Thought exercise

Select one game from each list and play them. While playing make a note of the types of opportunities and activities the game provides you with throughout. Compare and contrast the games, see how each offers you different experiences.

NON-LINEAR	LINEAR
Animal Crossing	**The Legend of**
Sim City	**Zelda: The Windwaker**
The Elder Scrolls	**Metroid Prime**
Gary's Mod	**Myst 5: End of Ages**
Grand Theft Auto	

Ask yourself the following questions:

- How many different ways are there of achieving your goals?
- Can you 'play' the game without reference to the central story?
- Is there a central story?
- Does the game have an end?
- Are both types of games enjoyable for different reasons or the same reasons?
- What factors have been designed in (game mechanics) to provide this experience?
- What choices have the designers made when creating their games?

In analysing and examining these two types of games you should begin to get an idea what different gameplay types there are and how some or all of the features are present in certain games. As a follow-on from this, create your own lists of types of games and discuss your choices with other gamers.

Case studies

Game structure

▶ Case study 1: **Linear structure**

There are many games which could be said to have a linear, or objective-driven, structure. Two excellent examples are God of War and Resident Evil 4™. As well as being classic examples of the linear structure these two games are interesting to compare with each other.

Both games guide the player along a fixed route – with minor asides – and line up groups of generic opposition characters, followed by set-piece battles with much larger or more powerful opponents, usually with particular attack-patterns and weaknesses. Both games also allow the player some customisation of ability and/or weaponry, and some degree of freedom over the way this is done. The games often force the player to annihilate the current set of enemies before being able to continue to the next section. They also make extensive use of cut scenes to inform the player of the goals, level layout, level access changes, and key points of call necessary to complete the section.

All these elements are typical of linear games, and linear games are often – if not always – defined by a series of objectives. But though they share such a lot of similarities, God of War and Resident Evil 4™ feel and look like very different games. It might not be obvious they are both using

similar design solutions. They have different combat and movement mechanics, different camera systems and very different settings and styles, but underneath all these superficial features, the structure is essentially very similar. They even have identical save systems, using fixed points on the map which must be reached to store progress.

An objective-driven, linear structure such as this allows the developers of a game to spend time making each section of each level work. Both God of War and Resident Evil 4™ show evidence of this, being highly polished, well-crafted games which provide a good variety of challenges and many hours of play.

1 Opponents
Levels in God of War are punctuated by opponents which the player must defeat to progress.

2 Order of events
In Resident Evil 4™, the player progresses through a set order of events, and items collected in the game are made available later on.

GAMEOGRAPHIES

Title God of War
Developer SCE Studios
Key features
- Third-person combat
- Puzzle-solving elements
- Intuitive controls
- Unique mini-games

Title Resident Evil 4™
Developer Capcom
Key features
- Third-person shooter
- Cinematic style
- Context-sensitive controls

Case study 2: **Sandbox structure**

There are far fewer games with open-ended, or sandbox, structures than there are games with linear structures. A good example of a game with a truly open-ended structure is Animal Crossing. It has an implied goal – to get a big house and furnish it stylishly – but presents the player with many ways of achieving this, and no time restrictions at all.

Animal Crossing is ingeniously designed so that there is always something going on. Even when you aren't playing, things are happening (or at least will appear to have happened when you play again). Each day there are new ways of making money and opportunities to discover new things. Each hour the game changes in subtle ways. Every night the game changes again; and certain tasks can only happen at night. All the time things are growing

and dying, leaving and arriving, chatting and snubbing, trading and stealing, changing and discovering.

All this happens through a simple interface consisting mainly of talking and asking set questions, fishing, digging, planting, mailing, buying and selling. For example: When you are fishing, you'll get different fish depending on what time of day (or night) it is, where you fish, what time of year it is, and what the weather is like. The end result is that you'll always get a fish (or possibly a boot, or squid), but you can keep the fish for display in your house, sell it, or donate it to the museum. Some fish are rarer than others, and they sell for more. This system drives most of the 'collectible' part of the game. The structure works because the activities, although repetitious, often result in surprises, and all activities nudge the player toward the implied goals of the game.

GAMEOGRAPHY

Title Animal Crossing
Developer Nintendo
Key features
- Open-ended
- No linear structure
- Many different opportunities
- 'Living, persistent gameworld'

1 Clothing design
One aspect of Animal Crossing is to create designs to go on clothing.

2 Graphics
A drawing application lets the player design graphics for inclusion in the game.

3 Other characters
The non-player characters in the game have their own 'lives' and react to the player's input. They often give the player jobs to do in return for items.

4 Text input
A text-based input can be picked up by the non-player characters and used in conversation with the player.

Single-player v multi-player

Know your opponents

A single-player game involves a player competing or cooperating with non-player characters (NPCs) and objects controlled by the computer. A multi-player game is when the player plays against or with other human players, either on the same computer, a Local Area Network (LAN) or over the Internet. The difference between the two can be subtle or dramatic and both have advantages and disadvantages.

Single-player games

In a single-player game, the focus of the designer is to entertain the player. The designer is free to create opponents and characters which are entertaining to interact with and play against but which would be dull or unrewarding for a human to control.

Until recently, most enemies in games would have been very boring characters to play, such as the invaders in Space Invaders or the Barnacles in Half Life 1 or 2. The designer has the opportunity to create unbalanced opponents so that a variety and combination of challenges can be orchestrated to get the player to perform in a particular way. For example, a very small, weak – though moderately fast – character might be fun to play, but it wouldn't be a very fair match if pitched against a well-rounded opponent. However, many different opponents all controlled by the computer can be placed in a way that presents an entertaining threat requiring a particular tactic to defeat them.

Multi-player games

A multi-player game is almost always set up so that the players involved are given equally able toys (characters). The reason for this is that players usually want competition to be based on their relative skills, so if all players are equal, winning or losing can only be down to player ability. A good example of a multi-player game which neatly fits this system is

DOOM. In the multi-player game of DOOM each player is given identical marines, which, to begin with, have an equal amount of health (equipment and power). Play-balance is altered slightly by picking up certain weapons that suit particular situations and level designs.

▶ ▼ **Simple foes**

Space Invaders' attacking motion is crude yet devastating. The player must destroy them before they destroy him. The Barnacles in Half Life 2 do nothing but hang from the ceiling, waiting to grab the unwary player. Simple foes, but lethal if unnoticed.

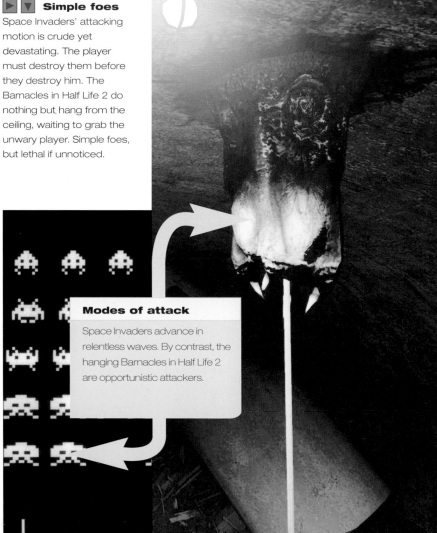

Modes of attack

Space Invaders advance in relentless waves. By contrast, the hanging Barnacles in Half Life 2 are opportunistic attackers.

Deathmatch

DOOM coined the term 'deathmatch' which has become a multi-player standard. A deathmatch is a multi-player game in which all players are enemies and each one killed is added to a kill total. When a player is killed there is a short time penalty – and sometimes a kill-total penalty as well – before the player is 'respawned'. (Spawning refers to something being created in the game. Respawning is when something is recreated.) Usually players, enemies and items are spawned when the game begins so that it looks as if the game was 'alive' before the player joined it. In multi-player mode, respawning is a simple way of keeping players playing even though they have been killed.

Development time

There are differences between developing a single-player and a multi-player game. Multi-player games rarely require any AI because the opponents are all controlled by people. They often centre on short, intense action between a few players at a time. Single-player games typically require much more design time in order to create exciting gameworlds and opponents.

◀ **Demonic enemy**
The enemies in Doom 3 are demonic and bestial. Sophisticated AI makes them challenging foes.

▲ ▶ **Unpredictable**
Whether controlled by another human player online, or the in-game AI, the characters the player encounters in World of Warcraft (a MMORPG) make for a challenging game. Friends and foes have the potential to be equally unpredictable.

◀ **Teamwork**
In City of Heroes, players work together to defeat a number of computer-controlled super villains.

MMORPGs

Massively Multiplayer Online Role-Playing Games (MMORPGs) such as World Of Warcraft and City of Villains are exceptions to many of the previous rules. Often players have characters with different abilities and powers. Character power is usually a measure of how long they have been playing rather than actual skill, clever tactics or strategy. Computer-controlled AI characters are needed to fill the world up, issue quests, trade and provide other opponents.

Case studies

Multi-player/single-player

▶ Case study 1: **Multi-player**

World of Warcraft and Counter Strike are different types of games in some ways, but are equally good examples of the multi-player genre, with particular features in common.

World of Warcraft, initially released in 1994, is a MMORPG, with millions of subscriptions from players around the world.

Players control characters and can explore the gameworld and fight monsters, either individually or as part of a team or 'guild'. They seek to improve their skills and power through gameplay. As their ranking improves they can buy equipment to help them in the game.

Players can select 'realms' to play in – this influences the mode of play. For instance, PvE – Player versus Environment; or PvP – Player versus Player.

Counter Strike may be the world's most widely-played online FPS ever. First released in 2000, it has remained popular despite gathering criticisms of certain key features.

Players can choose between two teams – the terrorists or counter-terrorists – and play rounds in order to win money to upgrade weapons. Different game types exist, presenting the teams with different objectives depending on the option chosen.

One major problem with Counter Strike's gameplay is that whilst players are injured, they cannot play the game but are still able to observe the action. They are then able to communicate to 'live' players the whereabouts of enemy positions, by telephone for example – though this is thought of as cheating and is generally discouraged by the gaming community.

GAMEOGRAPHIES

Title World of Warcraft
Developer Blizzard Entertainment
Key features
- Departure from RTS style of other MMORPGs
- Attainment levels influence gameplay

Title Counter Strike
Developer Valve Software
Key features
- Varied missions; team-based adversarial
- Large number of tactical variations possible

1 Interaction
World of Warcraft is a multi-player phenomenon. Players enter the mythical world and find many, varied creatures to interact with.

2 Teamwork
Counter Strike is an old multi-player game that has seen several updates. The degree of teamwork necessary defines it as a classic multi-player.

► Case study 2: **Single-player**

Ico, released in 2001 for PlayStation 2, is a wonderful and emotive single-player game designed by Fumito Ueda. It draws upon many design ideas from early single-player games and combines them with innovation and modern expectations.

In Ico, the player takes the role of a young boy with horns who must escape from an elaborate castle with a young girl, Yorda, whom he must protect. The castle is essentially a huge collection of puzzles, traps and hazards which must be overcome. Yorda is a computer-controlled character who follows the player character around. She has limited abilities, requiring the player to perform various actions in order for them both to progress.

Purely from a game mechanics perspective, Ico has two major features which are very common to single-player games – puzzles and sub-class enemies.

Puzzles in games maintain a player's interest because they provide a challenge that the player knows has a solution. They also represent a challenge to the designer. Consistency is important because without this the player will feel cheated by the logic and the game is unlikely to hold interest. It is important also to restrict actions and activities, because every new action complicates the logic of the game, and the code and testing needed. For example – imagine a game designed so that the player character can only push and pull boxes. Later, a decision is taken to

add the ability to climb over boxes. This would mean that all the previously designed puzzles are rendered trivial.

Sub-class enemies are a typical way of adding hazards and challenges to single-player games. The term 'sub-class' is used to classify enemies which have fewer actions than the player's character or inferior attributes. An Invader in Space Invaders is a perfect example of a sub-class enemy. In Ico, shadowy forms appear and attempt to capture Yorda. It is up to the player to fight them off and save her. As with many other single-player games the enemies attack in groups, and there are a few different types with different abilities to contend with.

Shadow of the Colossus was also developed by Fumido Ueda, designed as a prequel to Ico. It employs similar features in a sparser, extrapolated form. There are fewer – though massively larger – enemies, and each enemy can be treated as a kind of puzzle. Shadow of the Colossus also uses an equally arresting graphic style to draw the player into the gameworld.

GAMEOGRAPHIES

Title Ico
Developer Sony Computer Entertainment
Key features
- Individual style with washed-out colours
- No head-up display
- Made-up language

Title Shadow of the Colossus
Developer Sony Computer Entertainment
Key features
- Strong story
- Complex tests of player's abilities

1 Responsibility
Yorda, the princess in Ico, follows the player character around. The player must act to save them both.

2 Strong aesthetic
Shadow of the Colossus is an aesthetically and mechanically outstanding single-player game.

Platform-specific design

Targeting your game

As a games designer, when planning your game it is more than likely you will be targeting one of four platforms: console, PC, hand-held and mobile phone. Each platform has strengths and weaknesses that need to be considered when planning a successful implementation of your design.

Console

Console is considered the most 'glamorous' of all target platforms. It has the marketing budgets and the big names, and generates the most revenue. But while console games can reap great rewards, it is also the riskiest area of games development.

Consoles also offer a standard input into your gameworld via the controller. While form factors differ from console to console, in essence they all do the same thing. This allows you to tailor the game controls perfectly and be sure that every player is experiencing your game exactly as you intended. The downside to console development is the spiraling costs of producing a commercially viable game. Development teams increase in size with every hardware innovation. The industry has gone from three-man teams to 12, to 30, to 100-plus in the space of 15 years, yet the cost of the final product has become less expensive for the consumer.

To make console development viable, publishers play safe with killer licenses (Lord of the Rings, 50 Cent) and established characters or brands (Metal Gear Solid, Need for Speed). Radical and very original game design very rarely happens. This can sometimes be frustrating for designers who may feel creatively stifled by the minutely incremental advances in gameplay, or the 'Grand Theft Auto meets Halo' pitch sessions.

Ultimately, market forces drive console development. It may be glamorous but if you're hoping to revolutionise the games industry you might want to rethink your target platform.

▶ **Glamorous hardware**

The big advantage of console development is that the hardware is static. When a new console is released, the only changes to it over the next five years will be purely cosmetic. Because of this, as a designer you can be sure that the experience you are creating will be viewed in its unadulterated form by everyone who plays your game. Shown here are three rival computer game consoles: Nintendo Wii (left); Xbox 360 (centre); Playstation 3 (right).

 Successful format

The new PlayStation 3 controller follows a tried and familiar format.

 New generation

The Nintendo Wii controller goes beyond the usual button interface, and will recognise the user's gestures.

▲ **Strengths and limitations**

Games for PCs are often relatively experimental and can reach a huge audience. However, PCs have control limitations and the user experience cannot be accurately predicted.

Cross-platform

Big name games are usually released across all platforms – console, hand-held and PC. Whilst the design and visualisation is similar for all, the requirements of different machines mean that a lot of the modelling, texturing, animation and coding is specific to each platform. This can make the development task even more complicated and requires considerable investment.

PC

PC development often has crossover with console development, with the big franchises being ported to the PC. However the PC is also home to a wide range of original content with equally wide budgets and exposure.

Unlike console games, PC games don't have to be huge cinematic productions. A crazy puzzle game can sit easily alongside the next big-budget FPS, and potentially sell just as many units.

If you want to revolutionise the games industry, consider the PC as your target platform. Innovation is relatively commonplace, with games like The Sims selling an incredible number of units and finding a market far wider than that of a console game.

PCs do have a number of issues that need to be considered. No two PCs are exactly the same – you must consider a huge range of possible target devices. As a designer, you have to compromise. This might be graphical finesse at the cost of frame rate – which in turn will directly affect how your game plays. PC games also have to work with a keyboard and a mouse. Some genres work best with this setup, which is why the PC market is full of FPS and RTS games.

On the upside, PC games can be sold over the web on dedicated portals, distributed as shareware, or sent out on the cover of the latest PC magazine. This means a three-man team can still develop a niche game, distribute it and make money.

Apple Macintosh

Mainstream games for the Mac have always been the last to be developed, if at all. However, this seems set to change with the move to Intel processors in Macintosh machines. Many new games now come to the Mac platform at the same time as their PC counterparts and the ability of Macintosh machines to run the Macintosh OSX operating system or Microsoft Windows XP opens Macintosh machines to the wider gaming world. The Macintosh platform has always had a reputation for innovation and engaging quirkiness. This may yet have a positive effect on the games developed from the Macintosh platform.

Hand-held

Hand-held gaming is very popular, and thanks to the Nintendo GameBoy, gamers everywhere consider computer games as a great way to pass the time.

There are three main hand-held platforms, but unlike the console platforms, each one is very different to develop for.

The most established hand-held is the GameBoy Advance. The hardware is incredibly basic compared to the PC, consoles, and even other hand-helds, yet its strength lies in its vast catalogue of games, simplicity of input and extremely long battery life. Developing for the GBA is cost-effective and small teams can quickly produce titles. Because the GBA is not the most technically advanced platform, often the best-selling games are examples of excellent games design, not technical prowess. Like all hand-helds, the range of games on the GBA spans the quick-fix games like Wario Ware to huge 80-hour-plus RPG epics like Final Fantasy Crystal Chronicles.

Nintendo has a second hugely successful hand-held in the Nintendo DS. The DS is a very different device from the GBA, having two screens, one of which is touch-sensitive. This has led to a number of unique games being developed for the device. However, if you are designing a game specifically to work on the DS, be aware that it will be difficult to adapt to any other platform.

Sony entered the hand-held arena with the powerful PSP. Development for the PSP is almost

◀ **Nintendo hand-helds**

A selection of Nintendo hand-held games consoles of different ages.

▼ **PSP**

The PSP has been sold on the glamour of the hardware. The expectation to deliver games close to PS2-quality in terms of production values is high.

on a par with a smaller console game. All that power allows the PSP to host games that would be impossible on the GBA and DS. Not just graphically—the PSP is endowed with the UMD drive that can store a large amount of game data, as well as music and video.

Choice of hand-held platform

Your choice of development platform for hand-helds is truly governed by your idea. If you have a simple game idea that hinges heavily on design, not technology, try the GBA. If your game requires a different form of input than the standard D-Pad, go for DS. If your design requires a large amount of data, look at developing it for the PSP.

◀ **Gaming device**
The line between mobile phone and handheld games device is becoming more and more blurred.

Mobile phone

The mobile phone platform is the largest growth area in computer games, with all the major manufacturers looking at mobile phone games as a way to increase revenue. Mobile phone games cover a massive range of products, from SMS-based text games to high-end, console-style titles. They tend to use one of two different development environments: Java or 'native'.

Java games

Java games are small in size (on average 64k) and because of this size limitation are often simplistic in nature. They are usually quick-fix games, ideal for those wishing to fill a little time. They are often inexpensive to buy and can be downloaded from portals provided by the network operator. Because Java games are generally low-cost to develop and to purchase, they are appealing to small development teams since the overall risk for a project is greatly reduced. However this has led to a vast number of Java games being developed and you really need something that will stand out from the crowd to pull in those downloads.

'Native' games

The alternative to developing a Java game is to produce a 'native' game. This is a game that has direct access to the device's operating system. The main native platforms are Brew, Symbian, Windows Mobile and Linux. Going native gives the developer the opportunity to really open up the capabilities of the mobile device. Download sizes are much larger (often as much as 2.5mb). Because of this a lot of operators only offer native games over a 3G network, increasingly with a flat rate for data usage.

Importance of interface

Whatever platform you choose to develop for, when designing your mobile phone game, the interface to the game is of paramount importance.

The phone interface, while standard among most handsets in terms of function, differs widely in both quality and implementation. This means that as a designer you really have to come at the issue of game input from a more abstract approach. There's no standard analogue stick and action keys (yet), and the D-Pads on most phones are not designed with games in mind.

Potential market

The main reason most publishers are excited about mobile phone gaming is simply that most people have a mobile phone. The potential market for your mobile phone game is huge, yet overall development costs and expectations are still relatively low when compared to other platforms.

▲ **Graphic quality**
Mobile phones now include 3D accelerator chips to increase the quality of the graphics.

Realism and abstraction

Faithful simulations and surreal new worlds

In one respect all games are abstractions of reality – no matter how good the graphics and sound are, you are still sitting in your home playing a simulation via a control pad or keyboard. In game terms though, there are two poles of definition: abstract games and simulation games. In terms of presentation of the game there is a trend, particularly among first-person shooters and role-playing games, for visual and aural realism rather than abstract representation. Yet alongside this there is a strong tradition of games which do not attempt to mimic the real world and rather invite players into their own little areas of existence.

Modelling reality

Microsoft Flight is a game which gives the player the experience of flying airplanes, particularly commercial planes, as accurately as possible. The player is presented with all of the controls present in a normal plane, and the physics of the game engine require the player to operate the plane as he would in the real world. The views of the plane and the surrounding scenery are accurate portrayals of real-world machinery and places. Still, this game is played on a PC with a standard keyboard and a joystick; its realism is in the way the player interacts with the game in order to achieve a steady flight. These games maintain their popularity and give the player a chance to interact with airplanes in a way that he couldn't in the real world and to master a set of skills not easily gained. The sense of achievement in these games when they play according to your will is considerable.

 Realism

Microsoft Flight Simulator allows the player a huge choice of aircraft, both historical and modern. The player can also select their route. The game features weather effects, with real-life updates when connected to the Internet.

Sound and vision realism

The introduction of the next-generation consoles has seen the level of detail in the visual and sound modelling of games move to a yet more realistic level. For most of these games you would need a high-density television to see all of the detail. Games such as Far Cry Instincts, Project Gotham Racing 3, and Elder Scrolls IV: Oblivion provide compelling visuals and convincing sound effects, but are still not the same as observing a movie, or actually being there. The attempted realism is undeniably engaging; a player who participates fully in the game, suspending his disbelief, is rewarded with a near-realistic experience. Modern PCs and consoles push the boundaries of realistic representation in an attempt to draw the player ever deeper into the gameworld. These games rely heavily on cinematic tricks such as cut scenes and sophisticated camera angles. Players become used to seeing action scenes presented in this way through film and television. They accept this representation of the real world as reality, when in truth it is just a designer's fantasy.

Simulating reality

Real-time strategy games seek to provide players with a realistic challenge, by pitting them against the machine's AI, usually through a game of mass combat such as Rome Total War, Civilization IV or Warhammer 40,000: Dawn of War. In these types of games you are given a godlike overview of either armies or nations and are required to manage the resources and development of your forces in order to overcome your opponent, either by destruction or control of the playing area. Units in these games do not always explicitly follow your orders and the information you have about any given situation is not always complete. These game mechanics aim to mimic reality in that, despite a leader's best planning and intentions, things often do not go to plan due to factors beyond your control. The realism here lies in

Surreal
In Katamari Damacy, the player is given the surreal aim of creating a giant rolling ball of objects.

the fact that it is impossible to completely know or control a situation; it also happens in real time, so if you sit back and ponder a situation the machine's forces will defeat you. This type of realism challenges the player with a clever opponent and complex, ever-changing situations.

Abstract games

Abstract games present the player with a make-believe world; a surreal representation of somewhere else. Zelda Windwaker, Oddworld: Abe's Oddysee, Pikmin, Katamari Damacy, Darwinia and Vib-Ribbon (to name but a few) are all examples of gameworlds that are abstracted to a greater or lesser degree. Characters, places, game mechanics, and aims of the game are all different than we might expect in normal life. All of these games have received positive critical reaction from players, who find their twisted and surreal worlds exciting and engaging. In one respect they are pure games because they do not rely on a representation of the real world; rather they invite the player into their world and make him assume contrary viewpoints in order to play them. These games are compelling due to their contrary nature; players delight in mastering these dream worlds and seeking out all of their challenges.

Abstract or real?

Do you attempt to model realistic situations and present the player with experiences he might not otherwise get? Or do you invite him into a different gameworld of your creation, where some aspects might be unique? The expectations of the player are very important in this design consideration: to present

him with a realistic game you must convince him of this reality with subtle tricks and visual sophistication. Realism in game mechanics is important too. In reality the player might not be able to fly a plane or drive a high-performance car at speed, but a finely crafted game will provide him with that illusion. Some players may seek harsh game mechanics where vehicle controls are complex and difficult, or the requirement to make quick decisions and master complex and fluid situations is necessary for success.

Abstract games remove the need to model reality; often a difficult task, and demanding on the machine. They reward the player with novel and entertaining experiences. The designer faces the challenge of a scriptwriter – if many people like your material then you may be successful, if not then your game is doomed to obscurity. It is therefore of the highest importance when working on game concepts to identify at the outset whether the game is going to be realistic or not and consider this in all your planning.

Abstract inspirations

- Magnify absurd activities into compelling tasks.
- Give animals and objects personalities and aspirations.
- Imagine the real world from a different viewpoint.
- What if fairy tales and nursery rhymes were real?
- What if the intangible became tangible?
- Think of the pointless activities you do while you are waiting and daydreaming.

Abstract
In Vib-Ribbon, the player must move Vibri the rabbit in time to the beat and help her evolve into a winged princess.

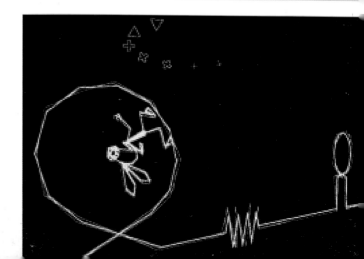

2D and 3D games

Into the third dimension

Gameworlds have developed in sophistication as technology has improved. Early games were flat, with the action being up and down or left and right. The third dimension was not present. As processing power became greater, three-dimensional gameworlds became possible, with the player having to consider the possibilities of that extra dimension. However, in the rush for technological advancement, designers should not forget that some games still work better in two dimensions, and that the limitation of a flat playing area can provide inspiration and challenges.

What is a 2D game?

A 2D game simply has actions and activities that work in two dimensions – but that's quite an ambiguous answer. It's sometimes difficult to tell from screenshots as there are many 2D games which use 3D graphics, such as Mutant Storm and Viewtiful Joe™. Animal Crossing could easily be categorized as a 3D game as it has a colourful, three-dimensional environment but, with very few exceptions, all the activities within the game are essentially two-dimensional in nature. Perhaps the best test to categorise a game is to consider whether it could be played using 2D graphics and simple 2D camera movement with little or no changes to game mechanics. Certainly Animal Crossing could be played in this way. Games such as Zelda: The Minish Cap and Grand Theft Auto 2 confuse the issue by including representations of playfields at different heights which overlap each other.

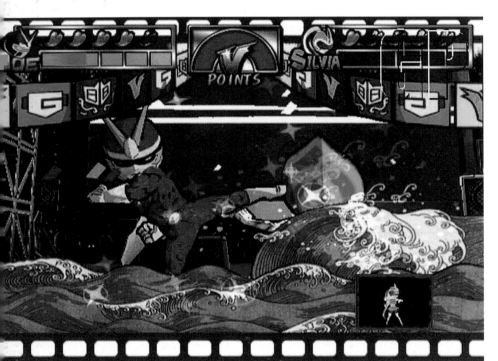

▲ **Cinematic 2D**
The exuberent cartoon nature of Viewtiful Joe™ makes it ideal for 2D.

▶ **Complex 2D**
Mutant Storm draws inspiration from the oldest 2D shoot-'em-ups and incorporates 3D graphics to deliver complex, demanding gameplay.

◀ Virtual city
City 17 is just one grim location in Half Life 2. The gameworld is as twisted and challenging as a real city would be.

What is a 3D game?

A 3D game takes place in three dimensions. Elite, Descent and Homeworld all fit this definition as they have full 3D movement and game mechanics. FPS games, such as Half Life 2, are also 3D games as they require full three-dimensional movement and views. It would be impossible to represent these games in two-dimensional worlds without major changes to the rules and mechanics.

Implications of 3D

The introduction of 3D games highlighted the role of the camera in the game experience. Designers faced the problem of having to place and control a camera so that it didn't interfere with the player's actions, but at the same time allowed him to see what he wanted to see. Early 3D games made use of the first-person camera perspective which means the player is essentially seeing through the eyes of the character he is controlling. This meant that the controls naturally moved the view, and that the player's character didn't have to be shown on-screen, which saved on asset production and processing time.

Other perspectives

Second-person perspective is almost never used as it means seeing your character from the subjective viewpoint of another character. Third-person has become the standard in most games – it means seeing the character you control from an objective viewpoint; not through the eyes of another character. 3D games with third-person views are often plagued with camera problems as there is rarely any perfect solution to balancing flexibility of camera control with a minimal input control system.

Deciding between character-relative or camera-relative controls can be complicated. Character-relative controls can be confusing when the character is facing the camera, as pushing left

will make the character move right on the screen. Camera-relative controls ignore the orientation of the player's character and use screen-space to direct the character. This is more immediate but can get confusing if cameras switch to different views, or move significantly.

3D reinterpretations

There are many people who have tried to make a 3D Tetris game. Some of these have been released, but the results are often confusing when compared to the purity of the original. Grand Theft Auto is widely considered to have made the jump from 2D to 3D successfully, although many feel that the police chases fall short of the excitement of the 2D versions.

3D games can be easier to market – the screenshots and box covers of 2D games tend to be less visually appealing. In a market where looks and licenses seem to have more impact than gameplay, 3D quickly became a priority for companies wanting hits. But with the rapidly growing casual gamer market, the industry is rediscovering what can be done in 2D.

▲ ▼ Exploration
In Sentinel: Descendants in Time, the player must solve puzzles to succeed. The game allows for a slow, methodical exploration of a beautiful 3D gameworld.

Case study

2D and 3D games

▶ Case study: **Worms**

This case study focuses on the transition of Worms from 2D to 3D. Worms was originally created using BlitzBasic by Andy Davidson, for a competition in 1994. He won the competition, and Team17 made a deal with him to create a commercial title for the Commodore Amiga. It became a hugely popular game and was successful in a 2D format for years. However, when it later made the transition into 3D, this highlighted considerations associated with such a move.

The premise of the original 2D game is that the player has control over a number of worms, each of which has access to a vast range of weaponry. The players take turns to move their worms around and attack. The aim of the game is to destroy all the opponent's worms before they destroy yours. It is particularly good in multi-player mode as it encourages alliances and negotiation (rarely honoured) between players – even when it isn't their turn.

Simple mechanics

The mechanics of Worms are quite simple, in that each worm can move left or right or fire a weapon. Most weapons have to be aimed and different weapons are useful in different situations. The 2D view supports the game mechanics perfectly, because at any time you can see most of the playfield and opponents and so work out a strategy. It's also quite easy to predict where things will go and how they will behave which is important to the strategy you use.

Winning formula

The combination of simple 2D view, variety of weapons, destructible scenery, simple but skill-based mechanics, silly graphics and replayability made Worms extremely addictive. Many follow up games were made and a few other companies copied the formula with different themes – pigs, snails and so on – and less success.

3D game

In 2003, Worms 3D came out. It excited a fair amount of interest in the games industry because

dedicated gamers were fascinated to see how such a simple, yet almost endlessly compelling 2D game could be reimagined as a successful 3D game. But many critics considered that the Worms franchise lost some of its charm following its transition into 3D.

Challenges

There are two main problems with Worms 3D. First is the controls – to navigate a 3D environment and fire at targets requires either a clever design, or lots of fiddly controls and compromises. Anyone who loads the Worms 3D demo is likely to struggle with the controls at first because they just aren't intuitive enough. There is not nearly enough action for the effort.

The second problem is the camera view – a camera in a 3D environment can only see so much. This means that it is much more difficult for the

player to know where he is in the gameworld, and where everything else is. Even a relatively simple task such as finding the best target to attack is quite difficult. Because the direction of the camera is controlled by only one player, the other players can no longer negotiate with each other about future moves. This means that a multi-player game on one computer isn't really an option. This problem is compounded by the fact that the camera can rotate independently of the worm and the direction it will fire, so the camera is decoupled from the aiming. Sometimes, the camera collides with the scenery, making it impossible to set up a valid shot.

Finally, shooting is far more difficult than in the original game, as shooting at a point on a highly varied 3D environment using projectile weapons is very difficult.

Design exercise: **Discussion**

Following on from the ideas put forward in this case study, discuss with a group of friends whether Mario, Zelda or Grand Theft Auto could be considered to have made the transition to 3D effectively, and the reasons for your conclusions. Which is the most successful, and why? Or, analyse and compare other examples of games that moved from 2D into 3D.

GAMEOGRAPHIES

Title Worms

Developer Andy Davidson

Key features
- Turn-based strategy
- Seamless game objectives and mechanics
- Huge array of weapons

Title Worms 3D

Developer Team 17

Key features
- Deformable 3D landscapes
- Detailed and humorous graphic style

Considerations

Worms 3D has been enjoyed and praised by many people, but successful as it is, it does highlight the difficulties associated with transferring a game from 2D to 3D, and some of the main considerations that need to be made from the outset.

1 Strange objects

The cartoon world of Worms gives the player access to many strange objects to cause mayhem with.

2 Movement modification

A can of energy drink can be used to modify the movement abilities of the player's worm.

3 Surreal gameworlds

The combat takes place in many surreal gameworlds, each with their unique twist on reality.

4 Saturated colour

The saturated colour of the cartoon world of Worms makes it instantly recognisable.

5 Shooting in 3D

As a counter-example to the problems of aiming and firing a weapon in a 3D game environment, Wild Metal Country manages this very well.

5

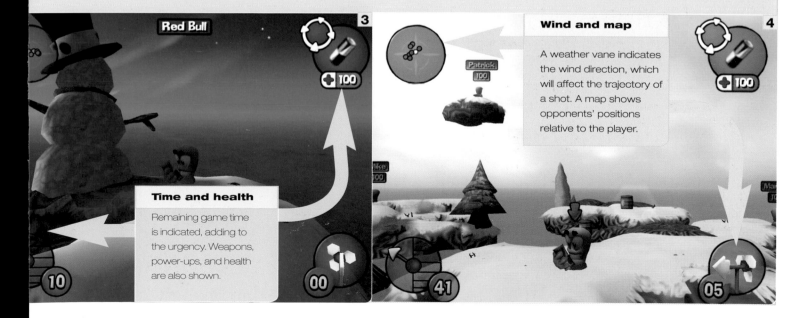

Red Bull

3

Time and health

Remaining game time is indicated, adding to the urgency. Weapons, power-ups, and health are also shown.

Wind and map

4

A weather vane indicates the wind direction, which will affect the trajectory of a shot. A map shows opponents' positions relative to the player.

First person v third person

The player's point of view

The terms 'first person' and 'third person' are used to describe the view of the gameworld the player has. A first-person viewpoint simulates the world as if seen through the eyes of the player-character. A third-person viewpoint gives the player a distanced perspective on the entire scene – including their own character – as if seen through a camera. Half Life and Halo are examples of first-person games; Grand Theft Auto and Prince of Persia are typical third-person games.

When designing your game, the type of experience you are intending to deliver to the player directly governs your choice of perspective. If you are planning a platform game with perilous drops and a dexterous lead character it would be a brave designer who would suggest this be done as a first-person game. Similarly, if you are planning a game that involves pinpoint accuracy of shooting in an immense universe, a first-person view will undoubtedly offer you the best perspective on your gameworld.

First-person view

Third-person view

Controls

Controls play a part in your choice of perspective. A PC's mouse and keyboard are not suited to third-person games but provide the perfect interface for a first-person game, in which the player is constantly in control of both movement and view. In a classic PC setup the mouse controls view (or head rotation) while the keyboard handles movement. This has become the standard control configuration for first person shooters on the PC.

Mapping this configuration to a 'dual-shock' controller means placing movement on the left analogue stick and view on the right. Generally there are also tweaks and assists going on in the code to make this configuration as comfortable as possible. First-person games on console live or die by their control implementation. Good examples are Halo 2 on Xbox and Metroid Prime on GameCube. Since the launch of the N64, players have enjoyed the subtlety of analogue controls. These allow precise control, and most games function well with the left analogue stick controlling the primary player navigation.

The playing experience

Beyond the technical implementation of first- and third-person games, there is one consideration that overrides all: what kind of experience do you want to give the player?

If you have a very character-centric game with a lead character who can perform a huge range of varied and cool-looking moves, you'll almost certainly want the player to see these moves in action. However, if you want the player to feel like he *is* the lead character, first-person games offer an absorbing perspective into your gameworld.

There are a few games that combine both first-person and third-person perspectives to great effect. Using third-person for the environmental puzzles and first-person for exploration and combat, Chronicles of Riddick is an excellent example of how these two very disparate perspectives can be brought together through clever, thoughtful game design.

▲ **Different views**

These two contrasting illustrations show the difference between a first-person viewpoint and the equivalent third-person view. The most obvious difference is perhaps that in the first person, the player character is not visible. Both types of view have advantages and disadvantages – the trick is to make the view you decide on work in the context of your game.

▶ Case study 1: **First-person**

GAMEOGRAPHY

Title Half Life 2
Developer Valve
Corporation
Key features
- Incredible storytelling
- Realtime gameplay
- Detailed facial animation
- Superb game physics

The original Half Life was a breath of fresh air in the world of the first-person shooter when it was originally released. It brought immersive storytelling and puzzle-solving to a genre that had been almost exclusively about firepower.

The promise of Half Life 2 made it one of the most anticipated PC games of all time. Half Life 2 created a gritty, dystopian world for the player to explore. It was some way into the game before you even had a weapon – a decision that distanced the series even further from the shoot-'em-up roots of the FPS genre. The first-person perspective brought the player directly into the action. Story sequences were played out with characters looking at the player-character while they were talking, drawing the player deeper into the perfectly pitched atmosphere of the game.

Half Life 2 innovated in all areas – even its distribution through the 'Steam' download system – and was a fine example of just how far first-person game design can be pushed.

▶ Case study 2: **Third-person**

GAMEOGRAPHY

Title Devil May Cry™
Developer Capcom
Key features
- Array of fight styles and moves
- Gothic tone complemented by music

Capcom's Devil May Cry™ series was about one thing from day one: kick ass and look cool doing it. The game even rated you on how cool you were at kicking ass. Because of this it was a perfect example of a game that excelled in the third person.

When you're being cool you want to see yourself being cool. Devil May Cry™ used a filmic approach to its camera system, cutting the camera to the best angle for the environment instead of a simple 'follow cam'. The lead character, Dante, had a huge range of attacks that allowed him to switch effortlessly between a katana and a firearm. This gave the player a wonderful sense of achievement when viewed from a dramatic third-person viewpoint.

All that jumping, weapon-switching, evil hordes attacking from all sides, and – most importantly – looking cool, would simply have been too much information to handle from a first-person perspective, making Devil May Cry™ a perfect example of a game that could only work in the third person.

Real world to gameworld

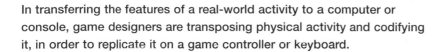

Replicating reality

In transferring the features of a real-world activity to a computer or console, game designers are transposing physical activity and codifying it, in order to replicate it on a game controller or keyboard.

Sporting games

Running around or kicking a soccer ball is not the same as moving an analogue controller; skateboarding requires a skateboard not a keyboard; and even with a steering wheel controller, driving a real Formula 1 car at 200mph is a very different experience from 'driving' one in your own home. Though games developers use words like 'realistic' the truth is that soccer, skateboarding and racing games are far removed from the actual experiences.

So what are designers trying to achieve by creating these games? And what are they giving the player that he cannot have if he is actually taking part in the sport? If you ignore the advertising hyperbole for a minute you can see what these games deliver is a representation of the real-world experience translated into a digital medium. The player is not physically engaging in the sport, but rather playing a digital game which embodies the activity.

Embodiment of spirit

If you are actually skateboarding then your mind and body are working on several levels and you are not conscious of many of them. You are flexing your muscles in an exact fashion in order to keep your balance and guide the board. Your mind is constantly plotting where you intend to go and how to use the terrain for your next trick. This delicate and intuitive balance is the experience of skateboarding.

In the Tony Hawk series of skateboarding computer games there is a demand for quickness of thought and manual dexterity – slightly different skills than actual skateboarding demands. But this is still considered a good skateboard game. This is

◄ Challenges

The complex control sets in Tony Hawk's Skateboarding (far left) aim to give the player comparable physical challenges to those he would experience were he skateboarding for real (left). He must master these controls to achieve complex stunts.

Scoring

Scoring does not generally take place in real-life skateboarding. In the digital version the score gives the player positive feedback on his performance, such as he might receive from his friends if he were actually skateboarding.

SCORE: 3648

Stunt information

Faithful to the language of skateboarding and the potential repertoire of stunts, on-screen information provides commentary and targets to achieve.

1440 X 2
Spine Transfer ◆

◄ **Adding realism**
The Nintendo Wii (far left) has innovative controllers that allow the player to use gestures as well as pressing buttons. This is used to add realism in The Legend of Zelda: Twilight Princess (left), but an aiming HUD is still used to help show the player their target.

Ranking

To push the player to even greater heights of achievement, goals are set and the player's skill in reaching them is ranked.

because the game designers have embodied the atmosphere and attitude of skateboarding within the game. However, this on its own is not enough. If it were simply the controls and the gamespace, it would be a pale imitation. The games work well because they include other aspects of skateboarding that are peripheral yet important. They feature extensive soundtracks from bands associated with skate culture. The characters are not simply representations of real-life skaters but also larger-than-life skater caricatures. Finally, in these games you are also offered the opportunity to skate where skateboarding is not normally allowed or even conceivable. The reason why these games and other sporting games work is that they not only provide the player with a representation of the sport, but they accurately embody the spirit and the culture of the activity within the game.

First-person games

In first-person games the representation of reality is an important issue. The designer is faced with the challenge of representing movement through a representation of a physical world in a digital gamespace. What happens, for instance, when the player character runs, jumps, or falls? How should the designer portray the character getting hurt or ill? How should the player character interact with the environment, equipment and other people around him? Whatever game mechanic is used, it can only ever be a representation of the real world and not an actual action.

What's going on?

There are many tools and methods available to enable a designer to get around the problems of replicating reality. Constantly improving technology allows for better graphics and sound, which both make a huge difference to the realistic effect. But one of the most important factors in making any game appear more realistic is a mechanic that allows the player to keep account of his character's actions and status. This feedback to the player is commonly referred to as the head-up display, or HUD for short. The HUD often appears on-screen as if magically superimposed over the player's view. A shortening bar or a percentage number might tell you the player how well – or wounded – he feels. An icon in one corner might tell him what type of gun is in his hand and how many rounds are left in the magazine. A superimposed map might be available to show the surrounding areas, possibly with markers for enemies. These user-interface devices make up for the real-world feelings or knowledge that a player would have if he were taking part in the scene for real. Usually, the removal of them, for whatever reason, makes the game considerably more difficult as the player effectively loses a 'sense'. These game mechanics are not a literal representation of a real-world situation, but are a contrivance to deliver the atmosphere and drama of a situation within the confines of a game.

KING KONG

1 The action occurs all around the character; they are not just watching from a distance.

2 Other computer-controlled characters play an active role in the action.

3 True to life, if the player has a weapon they have no magic aiming point (or sights) to shoot.

 Realism

Though the story of King Kong is fantastic, the game developer has attempted an air of realism in what the player sees on the screen and how they have to interact with the game. The usual on-screen scores, maps and so on are absent.

Head-up display

The HUD in a computer game may appear superimposed over whatever action is taking place on-screen. This follows the precedent of fighter jets or advanced cars, in which information, such as speed, is displayed on the windscreen. This allows the pilot or driver to access critical information instantly, without taking their eyes off where they are going. In a real-life context, this type of interface can save lives.

It is interesting to note that at least one game makes a notable attempt to explain the HUD and that is Metroid Prime, which has the HUD projected on the inside of the helmet of the character named Samus. As the game is set in the future this is an easily acceptable feature, more so than with a World War Two game which should not (in theory) have such a help. Recently some games, notably Peter Jackson's King Kong, have begun to eschew the HUD as a game mechanic, making the player rely on his wits in interpreting character dialogue and the game environment for the clues to his status.

More realistic than ever

One of the effects that improved technologies have on games is their greater processing power. This is the ability of the PC or console to undertake the high level of computing needed to present detailed visuals, complex sounds and credible artificial intelligence for opponents.

As a result of this power, designers can make greater use of real-world references for the game visuals. Textures on game models become almost photo-realistic. The locations can be real-world locations or can be fictional yet convincing hybrids of

real places. While visual realism is not always the defining mark of a great game, when it is used in conjunction with stunning design it maximises the player's suspension of disbelief and immersion into the game.

Enhancing experience

Sound designers can provide incredibly detailed sound. Not only the noise the character and equipment makes, but ambient sound such as wind and rain or the echoing of footsteps all add to the realistic experience. It is an interesting experiment to watch a horror movie with no sound – usually it stops being scary. However, if you leave the sound on but close your eyes and listen to the sounds, particularly the sound effects, it may be even more frightening as your imagination fills in the images to the sounds you are hearing. This experiment underlines the importance of sound in a computer game.

Complex situations

One of the most effective uses of processing power in the newest machines (in game terms) is the increased ability to run advanced programs which enable the game to model complex situations. An obvious manifestation is the game physics (how inanimate objects act in the gameworld), for example how gravity works or how things can be broken. The closer in behaviour these are to our own world, the more realistic they seem. The apparent intelligence and abilities of the opponents provided by the game is helped by new technologies. In the best examples, opponents do not stand idly until the player is in front of them; rather they seek the player out and track him by noise or movement in order to confront him. Some game characters might even appear to engage the player in a 'conversation', which is dependent on how the game has played so far and gives the illusion of a conscious person talking to the player.

The designer's role

In achieving all of this the designer is faced with two problems: how to design a game which captures the spirit of the sport or situation in question and seeks to provide the enjoyment and challenges of the sport; and what game mechanics to develop to allow the player to experience the sport or situation features through the traditional medium of a controller or keyboard interface.

Remember that the game you are working on is an emulation of a real situation, and that it can never be a replacement for the real thing. This need not be a limitation, though – as a designer you can work this to your advantage. Aim to add features that enhance the experience in a positive manner for the player, whilst continuing to embody the spirit of the original activity.

Above all remember that the player wants to engage in a fantasy – he may not actually want to be a professional skateboarder, or battling for the safety of humanity in real life, but he would like to feel that he is doing this for the space of time in which he plays the game – and that he is having a rewarding time doing so. All games should be enjoyable; if they are too literal in the interpretation of reality they may not be satisfying to your players. Fail to strike this balance and your game risks being a critical and commercial failure.

▲ **Sensory assault**
Silent Hill not only assaults players with terrifying images, but juxtaposes these with a soundtrack that is equally disquieting. Together, sound and vision make for a convincing, frightening game.

Storytelling in games
Narrative structures and implications

A major factor in the evolution of computer games – after obvious technological improvements – is the increasing importance of storytelling. While storyline implementation may have stumbled and tripped along the way, the sheer ambition to progress interactive storytelling in games has pushed designers to become ever more inventive.

The earliest computer games had no narrative as such, but still had scenarios. Space Invaders, for example, is a 'story' of an alien invasion, while Mappy is a cat-and-mouse 'tale' about theft. But only with the arrival of home computers and games consoles did storytelling in games begin to be explored. Early text adventures such as Infocom's Zork introduced interactive fiction, and soon all games had a backstory at the very least.

'My game needs a story'

The big question is: how much? This has a direct effect on the design of your game. Some games, like Metal Gear Solid and the Final Fantasy series, are often more story than game – which is what attracts fans of these games. Other games simply use basic mission introductions to get the story moving and allow it to play out in the action.

A good 'compare and contrast' exercise is to play Metal Gear Solid and Splinter Cell. Both are sneaky, mission-based games (Splinter Cell is even 'endorsed by Tom Clancy') yet the level and style of storytelling is completely different.

'Does my game need a story?'

If you're planning a sports game, Virtua Tennis for example, little or no story is needed – yet even sports games usually have a 'career mode' where your route to stardom is plotted with rival players. Your game may not need a story, but it does at least need context. All but the most abstract of games need some kind of justification for their existence.

◄ **Comparison**
Tom Clancy's Splinter Cell (left) and Metal Gear Solid (below) belong to the same genre, yet their level of narrative is very different. Metal Gear Solid is much more story-centred.

© Sega

◄ **No story**
As Virtua Tennis focuses on a series of professional tennis matches, no story is needed. The game is all about the players' skill.

'I don't want a lot of story'

This decision will save you millions on your budget.

The simplest structure for a game with a basic storyline is the same as for many movies, with a three-act structure. Act 1 sets up the story; act 2 is the main action; act 3 is the resolution. In a game, 'stage intro' is act 1, 'game' is act 2, and 'Boss' is act 3. Simple game story structure usually differs from movie structure in that it is essentially made up of lots of three-act 'movies' strung together to provide a stream of action.

Some movies can be re-imagined easily as computer games. For example, whenever James Bond flies off to his next exotic location, a new 'stage' is 'loaded'. An even better example is a movie like *Kill Bill*, which is effectively a series of boss battles.

This simple structure gives players a sense of progression and achievement. Imagine a game with no bosses and one location played out over 20 hours. The player would lose the will to live.

◄ Boss battles

Kill Bill is a movie structured like a computer game that was based on the structure of a typical three-act movie. In other words, rather than following the typical movie structure of 'Act 1, act 2, act 3', it is a series of three-act parts joined end to end. Each part contains a 'Boss battle' in which the heroine takes her merciless revenge on a character.

'I want lots of story'

If you're planning a heavily story-based game, be sure that you have a great story to tell, as well as the budget to back it up. Games such as FINAL FANTASY are all about the story. Every action taken, every battle fought, is designed for one thing – to find out what happens next.

'Plot points' in story-based games are sections of story that progress the stage. For example, if the story for Stage 1 is to break into a museum and steal a diamond, Plot Point 1 might be when you've got into the museum and are checking out the security system. Plot Point 2 might be finding the room with the diamond, and so on.

Games with lots of story can polarise players. Ask around and see how many people like Metal Gear Solid and how many don't – the story divides opinion. Yet the sales figures prove that there are a large number of players who enjoy story-based games. Like them or loathe them, stories in games are here to stay.

Must-play narrative games

- Broken Sword: The Sleeping Dragon (Revolution Software)
- FINAL FANTASY XII (Square Enix)
- Deus Ex (Eidos Interactive)
- Max Payne (Gathering of Developers)
- Metroid Prime (Nintendo)
- Tomb Raider Legend (Eidos Interactive)
- Lego Star Wars 2 (Lucas Arts/TT Games)

◄ Complex story

There is a rich and detailed storyline to all the FINAL FANTASY games. Not only the stories experienced by the player; the backstories of other characters and creatures met in the game are included as well.

Cut scenes

Telling the game's story

A cut scene is part of a game that progresses the game's storyline and is non-interactive. Some games are cut-scene heavy. The FINAL FANTASY and Metal Gear Solid games often employ lengthy cut scenes. Other games, like Grand Theft Auto, use short story sections to give the player mission briefings or status updates.

A useful rule of thumb for using cut scenes is 'play action – show story'. This means not using a cut scene to show the hero defeating the boss, which would cheat the player of action. Instead, use the cut scene to introduce the boss; get the player really involved so he can't wait to jump in and defeat it.

Boss death scenes

Boss characters are often placed between a 'boss intro' cut scene and a 'boss defeated' outro. Sometimes these cut-scene boss deaths contain a large amount of action. Be careful – there are games where, after attacking a boss with a limited number of moves for five minutes, the boss-death cut scene kicks in and the player character is jumping around the screen and pulling off moves that are inaccessible during normal play. This cheapens the experience and exposes holes in the game mechanics.

Intro cut scenes

There is one exception where action can be used successfully in a cut scene – the intro. At this stage, you want to engage the player by showing off the awesome gameworld and the possibilities of the main character. Onimusha 3 has an amazing intro cut scene that still accurately reflects the main character's abilities.

◀ Intro cut scene
This scene, from the intro of Onimusha 3, is not controlled by the player, but develops the game's story and adds important information.

Cut scene methods
There are two main ways cut scenes are played back in computer games – either dropping to video for a pre-rendered scene, or using the in-game renderer to produce a real-time cut scene.

Video cut scenes
A video cut scene is usually an animated sequence rendered out and encoded as a video stream to be played back during the game. There are two main advantages of using video. The artists can generate a scene using all the rendering techniques available with a package such as 3D Studio Max or Maya. They are not restricted by the number of polygons, lights or particle effects that the game engine might have, so video cut scenes can have a quality akin to cinema. The FINAL FANTASY games are great examples. In addition, the scene will look the same on all hardware. Video playback is easily achievable on everything from a mobile phone to the latest-generation console.

However, the downside is that there may be a jarring of quality between game and video assets. Video scenes will always look better than the real-time game. Producing high-quality video can also cost a lot of money. Often, video cut scenes are outsourced to specialist studios to ease the pressure on the development team.

 Story overview

Cut scenes may borrow from cinema and have multiple points of view, to give the player a better impression of a critical part of the story, as this scene from Metal Gear Solid demonstrates.

Real-time cut scenes

Real-time cut scenes are played back using the same renderer and assets as the main game. As a result there is no jarring of quality between the game and the cut scenes. A game like Metal Gear Solid uses real-time cut scenes for all its story sections, and this is one of the main reasons why the game feels so consistent. Production of real-time cut scenes is more complex than video and usually relies on in-house tools to allow animation data to be exported directly from the animation package of choice for direct playback in the game engine.

The big disadvantage of this is that what the animator sees in Maya, for example, will not be exactly what is seen in the game. A lot of time can be spent tweaking animation data to get the desired results, exporting and re-exporting the data until it's just right. Because the rendering of the cut scene is all handled by the game engine the quality and frame rate may change based on the target platform. This can be something of an unknown variable with PC development where the player's PC spec may be significantly different from the spec desired.

*: I'm sorry but I've got a business to run. This, er, haphazard fortune-telling of yours is costing me a fortune in free drinks!

*: Get out! Get out, monster! You're not welcome here!

Rosalind
You will stop this foolishness this instant! You are a young lady, not a warrior!

Dialogue

Cut scenes provide an opportunity to present spoken or written dialogue, which enhances the player's experience, as in these screenshots from DRAGON QUEST.

Scripted cut scenes

There is one other, simpler type of cut scene that many games rely on – the scripted cut scene. If you simply want two game characters to meet and exchange some dialogue, it is often simpler, easier and more cost-effective to use a scripted cut scene. These are scenes played back using the game engine and are created using the same scripting language that is controlling your game. Here is an example of the code for a scripted cut scene:

```
SetCamera CameraIntro, player
PlayAnim player, Idle
Print 'How's it going?'
Wait 30
SetCamera CameraIntro, enemy
PlayAnim enemy, angry
Print 'I'M GONNA KILL YOU!' ...and so on
```

With a sophisticated scripting system in your game engine – and a lot of patience – you can actually build up reasonably complex sequences using this system. Even elaborate games like DRAGON QUEST use this technique a lot when the player chats with the other characters in the game. DRAGON QUEST actually uses a combination of all the techniques discussed here and is a great example of where and how to use video, real-time, and scripted cut scenes. Play it and try to spot which sections are which.

Motivation and objectives

Analysing the need to win

All games, not just computer games, are driven by motivation and objectives. In sports, people are motivated to be the best, to become legendary for their talent; while their objective is to win the current match. These principles translate directly to the world of computer game design.

Why play?

Motivation: the need to get the girl, kill the baddies and save the entire planet because some invading force is threatening you.

Objectives: the challenges, stages, mini-bosses, bosses and so on along the way.

Motivation types

Motivation in a game can be split into distinct types, with the emphasis placed on the main character (personal motivation), or the planet (global motivation), or both ('having a really bad day' or 'Die Hard' motivation). The threefold illustration (right) demonstrates some examples.

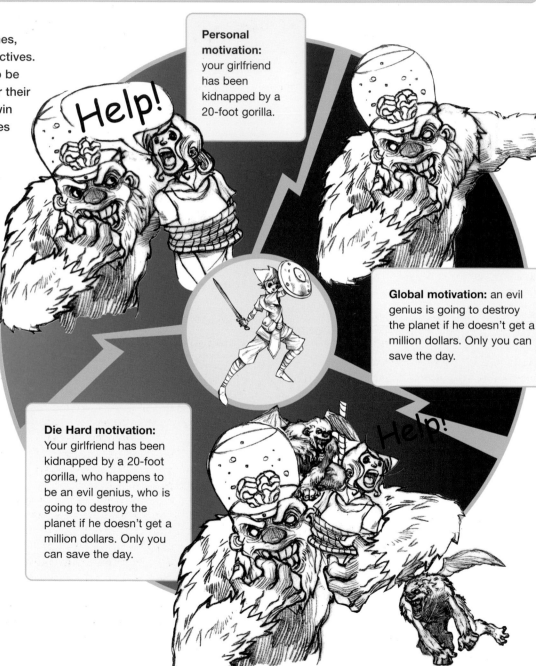

Personal motivation: your girlfriend has been kidnapped by a 20-foot gorilla.

Global motivation: an evil genius is going to destroy the planet if he doesn't get a million dollars. Only you can save the day.

Die Hard motivation: Your girlfriend has been kidnapped by a 20-foot gorilla, who happens to be an evil genius, who is going to destroy the planet if he doesn't get a million dollars. Only you can save the day.

| LEVEL 1 | MINI-OBJECTIVE | FIGHT BOSS | NEXT LEVEL |

Die Hard motivation is the best

Make the motivation personal and global (Die Hard) and you create a great impetus for your character to act. Nearly all successful action films follow the Die Hard motivation pattern. But even supposing the planet is about to be destroyed and your girlfriend is being held captive by a giant simian; what's to stop you from just going back to bed and not even trying to face these insurmountable odds? Well, as in many great stories, your character is forced into action.

Forced action

Your character wakes up after being drugged to find his girlfriend gone. Initially confused, he finds in his hand a TV remote with a note attached to it with the words 'Press me' written in terrible handwriting. Your character pushes the 'play' button, and on a TV at the other end of the room a DVD plays. It turns out that a 20-foot gorilla has kidnapped your girlfriend and is going to destroy the planet if he does not get a million dollars. Oh, and just for fun, he has surgically implanted a thermonuclear device in your stomach that will go off in 12 hours unless you personally deliver the money.

Your character gets out of bed. Self-preservation is the ultimate motivation.

Objective types

Objectives are the obstacles between the player and his ultimate goal. A structure for game objectives developed early on: reach the end of a level, kill the boss. This basic structure prevails, though it may be masked by complex storytelling and graphical finery.

Players need to feel a sense of progression. The boss-battle is a sign to the player that he has successfully completed part of the game. In Greek mythology terms, a computer game boss would be called a 'gatekeeper'. These gatekeepers would try to stop the hero from progressing on his worthy mission. Defeating the gatekeeper allowed him to continue his mission and prove he was up to the task. In modern computer games the gatekeeper (or boss) does not have to be human; it could be environmental. However, people do tend to respond to and remember characters best.

Mini-objectives

Within game levels, a useful device is to have mini-objectives. Mini-objectives help to maintain the player's interest by offering intermediate challenges before the eventual face-off with the boss. These mini-objectives could be as simple as 'break into the museum', 'steal the diamond' or 'get out of the museum'. These examples are fine, but as with the motivation example, the more incentive you can throw at the player the better.

For example: maybe the kidnapping gorilla has an army of mind-controlled monkeys who have been sent out to stop you getting the diamond. They let you get into the museum, but then start to trigger the alarms and generally cause chaos. Just as you are about to retrieve the diamond, a monkey swings down from the ceiling and steals it from your grasp. The mini-objective switches to getting the diamond back from the mind-controlled monkey, and so the play progresses at a high level of excitement.

Checklist

- Make the mission personal to force the player to act.
- Bosses help players feel a sense of progression.
- Mini-objectives maintain the player's interest.
- Combine both personal and global threats for maximum effect.

Players' roles

Hero, anti-hero or god?

The player's role in general is to re-balance a world that has fallen into chaos – he is the 'hero'. This archetype is true of the majority of games, the exception being pure sports or simulation games. In titles such as FIFA, Gran Turismo, or Microsoft Flight Simulator, the player's primary role is personal development. As the player you want to get the better car, be top of the leader board, or win the World Cup. The player is still the hero in these games, but there is no external pressure beyond the need to win driving the player's progress – his world is not in complete disarray.

Chaos dynamic

It's possible to apply the 'world in chaos' dynamic to sports and simulation games too. For example, you are the driver for a NASCAR team which is down on its luck. If the results don't improve, the team is going to be bought out by Hyperglobal Evil Corp. You're the fresh-faced rookie, and the team's last hope. If you win all the races, the team will be saved. Any sports movie worth its salt exploits this model. It adds an additional dynamic to the piece and cements the player as the true hero.

Heroes and anti-heroes

In Super Mario Sunshine, Mario's holiday island is in chaos. Mario has been accused of defacing the island with graffiti. He must clean up the island and find the real culprit, in order to restore normality. He does this selflessly, risking life and limb. This makes Mario a hero.

The Grand Theft Auto series is an excellent example of a different type of 'hero' scenario. The technological and artistic achievements of this series have been recognised by millions of fans worldwide. The freedom with which gamers can play within GTA's interactive environment enables them to explore increasingly sophisticated and immersive virtual worlds.

After the player's character has been betrayed and left for dead, he is arrested and locked away, until he gets caught in a prison break. While on the run, he sets out to take his revenge and rise through the ranks of the city's criminal underworld.

◀ **Anti-hero**
In GTA the player plays a hero, but one with a criminal mission.

▶ **Unlikely hero**
Mario started life as an unlikely hero, but is now often called upon for help. In Super Mario Sunshine he is wrongly accused and must clear his name.

Playing god

There is another genre of game that uses the idea of restoring balance to a world in chaos, but approaches it from a slightly different angle. In a 'god game' the world starts in balance and it is your job to maintain this balance or restore order if the world becomes chaotic. In Sim City, for example, you are constantly balancing multiple variables to make sure your citizens are a happy bunch. You battle everything from power outages, natural disasters, and even an occasional random attack by Godzilla. If you maintain order and refuse to let chaos reign, you're successful.

Taking this one stage further, there is no real reason why this dynamic of balance couldn't be applied to a game like Super Mario Sunshine. Instead of the player reacting to events, you could twist the Mario game into a proactive game. In Super Mario Sunshine, the damage has already been done – the graffiti is already on the walls. If this were twisted slightly you could change the dynamic, so Mario had to stop the island from becoming a mass of spray paint. If you managed to stop all the graffiti artists, balance would be maintained. However, if the street art got out of hand, the island's inhabitants might turn on Mario, shifting the challenges of the game from policing to protection.

Whatever your scenario, one thing stays true – even for Microsoft Flight Simulator. The player is the most important person in the gameworld and the centre of all the action.

Godlike view

With a god-like overview and the capability to affect the world on a massive scale, Sim City allows players to exercise their whims and fancies over the urban landscape. Styles of management result in differing outcomes – grimy, industrial dystopia (left) or gleaming, well-run metropolis (right).

FLIGHT SIMULATOR

In simulators, the player's role is to be 'himself', but engaged in an activity he may never have access to.

1 Difficulty
The difficulty level affects the degree of satisfaction the game provides.

2 New pilot
Create and save pilot details based on existing parameters.

3 Career path
The player can plot his career path, with implications for goals and level of difficulty.

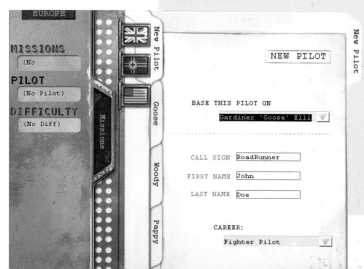

Difficulty curves

Testing the player over time

When considering how to pace the level of difficulty in a game, the general rule is 'start easy and end hard'. This means that most players will be able to play most of the game. It also means that the player is given time at the beginning to learn all his character's moves. It also means that the game will have some longevity, as it may take many attempts to complete the final stages.

Varying the approach

A simplistic approach to pacing the difficulty level in a game is to gradually increase it as the game progresses; this is quite often successful, but there are alternatives. One simple variation is to introduce dips in the difficulty curve to give the player some time to relax and prepare for the next rise. This can increase the tension and drama in the game, especially if the player begins to recognise the pattern – introducing an anticipatory feeling of calm before the storm.

Quality Assurance

When designing a game it will probably feel like a fairly natural process to increase the difficulty as the game progresses, adding more features and harder challenges toward the end of the game. It is often common for designers to make early levels too hard though, because as they develop a game they often get very good at it. This is where Quality Assurance (QA) becomes invaluable. QA is the team of people who test the game for bugs, inconsistencies and for how well it plays. They provide the development team with constructive criticism and feedback from an objective point of view.

The QA testers log their findings on a questionnaire, an example of which is shown on the right. The details are important to provide consistent, comparable feedback.

QA test sheet

Tester
Who found the problem? They may need to demonstrate it to others in the team if it is hard to spot.

Developer/Publisher contact
A tester may be working for more than one developer or publisher. The developer or publisher might specify a point of contact.

QA test sheet

Name
The name of the game. The team may be involved in testing several.

Date
The date is particularly important in relation to the development milestones of the game.

QA test sheet

Issue
A brief description of the problem.
Location
Where it occurs in the game.
Severity
What level of seriousness is the bug?
Explaination
A full explanation of the fault.
Resolution
The tester may record a suggestion as to how the problem may be fixed.
Refer to
The tester may record whose responsibility it is to fix this problem.

Game: Relentless

Date: 02/02/07

Tester: C. Ryan

Developer contact: E. Smith/Imagination Gam

Publisher contact: R. Kostos/Gamevision

Issue: The player character becomes stuck and c complete a level resulting in the game being unfinish

Location: Beginning of level 5.

Severity:
Critical / ~~Severe / Minor / Cosmetic~~

Explanation: The player character is requir place objects in such a way that they can esca a room. By moving these objects they inevitably become blocked in.

Resolution: The positioning of the objec needs to be re-thought.

Refer to: M. Clinton

Choices

Non-linear games such as Grand Theft Auto and Elite offer a differing difficulty experience, because they give the player more choice in how they play the game and what they do. To a lesser degree, level-based non-linear games, such as Burnout 3, give the player choice too, by allowing him to select one of a small number of levels to play. However, Grand Theft Auto 2 is particularly interesting in this area as it allows the player to choose the difficulty of the missions by selecting different telephones within the game itself. This complete integration of difficulty choice into the gameworld really opens up opportunities for the player in terms of how he wants to play the game. It forces the player to question himself about how skilful he actually is, and how much effort he wants to put in. This self-questioning element could be considered a game on its own – but is lacking from the more recent GTA titles.

▲ ▶ **Dips in the difficulty curve**

Shadow of the Colossus takes the concept of pacing play through dips in the difficulty curve to extremes, as the game consists entirely of a few huge 'boss' opponents, and the rest is almost empty, but beautiful, scenery. The player has little to do but ride around until he finds a Colossus. This then leads to a period of intense, kill-or-be-killed action between the player character and the much larger Colossus.

Adaptive play

A good way to play with difficulty curves is by monitoring what the player is doing and how well he does at particular tasks. If he seems to be particularly bad at one activity then it may be possible to make it easier. If he excels at an activity it can be made more challenging. This process is sometimes known as the adaptive difficulty system and has been used in games such as Rainbow Islands. It is a neat idea in theory and has many advantages for the player. For the developer it is trickier because all games need to be tested thoroughly, and adaptive play means that comprehensive testing of all permutations is difficult or even impossible. Developers have to be very careful; the parts of the game the player enjoys most must not be too hard, and the parts the player enjoys but isn't good at must not be too easy (the challenge of these parts may be the enjoyable aspect). Less importantly, but still something to consider, is that players comparing progress may feel cheated if the system isn't very obvious or carefully explained.

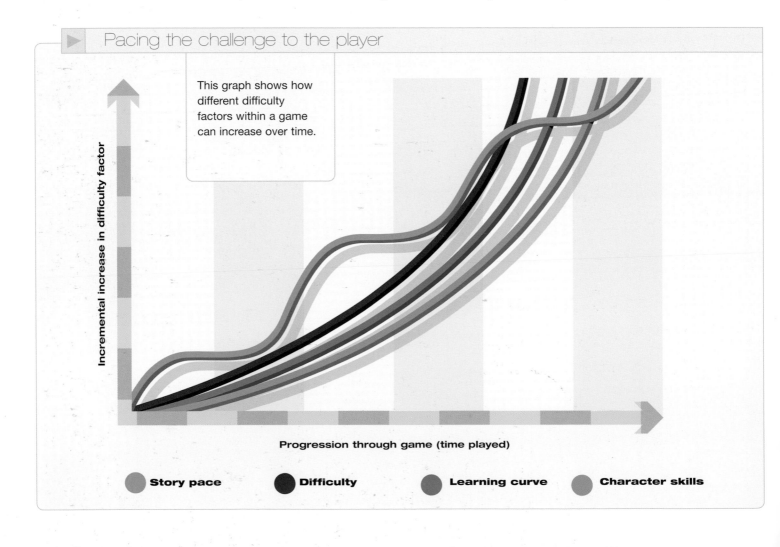

Pacing the challenge to the player

This graph shows how different difficulty factors within a game can increase over time.

Incremental increase in difficulty factor

Progression through game (time played)

● Story pace   ● Difficulty   ● Learning curve   ● Character skills

BURNOUT 3

1 Player position—as the player gains experience he learns that being first is not always the best position.

2 Lap counter—the player must interpret when in the race to make his move against his opponents.

3 The boost-meter is a reward for driving skilfully. Players can accumulate boost to accelerate faster.

4 Speed influences the outcome of manoeuvres. The player learns to judge when moves are viable.

▶ **Mastering the game**

Burnout 3 is a racing game that encourages you not only to race as an individual, but to actively drive dangerously and cause you opponents to crash. As well as mastering car-racing, the player must learn high-speed manoeuvring stunts in order to win, and cause massive pile-ups among his opponents. In mastering this game, the player must make extensive use of the on-screen help provided in the form of an HUD. The player uses valuable information built up as the game progresses in order to succeed.

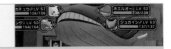

Game design catchwords

Exploiting industry standards and clichés

There are many possibilities facing a game designer. The challenge is to learn not to become overwhelmed by these possibilities and end up developing a confused and unsatisfactory game. In order to maintain clarity, a designer should always be aware of three useful catchwords to aid his gameplay design – simplicity, consistency and fairness.

▼ Internal logic

Though the strange environment in Shadow of the Colossus (left) is populated by giant fantasy creatures, the game has its own internal logic. Oddworld: Munch's Oddysee (right) is set in a bizarre world, yet the player can quickly accept this as the norm as the game makes sense on its own terms.

Simplicity

A phrase that may be familiar to you is K.I.S.S. or 'keep it simple, stupid' – a little insulting perhaps, but good advice. When designing games there can be a tendency to over-complicate issues, quite often with the best intentions. However, it is highly likely that a simple solution will be the most satisfactory one.

Consider the following example. Why force the player to go into his inventory, select a key, use the key, and then go back from the inventory to open a door? The player has the key, he wants to go through the door, so let him! In this case simplicity translates directly as 'interface ergonomics'.

Consistency

Players will immerse themselves in any type of behaviour, no matter how bizarre or ridiculous, within a gameworld, as long as it is consistent. Two important concepts for maintaining consistency are verisimilitude and suspension of disbelief.

Verisimilitude

When applied to games, verisimilitude means that once you have created a story or setting with its own internal logic, players will accept what is 'real' in your created world but will sense a fault if something unexpected appears. For example, players accept the existence of giant creatures in Shadow of the Colossus. These giants must be scaled by the player to find their weak points and defeat them, equipped only with a horse, bow and sword. But if a laser pistol were introduced – essentially another fantasy item – it would not seem right as it would be a technological item in a primitive game. Yet the whole thing is fantasy. It is the designers' skill in maintaining consistency when developing the story and the world the game takes place in that makes it seem real.

Suspension of disbelief

Suspension of disbelief refers to the readiness of the player to put aside his critical faculties and accept fantastic creations. Many games concern fantasy events – in terms of science fiction or surreal themes, or in allowing us to play in a familiar world but without societal constraints. If the player could not suspend his disbelief, he would not enjoy the troubled adventures of Munch in Oddworld: Munch's Oddysee. This world is quite different from our own. The trials Munch faces and how he deals with them are surreal compared to the player's experience.

Designers are therefore free to create quite fantastic worlds that may require extraordinary in-game behaviour to master, but as long as they are consistent in applying features to the gameworld, the player will willingly accept the game and enjoy the varied challenges and rewards it presents.

Fairness

Players should always be able to understand the reasons for things happening to their on-screen persona. As a player there is no worse feeling than being cheated. Whether this is by bad luck, or by the devious actions of an opponent, it usually means that the player becomes so unhappy with the game that he never plays it again. This can be disastrous for a computer game if players feel cheated by poor design or inconsistent in-game opponents. There is a fine balance between a game being fair and being challenging. This balance comes down to the skill of the designer. If the pace and challenge of the game seem too difficult then a player will quickly get the feeling that he cannot succeed no matter how hard he tries. Likewise, if there is an unavoidable pitfall, this could prove to be a disincentive to carry on with the game. Players will delight in challenges of all types depending upon the game, from the hidden sniper to the complex pattern puzzle. It is your job as a designer to make sure that they are entertained by your challenge and not dissuaded from play.

▶ Game design clichés

It's always handy to be aware of game design clichés, either to use them, avoid them, or even subvert them. Here are three examples.

A key opens a door

This design cliché is seen practically everywhere from very early games right up until now. The basic version is simple: a door prevents you getting any further; to get to the next area, you must find the key to unlock the door. But there may be more than one key and more than one door, each key only opening a specific door. The 'door' might not be a door at all – it might be a monster – but to defeat it and progress, you need to find a magic sword and use it on the monster. It's still essentially the same thing.

Collecting things

A simple way to add longevity to a game is to fill it with things to collect. There will always be a percentage of people who, if collecting is involved, want to collect everything. The collection mechanic works best if there are rewards for collecting certain percentages of the total in the game and strong information design (see page 118) to encourage it and show progress. Collected items may form an essential part of the game or be a completely separate component. It's a simple, easy, and successful design pattern, but it can be overused and unrewarding.

Upgrading and power-ups

Improving a character's abilities is an old industry standard. Pac-Man used this to great effect with the Power Pill, and Elite's incredible range of ship modifications gave the player reason to play well and allowed them some customisation of their ship. Things haven't changed much since then, the only real difference being the range of objects which can be modified and to what extent they can change.

◀ Collecting
In Pokemon, the player must collect all the monsters in order to succeed.

02: Design Process

Starting the design process

Organising ideas and resources

The 'design process' refers to the ideal way in which a computer game should come together – from first ideas to the finished code handed over for manufacturing. This process can be incredibly complex, even for a small game. There is no set order to follow to achieve an end result, and each company will have its preferred method of organising resources. Companies are continually changing and refining their development processes to suit specific games. The start of the design process comes when there is an idea for a new game. This initial spark can come from several sources.

Existing Intellectual Property

Working with an existing Intellectual Property (IP) means that the game is intended to embody a previously existing idea. Possible sources include films, TV, comics or even existing computer games. Development of an existing story or concept is quite a common feature of the modern game development world, perhaps chiefly due to the fact that it can be an extremely lucrative proposition. Competition for the rights to certain intellectual properties can be fierce. Intellectual property rights can cover all sorts of subjects from sports to comics, films to existing games.

Similar theme

So-called 'me too' products are another example of a common start for a game's life. For example, if game company A has a successful title concerned with classic racing cars, then as the director of game company B you might direct your designers to come up with a similarly themed game with enough differences to avoid copyright infringement. Though some may criticise this as demonstrating a lack of imagination on behalf of the second company, sometimes the second game is better than the first. This may urge the original manufacturer to make a better game and so on.

 'Me too'
Unreal Tournament (left) and Quake 3: Arena (right) were released within days of each other and both follow the format of an FPS with multi-player action. Each game has its own distinct flavour, yet the gameplay is remarkably similar.

▶ **Mix and match**
The musical, *West Side Story* (left), by Leonard Bernstein, Arthur Laurents, and Stephen Sondheim, set in 1950s New York is loosely based on William Shakespeare's play, *Romeo and Juliet* (right).

Mix and match

Seemingly new ideas can come from mixing together ideas from old genres. Sometimes these ideas stem from a 'what if?' conversation; the 'what if?' may be an alternative history or the transposition of one story into a different age or setting. We can see this in such films as *Outland* (directed by Peter Iyams, 1981) which is really a retelling of the cowboy story *High Noon* (directed by Fred Zinnemann, 1952) based in a science-fiction setting. This mixing and matching of ideas can breathe life into an old idea or spawn a completely new one. Games such as Lego Star Wars give players the chance to play through one of the most popular stories of our time in the form of Lego miniatures. Warhammer 40,000: Dawn of War offers a science-fiction RTS (real-time strategy) game, with space marines and blasters facing orcs and elves, more commonly seen in swords-and-sorcery fantasy settings.

Brand new idea

Brand new ideas are the rarest and riskiest propositions in game development. Few games designers have achieved both critical acclaim and commercial success with new ideas. As a result, managers tend to be nervous of these propositions – wary that gamers may not accept a game's concept, gameplay or characters. There are many puzzle games out there, but only one Tetris. There are quite a few comedy characters, but only one Mario. Even with these caveats, as a designer you shouldn't shun new ideas. Though few see eventual production, these are examples of creativity in its rawest sense.

Creativity can be likened to an aptitude for physical sport, and as such depends on being exercised. Though your whole concept for a whole new game may not be accepted, you might have conceived of new ideas which can be transferred into other development projects.

Structuring the process

In an ideal situation, game development teams would be structured so that they can work collaboratively. Having a designer involved at an early stage can generate some new concepts, while a programmer can point out technical opportunities that might be applicable. As a number of ideas take form and the teams expand, the majority of work is for the designers and animators, with the programmers closely following, developing the code to give the creations life within the game. As this process goes on, the need for design is replaced by a greater need for 3D asset generation, level design and the implementation of the programming which will make the game run. Moving on from this stage, the testers thoroughly go through the game to find any inadvertent faults before finally pronouncing that they are satisfied. Throughout this process, the relevant managers and QA staff monitor, guide and enable the process to its conclusion.

What if?

Iconic scenes from the *Star Wars* movies such as the two shown above lent themselves to being reimagined with the main characters played by Lego people, in Lego Star Wars. This potentially surprising fusion made for a rewarding and challenging game, using concepts from both sources.

Who is involved?

At the outset of the design process there will probably be one or two individuals, or small teams, working on developing the initial ideas. These might be senior designers within the company or specialist idea-generation teams who are tasked with developing new concepts.

Once an idea is approved for further development it might be assigned to a larger team. This team will consist of most of the following groups of people:

Designers

Game designers are responsible for the look and feel of a game; they generate the concept, story, gameworld, and mechanics. They are concerned with the aspects of a game that grab the public's attention and hopefully make it a success. Under the general term of 'designer' there are sub-roles such as game designer, scriptwriter and level designer. There will also be posts ranging in seniority, from junior positions to leads, who manage many staff.

Art and animation staff

Art and animation staff give visual form to the designers' ideas, from 2D drawings right up to fully realized 3D models and animations. These visualizations are necessary to develop the game's unique style. These roles can overlap with those of the digital modellers and animators who create the assets to be included within the game.

Sound and music engineers

Sound is an incredibly important aspect of modern game design, and the roles of musician and sound engineer are critical. These roles may cover the design aspects of the game as well as the more technical side, when incorporating the soundtrack into the game programming.

Programmers

Programmers create the code for the engines that deliver games. Despite coming from highly technical backgrounds, many programmers have a creative aspect to their skills. Though creating the code may be an unforgiving logic exercise, if it is to deliver the sound of a delicate breeze or the effect of a football kicked through the air the code must be created by a programmer with a sympathy for the subject.

The obvious roles in this category are software engineers and programmers, but these areas can be subdivided – possible roles also include artificial intelligence programmer or platform designer.

Quality Assurance and testing

QA professionals and testers make sure the game works, and that it meets its specifications. Testers have a pivotal role in achieving this, by playing early versions of the game repeatedly to see if it crashes, doesn't work properly, or contains loopholes that allow the player to cheat. Becoming a tester can be a good way into the games industry, if not always a well-paid one. Testers are the kinds of players who can familiarize themselves with every aspect of a game quickly and have broad knowledge of games to compare against. Feedback from testers can range from identifying simple technical bugs to flagging up unsatisfactory aspects of gameplay.

Managers

Developing games is big business, and so the whole apparatus of company and project management comes into play. There will be an overall head of development who may have a project manager, programming manager and art director beneath him. These roles are usually filled by very experienced staff as it is their job to oversee the entire project and make sure it is all running well and to schedule.

▶ Overview of the game development process

Start of process

End of process

Level of involvement

New game proposals	Multiple idea generation	Concept selection	Game development	Game testing	Game launch

Designer
• Develops game concept
• Develops game story
• Develops game levels
• Designs game mechanics

Artist
• Produces concept art
• Develops visual identity of the game
• Generates assets
• Makes digital models

Programmer
• Develops game engine
• Prototypes game
• Implements mechanics

Animator
• Makes digital models
• Rigs models
• Implements in-game animation
• Implements cut scenes

Sound engineer
• Produces sound effects
• Produces music

Tester
• Finds problems
• Gives feedback

Managers
• Different managers oversee different stages of the process

This diagram is intended to give a general idea of the phases in a typical game development project. It does not take into account that there may be more than one project running concurrently, or that companies may have different procedures or roles.

Design inspirations

Setting your imagination free

Inspiration for a game can come from the most surprising of sources. As a games designer you should consider almost anything as a suitable starting point for a game. As the games market becomes increasingly crowded with similar products, and producers seek to jump on the current bandwagon or release yet another version of the same game, it is becoming increasingly important that designers seek to identify new sources for games, their settings, and their mechanics. Design inspiration comes from many sources and it is useful to see how some famous designers found the inspiration for landmark games.

For the designers featured in the case studies (right), outside interests and personal experiences provided fantastic inspiration for their designs, and this in turn helped them develop innovative and exciting finished games which attracted great critical acclaim. Many designers have similar tales, and they share the same factor of informed inspiration.

Cultivating inspiration

The problem with inspiration is that the more you seek it, the more it can seem to elude you. There is no magic formula that you can follow to make you creative and give you the ability to have good ideas on demand. The best practice for any would-be designer is to seek out as many different kinds of experiences as possible. This doesn't simply mean playing a lot of games – you will only end up making more of the same – but entails looking far and wide into other cultural activities such as literature, art, philosophy, and history. Getting that illuminating 'flash' of inspiration is always a rare occurrence, but with research and preparation it is possible to give the sought-after insight a little help.

► Case study 1: **Real life and literature**

Warren Spector and Harvey Smith are the designers of Deus Ex, a critically acclaimed game that is often cited as one of the best examples of a first-person shooter/role-playing game to date.

Warren Spector started his career with tabletop role-playing games and it is easy to see the influence of these types of games on the depth of the story in Deus Ex. Throughout the game there are many references to classical and modern literature. Also some of the environments in the game are real-world locations such as a damaged Statue of Liberty, Hell's Kitchen in New York City and the Wan Chai District in Hong Kong. An innovative feature of the game was the fact that the players could choose violent or non-violent means of getting through levels, with the attendant moral choices. This freedom of choice had the effect of making the game seem more real than previous linear-style FPS games. To create such a physically and psychologically rich game, the designers drew upon all their non-digital gaming experience, the literature they enjoyed reading, and real-world locations, as inspiration.

GAMEOGRAPHY

Title Deus Ex
Developer Ion Storm
Key features
- Dystopian cityscape
- Hybrid FPS and role-playing game
- Cyberpunk feel
- Literary references

1 Real-life setting

A real-life-inspired setting from Deus Ex; a dirty, dark and threatening version of Hong Kong.

2 The violent option

The player has elected to proceed through this level by violent means.

▶ Case study 2: **Childhood bug-collecting**

Nintendo has a reputation for producing innovative and popular games which achieve commercial and critical success. Two of the main designers of Nintendo Games, Shigeru Miyamoto and Satoshi Tajiri, are held in high esteem by many designers and players alike. A look at their backgrounds provides an insight into the inspiration for their most famous designs.

Shigeru Miyamoto was born in Sonobe town, Kyoto, Japan. In his youth he often explored the countryside around his home, which had a wealth of striking natural features, lakes and concealed caves. This would later provide material for his design inspiration. In 1970 he enrolled in the Kanazawa Municipal College of Industrial Arts and Crafts, and though he graduated with a degree in Industrial Design he later confessed that he spent much of his time sketching his ideas. With his degree he managed to secure a position as a staff artist within Nintendo's planning department. The inspiration of the landscape and the idea of exploration can be seen in Shigeru's games such as Mario and The Legend of Zelda.

Later in his life, while he was gardening, the inspiration for Pikmin came to him, and he developed the idea of exploring a microcosm.

Satoshi Tajiri lived in a suburb of Tokyo. In his youth he took part in the popular hobby of bug and insect collecting from the surrounding countryside. His enthusiasm for the hobby led him to try to collect as many different bugs as possible and to try to design increasingly varied and ingenious ways of collecting them.

As he grew older, the encroaching city meant that the countryside was swallowed up by building development. While at technical school, he discovered his love of digital games, and this led him to form a games magazine with some of his friends. At this time, he became fascinated by playing games with the new Nintendo GameBoy.

All the inspirational factors were in place and Satoshi's desire to allow people to enjoy collecting weird beasts from the surrounding countryside and trade them gave rise to the concept of Pocket Monsters, or Pokémon, as it later became known.

1 Catch them all

Pokémon requires the player to collect a variety of monsters, train them and use them in battle against opponents.

2 Microcosm

In Pikmin, the microscopic world of the garden is transformed into an exciting and dangerous fantasy gameworld.

GAMEOGRAPHY

Title Pokémon
Developer Nintendo
Key features
- Collecting element—player aims to capture the range of Pokémon
- Though Pokémon fight each other they don't die, they only faint

Sketchbooks and notebooks

It is good practice for any designer to keep a sketchbook or notebook. This is a place for you to jot your ideas down as they occur to you. Whenever you are involved in the design of a game you will then have a rich source of personally collected information to draw on, which could help stimulate your creativity. A designer's notebooks should contain a wide range of material that has attracted and stimulated their attention over the years.

▼ Snippets

Collect interesting snippets of information and images. They may not be immediately useful, but will be there to refer to later on.

▶ Real life

Sketching and photographing real life can help to inform and inspire your character designs and animations, and make them more physically credible; even if the eventual character does not take human form.

▶ Details
Work up details for quick comparison and reference. Anything you don't use now may be useful later.

▶ Sketchy ideas
A sketchbook or notebook is a place where you can let your imagination run riot. There is no need to feel pressured into making a finished design or showing your work; just experiment and see what happens Anything that seems interesting can be developed over time into a concept for a game, environment or character. See pages 92–101 for more on developing concepts.

▼ Working drawings
Use your sketchbook as a place to work out hidden structures. Designs will be more credible if you know them inside out.

▲ Photos
Use your sketchbook as a place to gather cuttings and photos that inspire you.

Question the status quo

While searching for inspiration it is all too easy to crush new ideas before they have a chance to develop. The 'seen it before' response is most damning for a new idea. Often it is a true response, though – most games designers love games, and have played hundreds of them from all different genres and platforms since they were old enough to grab a controller. They can seem doomed to repeat what they have already seen when trying to come up with new ideas. To counter this it is a good idea to force yourself to think of different responses to familiar situations – to think laterally.

For instance, the designers of Activision's Call of Duty 2 recognised that the concept of the health pack was an artificial mechanism in their earlier games. Simply moving over a green first-aid box was not a very realistic representation of getting first aid for gunshot wounds. Obviously the game would become pretty boring if the player simply became incapacitated when shot (this is too real). So their solution was that when a player was hit by an enemy bullet, the edges of the screen would flash red and the player's vision would blur, his movement would slow down, and his ability to aim would be reduced. On top of this, a sound effect of the player gasping in pain left him in no doubt that he was in trouble! If the player received no further damage then he returned to normal health. This innovative mechanic variation made significant changes to the FPS gameplay, by making the player think more tactically and use the available cover more effectively, rather than charging in, getting wounded, and hoping to stay alive long enough to run over the 'magical' health pack.

This type of solution must have arisen from designers asking basic questions such as 'why are there health packs in games?' and 'what if there weren't any?' The answer is an innovative approach in Call of Duty 2, not seen in other games at the time. If you can learn to ask these 'awkward' questions and then seek to answer them, you will find that it can drive you toward innovative answers.

▼ **Shock system**
In Call of Duty 2, the usual method of measuring the player's health was replaced by a more 'realistic' system. When the player is shot, he feels the effects of his injuries, but gradually returns to normal if he avoids being wounded again.

▶ Independent games developers

Even though the games market seems dominated by large games developers, there are still many smaller, independent games developers. These outfits usually employ a small number of people and develop games either for web browsers, PCs, or the mobile phone gaming market. Because these independent developers are not tied to making large profits and therefore do not need to develop 'sure-fire hits' they can experiment by making games which explore themes that are not normally investigated.

The Independent Games Festival (www.igf.com) has been running since 1998. This festival gives a public platform to smaller games developers. It celebrates independent games, giving them access to a public platform that they would not normally have, and awards significant cash prizes to companies displaying the most innovative products.

Another significant event for independent developers is the Indie Game Jam (www.indiegamejam.com), an event held every year where games developers get together, develop radical off-the-wall ideas in a short space of time, and present them to their peers. Games such as Katamari Damacy, Rag Doll Kung Fu, EyeToy: AntiGrav, and Darwinia all have their roots at the Indie Game Jam.

Both of these events allow game creatives the space to develop and present ideas without the restrictions that big business can sometimes impose. Many of the concepts and games at these events later find their way into the mainstream, either as whole games, or game concepts and mechanics adopted into larger, more commercial games. See also Bedroom coders, page 178.

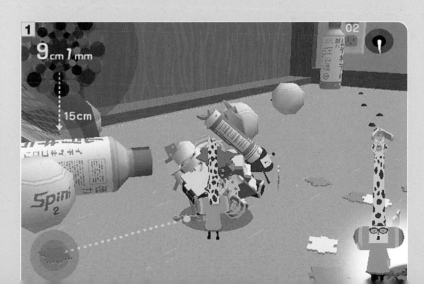

What if...

1 Your aim was to roll a big ball out of crazy objects? (Katamari Damacy.)

2 String puppets were Kung Fu masters?

(Rag Doll Kung Fu, created by Mark Heaton.)

3 You found yourself in a computerised universe, defending people from a deadly virus? (Darwinia.)

Research and development

Expanding the initial idea

Many people will have ideas for games; the first step on the path to that idea becoming reality is to undertake some basic research and development in order to expand the idea into a robust proposal. There are several simple considerations that the designer can make in order to turn the idea from a whim to a solid concept. A word of warning here – it may be tempting to jump straight into designing characters, levels, icons and other details. This is best avoided; if the basic premise of the game changes in the early development stages such work will be wasted. Good practice is to spend a relatively short but valuable amount of time at the outset making sure your idea has the potential for development. Undertake some basic research as outlined on the following pages.

Similar games

First look at games similar to the one you have in mind. Usually there will be something in the same genre, or comparable. If there is truly nothing similar out there then you may have a unique, brand-new idea. But even in this case there are likely to be games with analogous themes or game mechanics that you can look at. Having compiled a list of games, you should then play them as much as possible; while doing so keep notes about the good and bad aspects of these games. Particularly record which parts of the games fail to deliver the experience you expected. Look up the reviews of the games in the press or on the many game review sites on the web. Have all the reviews said the same thing? Do the reviews praise or condemn the same aspect of the game in question? By simply reviewing this information, and tempering it with your own experiences, you can begin to build a picture of what to include in your own proposal. Use this information to avoid the problems previous games have had, or to see which aspects were popular and therefore what details of your own concept need developing.

◄ Analytical study
Don't simply copy existing games, but truly study and analyse what they do well (and what they don't). Understanding how existing games work is an excellent first step to getting the inspiration for a new game.

News websites

News websites carry all sorts of interesting information, including social comment and technology news.

Wikipedia

Wikipedia is an ideal starting point for research. Its hyperlinked text makes it easy to broaden your areas of study.

Zeitgeist

Zeitgeist is a German word which has been appropriated into the English language; it literally translates as 'the spirit (Geist) of the time (Zeit)'. Put simply, it refers to what people are doing, thinking, using and generally enjoying at the current time. If you can pick up on a trend or interest which has not been fully exploited by the mass market, then you may have the opportunity to develop an innovative idea.

A good example is the popularity of World War 2-inspired games shortly after the release of several successful films based on that period. Extreme sports and 'urban' sports such as snowboarding and skateboarding have become popular, and particularly the counterculture associated with them. As a result there have been many games based on these sports. As an active designer you should constantly refer to as broad a range of material as possible – from news to culture, natural history to science and so on. This will keep you up to date with what is happening in the world and enable you to look outside mainstream game culture in order to bring in valuable new inspiration. Keeping your mind open to many and varied influences and sources of information will cultivate insight and inspiration when it is needed most.

Reusing game engines

Not every new computer game needs to start from scratch; quite often a new game can be developed by reusing an existing game engine. A game engine is the unseen code which drives the visual game action on screen. Within the engine are the 'rules' to the way the gameworld works, and how objects and characters behave. It is a fairly simple task to remove the visual aspects of a game, and replace them with other visual and model data, to create a new game which is very different.

Due to the fact that a game's code is usually very expensive to develop, the starting point of working with an existing game engine makes excellent financial sense for a game developer. An example of this is the re-use of Valve's Half Life 2 engine for Day of Defeat.

The next step

Having studied the factors described on these pages in relation to your own game, you will begin to get a broad idea about what features your game needs to include, what unique characteristics it may have, who might play it, and how it might be achieved. Now you are ready to begin to record some specific details about your game.

Game engines

Games with distinct engines, such as Rag Doll Kung Fu, can be valuable sources of inspiration. Using an existing game engine to empower your own ideas can be another valuable starting point, and this method was used to produce Day of Defeat.

Questions to answer

This might seem a strange way to begin the design process but there are several important questions to answer in order to give your concept form as a game and avoid a poorly defined idea. While some of the following details may change in the design process you still need to define the game at the outset.

Can you describe your game?

Can you describe the game concisely in one paragraph? If not, then your idea may still need refining until you can. This is particularly important as you will need to 'sell' your idea to others, either as part of a design team promoting ideas within a consultancy, or as an independent developer looking for a publisher. When you are selling your idea you need to grab and hold other people's attention. A good description will include the premise of the game, any unique features, and its potential market.

Example of description

Title: Celtic Awakening
This is a third-person action adventure game set within the culture of the ancient Celts. The player takes on the role of a young person who must complete several quests. The game draws upon mythology of the period. The game will feature historically accurate skills and activities. It will appeal to fans of adventure games, fantasy role-playing games, and those interested in this exciting period of history.

Can you summarise the story?

The story of a game is different from its description. A story summary should be a short paragraph which captures the essence of the story and allows others to appreciate and enthuse about it. A useful exercise to develop this skill is to practise briefly summarising your favourite films (you could set yourself a limit) while successfully communicating the story.

From this short paragraph, a person who knows nothing of the story should be able to rapidly understand its concept. In some arcade-style or puzzle games the story may not be as pivotal; in these situations you need only describe the nature of the gameplay and its challenges. The two paragraphs below describe familiar examples.

Story summary

In a distant time and place a young farmer discovers his family has a mysterious past. He joins up with a strange bunch of adventurers to seek answers. He travels to different worlds and faces many perils, which build his character and answer some of his questions but provide many more. He joins the resistance to the oppressive, evil Empire and helps with the destruction of their super-weapon, thus saving many millions of lives.

Star Wars IV: A New Hope

Puzzle game summary

Differently-shaped blocks drop from the top of the screen and pile up at the bottom. The player has to rapidly spin the blocks as they fall so that they fit together when they land. If the player manages not to leave gaps in a row of blocks then that row disappears, leaving room for more blocks. The blocks continue to drop with increasing speed and the game ends when they stack to the top of the screen.

Tetris

Which platform?

Platform consideration for games is extremely important. Some games are more suited to consoles, others to PCs. They may be designed specifically for hand-held consoles or even mobile phones. Games may work well on certain platforms and not on others. Some games would need extensive revision to work on two platform types. Many of these considerations are technical; while some are concerned with the market sector the chosen platform is designed to appeal to. At the outset of the proposal it's good to focus only on the platform(s) that would best suit your game idea and not try to stretch it to fit everything.

Platforms

- Console – Playstation, Nintendo, or Xbox?
- Hand-held console?
- PC/Mac?
- Mobile phone?
- Other niche platform?

Does it fit a genre?

Game genre, like film genre, is an easily understood and quick way of categorising your game. You are trying to firmly establish the game's provenance at this stage. Relating it to a genre will help you establish exactly what the game is about.

Genre types

- Shmup
- FPS
- Strategy
- Puzzle
- Sandbox
- Linear
- Action adventure
- Beat-'em-up
- Role-playing
- Platform
- Simulation
- God game
- Sports
- RTS

What's the target audience?

The types of people likely to make up your audience and their age range are extremely important factors in game design. Establishing the target audience will relate the development of the game to the players' perceived expectations. If you are going to meet, challenge and even exceed these expectations, you must have a clear vision of who the game's aimed at.

Age considerations are relevant for classification. The Entertainment Software Rating Board (ESRB) is a non-profit organization which provides international ratings for the entertainment software industry. As well as the audience age dictating what is admissible in a certain game it is also significant to note the size of the audience available to that rating. This is an important marketing consideration.

Establishing the audience

- What age range?
- What type of personality? Competitive? Curious?
- What type of games previously preferred?
- Platform loyalties (PlayStation, Xbox, PC, etc.)
- How to attract new players?

For future reference

By listing description, story, platform, genre and target audience in a concise document you will compile a quick-reference tool with which to answer questions arising during development about what the game should be be – and what it shouldn't.

Gathering material

Developing your ideas

Once you are committed to designing your game you need to consider the details. To develop the idea you must start to gather material that will inspire your work. These pages suggest some valuable reference sources.

Without a doubt, one of the most important research resources for a games designer is the Internet. The World Wide Web has made more information readily available than ever before. Using any search engine, you can look for written and visual references. Sometimes it is important to use a variety of search topics in order to throw out as many connected items as possible. If you find an interesting fact in your search then use that as a search topic in order to increase the scope of your research. Remember when searching not just to look at existing games as reference, but to be as broad as possible. There will be references concerning the information you are looking for directly, but also be prepared to look at connected information. Quite often it is the discovery of an apparently unrelated piece of data which can inspire a true creative insight.

Wikipedia, a free encyclopedia, is an excellent example of a site which covers a vast array of topics, all hyperlinked to similar articles within Wikipedia and elsewhere on the web. While the accuracy is sometimes disputed, it remains an easily accessed starting point for finding out information. You will probably find links to other subjects that you may not have originally thought about, and these often trigger whole new lines of investigation.

Game design sites

There are an increasing number of game-related sites—not only review and fan sites but also sites dedicated to discussing the profession, nature and sociology of games design. These sites are valuable when researching how similar games have been developed and received by players. A good source is *www.gamasutra.com* which often features insights into game-production from the point of view of the designers themselves.

▶ **Game post-mortems**
The Gamasutra website often has post-mortems of game production, written by game designers.

First-hand material

Gathering first-hand material is an excellent practice to develop. Captured images can provide invaluable reference for all kinds of realistic effects. Gathering information from your local surroundings, from the shopping mall to disused factories, can help inspire your fantasy creations too. Does the roof of that modern building look like a UFO? Perhaps that old memorial in the centre of town looks like a pillar in a dark dungeon. Use the environment around you, and not just literally – see how things might look put into different contexts, turned upside down, enlarged or reduced in size.

Real-life inspirations

Designers for Half Life 2 traveled to Eastern Europe to photograph environments for the game, while they found some of the inspiration for the characters walking down the street outside their offices. Steven Spielberg is reputed to have had the inspiration for the mothership in *Close Encounters of The Third Kind* while sitting in his car looking at the pattern of Los Angeles street lights at night. So grab your sketchbook and camera and get out into the world – it is there for your inspiration.

▲ ▶ Transferable fun
Could the playground climbing frame form the basis of a level in your platform game? Don't be afraid to let your mind play with ideas.

▶ Digital images
The availability of digital cameras makes capturing images for reference extremely simple. They can be invaluable for recording poses, textures, character references, environment references, objects and a whole variety of other uses.

Keeping references available

As your ideas begin to develop you will be influenced by a wide variety of sources. At the outset of the design process you should gather these inspirational items into one place and keep them available to remind you of what you are doing. During any design process it is essential to keep yourself inspired and fresh with your ideas.

Mood boards

A good idea that games designers can borrow from the advertising industry is to create mood boards. For example, if you were working on a game intended for a younger market, you might create a mood board incorporating children's cartoon characters, popular toys, play activities, and samples of intended colour schemes.

Each designer has his favoured method of collecting reference material and inspiration. Each new design challenge will provide a different emphasis on the type of material collected. The important factor is that this material is not only gathered but exploited fully in developing an exciting game proposal.

Reference resources

- Internet – search engines, Wikipedia and so on
- Gamasutra and other review/discussion sites
- Digital photos
- Sketches and notes
- Found material
- Cuttings
- Mood boards

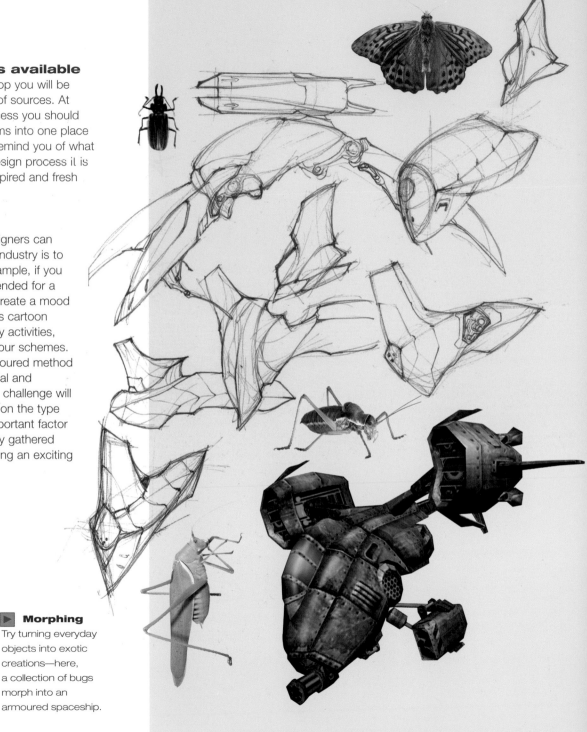

▶ Morphing

Try turning everyday objects into exotic creations—here, a collection of bugs morph into an armoured spaceship.

▶ Mood board

A mood board is a collection of images, and possibly words, selected to represent the ideals, styles, moods and aspirations of the project. The images can be sourced from anywhere and can be figurative or abstract.

Communication

A mood board embodies the the ideals of a project, captures its emotional and associated values, and communicates them quickly.

Abstract details

People tend to respond better to images than words because images (even fairly abstract ones) can convey a lot of information quickly.

Ongoing resource

A mood board can be returned to later to continue to inform designs and serve as a constant reminder of initial concepts.

Game concept

Shaping the vision

The proposal's been approved, and a wealth of reference material gathered; now is the time to develop the game concept. Rather than tackling the game as a whole, this entails breaking the idea down into its component parts and identifying their individual development needs. The six headings on these two pages will apply to most games, though each project will have its own unique emphasis. This development material will ultimately form the Game Design Document (see page 106).

Concept artwork
Concept art for an in-game asset – a creepy old mansion.

Asset artwork
Creating concept drawings of game assets such as characters, levels, vehicles and so on is a job for the designer or artist. This process is similar to the visual work undertaken in the film industry to develop the look and feel of a film. This activity will produce a great deal of concept art – both traditional and digital. This is later used by the modellers and animators when they are creating the 3D assets.

Interface
All digital games have an interface to enable the player to use them. At a basic level, this begins when the player loads the game and must navigate to the point where he starts to play. On-screen information is also presented to the player during gameplay – this is the graphical user interface (GUI). This may take the form of a head-up display, quite common in first-person games, or information such as statistics and hints. The design of this important information is crucial. A well-designed interface can add to the mood of a game before it is played.

For more on user interface and interaction design, see page 118.

Story

If the game is an adventure-style game with a story this will need as much care over its development as a film script or novel would. Game players can be very critical of poorly thought-out or naive plots with stilted dialogue. If the game is more abstract then the 'story' may take the form of a write-up of a typical game noting all the points a player may go through.

For more on storytelling in games, see page 58.

Level design

Games consist of stages, or levels. As the player progresses through a game, the levels generally increase in difficulty and the story develops. The designer must create a series of challenges for the player as he progresses through a level. This means that the design of individual levels is closely linked to the design of the game mechanics.

For more on difficulty curves, see page 66; for more about level design, see page 108.

Game mechanics

The mechanics of a game is a crucial factor in its design. There is always an opportunity to develop exisiting ideas for game mechanics, deploy them in different ways, or even develop entirely new ones. Remember though, that the game mechanics directly affect the way a player experiences a game – perhaps more so than other factors. Games with poorly designed or over-complicated mechanics are unlikely to be successful.

For more on game mechanics, see page 11.

Audio

Sound within a game is a critical aspect. There are specialist musicians and sound technicians working in the games industry, and it is their role to help build and implement the sound in a game. A designer's role at this stage is to suggest sound effects and dialogue to give the sound engineers direction in their work.

For more about audio and music, see page 160.

Character concepts

Populating the gameworld

▲ Concept
Character designs start life as concept drawings, to develop and assess their finished look.

▼ Complete
A character – Abe, from Oddworld – is modelled and posed to display its mannerisms.

Central to most first-person and third-person computer games is the character that is controlled by the player. Alongside this main character there are also friendly and unfriendly non-player characters (NPCs). It is the characters which populate the game and deliver its story. In the movie industry, casting the right actor in a role is of critical importance; so too with computer games – the difference being that games designers can create their characters from scratch. This allows for tremendous latitude in developing a persona. Many games are most memorable for their central characters, and even, in some cases, their enemies.

The development of a character is both visual and conceptual. As well as the many sketches that define the appearance of the character, the character's personality must also be considered. This will have a direct effect on the character's disposition and reactions to the situations they find themselves in. This is of course important if the character is an NPC and controlled by the game's AI, but it also has relevance if it is the central character to be controlled by the player.

Asking questions

A good way to start designing a character is to answer some questions about them, as you might for a real person. For example, what is the character's job or role in life? What is their previous experience? Answering these questions will give you some idea of the character's basic skills and abilities. Depending on the style of the game you begin to dictate some of the challenges. Is the character a skilled and experienced individual able to cope with the situation the game presents, or an unlucky individual in a situation unfamiliar to them, using their wits and raw talent to succeed? The latter is often used as a tool in all types of drama, such as the hero unexpectedly marooned on a desert island or the everyday common man suddenly faced with an alien invasion.

Back story

'Back story' refers to what has happened to the character before reaching this point in the game. As in real life, things that have happened to a character previously shape his current outlook and demeanour. A back story helps to give the player a greater understanding of a character. Back stories do not have to be too long or too detailed – just enough to give the player some reasons as to why things are as they are. One of the most famous back stories is in *Batman*. The murder of protagonist Bruce Wayne's parents drives him to become a ruthless persecutor of criminals. Very quickly the audience can appreciate what drives the central character. Back stories do not always have to be as tragic as that, and sometimes dramatic narratives can develop out of apparently simple circumstances, such as private detective Jack Walters being called on to track a missing person in Call of Cthulhu: Dark Corners of the Earth.

Behaviour and mannerisms

Once you know about your character's story and skills you can make additional decisions as to how these affect his behaviour. How does he speak? Does he have peculiar mannerisms? How does he dress? These details begin to make the character more believable and help the player to accept him.

◄ ▲ **Aura of lethal competence**
Sam Fisher, from Tom Clancy's Splinter Cell, is always shown in an athletic pose with his trademark triple-lens night-sights.

◄ ▲ **Clues**
Good game characters, such as the Fishman (above left) and Jack Walters from Call of Cthulhu (above) give the player clues to their personality, disposition and the world they inhabit. Their clothing and mannerisms all help to build atmosphere.

Importance of the character

The designer must be aware of any character's significance within the game. NPCs who are seen briefly do not need much character development, and may only need superficial details of their personalities worked out. However, the player character and major NPCs do need careful consideration. In your game you want to make the player react to the characters as if they were real. You want the player to fear for the central character's life through all the perils of the game; likewise you want the player to be fearful of their opponents.

Player characters

You may think that a player character needs relatively little in the way of detailed design, as his actions and reactions will be dictated by the player. This is not strictly true, as the basic nature of the character will affect the player's actions. If the character is knowledgeable and thoughtful the player is more likely to use their and their character's wit to resolve a conflict rather than charging in 'all guns blazing'. If the character has a strong moral code then they may seek non-lethal ways of resolving a situation. Encouraging the player to empathise with the character has a huge effect on gameplay. While everyone might enjoy a mindless rampage on occasion, it is possible to present far more subtle experiences in a game. For example, even though it is a militaristic game, Tom Clancy's Splinter Cell by Ubisoft requires the player to perform acrobatic levels of stealth and concealment in order to be successful. Attempting crude levels of violence leads to failure.

► FPS characters

Character design is important even in a first-person game. Even though gameplay is from the character's viewpoint, the player will still be presented with illustrations of the character in order to set the scene. In more sophisticated FPS games the NPCs will also be reacting to the character controlled by the player.

'Clothes maketh the man'. In Half Life 2, central (first-person) character Gordon Freeman's glasses, environment suit, and crowbar are often used even without him being present. These items have become instantly recognisable icons in the gaming world.

Appearance

As with designing any kind of visuals, it helps to begin with plenty of reference material. This is the point at which you decide how the character will look and dress. Normally you would start with the character's main body form – tall or short, fat or thin – and move on to more specific features. Then you can consider whether the character has any significant body features such as scars, hairstyles, missing limbs and so on. While you have almost complete free rein to develop the character as you wish, try to avoid making your character too outlandish unless the story requires it. Too many unique features may make a character become freakish and unbelievable.

◄ ▼ Defining a role

Clothes and personal kit add to a character's persona, and can become significant features. Lara Croft's distinctive clothing and hairstyle tell the player a lot about her no-nonsense, daredevil lifestyle. Her trademark twin pistols are never far from her hands and she is highly competent at using them. She is a character you shouldn't upset! Whether she is in polite company, tracking down clues for her next adventure, or leaping around an ancient temple, her physical strength and ability is reflected in her pose. All these visual clues help define her role within a game.

View considerations

When preparing the visuals for a character you should also be aware of the way they will be seen on-screen. If it's a third-person game, most of the time the player will see the back of the character, so that needs to be detailed. In first-person games, the player mainly sees the hands and the forearms of the character, so careful consideration is required there. NPCs usually need to be considered from all sides. However, the designer should keep in mind the relative importance of the NPCs and their time in view. More time should be spent on characters the player will see a lot of, rather than those who pass by quickly.

Longevity

Memorable characters sell games, and keep coming back. Any game with a much-loved (or feared) character is likely to have spawned many sequels. If the designer is lucky enough to hit upon a character that the audience loves to play (or defeat) it will probably enter the elite 'hall of fame' of characters cherished by game-players the world over.

As a designer you must remember that, just as you want to make players believe that they are in a different place by your creation of wonderful environments, you want them to find the in-game characters dynamic and credible. This is a key factor in the player's immersion in a game.

▶ Design exercise: **Character design**

Consider a historical time and a place; try not to pick the obvious well-worn areas such as the cowboy era or World War 2. Perhaps consider a Roman legionnaire or a 17th-century cavalier. A trip to the history section of your local library will refresh your historical knowledge and give you a starting point. For your selected period, design a heroic figure and an opponent for the hero.

For each character, undertake the following. With reference to the character, collect a series of images from magazines of persons of similar physique, facial types, relevant clothing, artefacts owned by the character and where the character lives. Be selective – about three to five images for each area should be enough to start.

Character building
Decide three positive character-building things that have happened in the character's history. Then decide on three negative character-building things that have happened in the character's history. Based on this history what is the character's present disposition? If you were to see them in a café or the street list what outward characteristics and mannerisms might you notice? Consider how they would respond if you were to ask them a question or for directions. Write out the main visual characteristics of the character and then sketch them, using the reference material to help develop your ideas.

Evaluation
By following this process for two characters you should begin to get a feel for how to bring a fictional person to life. If the character is to be a central figure in the game then you may feel the need to develop the story more. When you have completed this process, evaluate how believable the character is, particularly in relation to the situation. Ask yourself if you need to add more detail or take some away. Practice this type of exercise across different game genres and remember that not all characters are clear-cut good- or bad-guy types. Development of characters that are not immediately obvious requires careful thought. Once you have done this exercise you might wish to try it again, using a fictional time and place either of your own creation, or from existing sources.

Character concept: Polynesian warrior

POSITIVE TRAITS

• His father was knocked unconscious on a fishing trip. He navigated home; this experience made him independent and resourceful.

• He has always listened to the tribal elders; this has made him skilled in traditional crafts, especially those related to survival.

• His elder sister always teased and tricked him good-naturedly. He reacts with his mind rather than his heart in confusing situations.

NEGATIVE TRAITS

• Despite the positive effect of his family he can be hot-headed and often gets into fights.

• Despite being a skilled seaman he can still suffer from seasickness, which he is ashamed of.

• He has been troubled by dreams of 'shark men' since the incident with his father on the fishing trip when he was young.

VISUAL CHARACTERISTICS

• Powerful Polynesian build, coupled with an agile grace.

• Simple, traditional clothing such as sarong; lots of pouches, bags and belts that hold useful tools.

• Face betrays emotions. Beaming smile, terrifying when angry.

Environment concept

Spaces for playing in

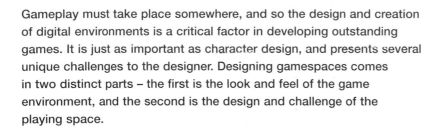

Gameplay must take place somewhere, and so the design and creation of digital environments is a critical factor in developing outstanding games. It is just as important as character design, and presents several unique challenges to the designer. Designing gamespaces comes in two distinct parts – the first is the look and feel of the game environment, and the second is the design and challenge of the playing space.

Once the general concept and the setting of the game have been decided on, work can begin on developing the look and feel of the game in more detail. As with film and television, the environment is a key factor in determining the overall mood of the finished product.

Atmospheric effects

Atmospheric effects play a vital role in environment design. An old building can look perfectly normal by day but in the fog it can take on a sinister appearance which hints at drama yet to unfold. Weather can also be a game mechanic; not only do fog and rain make environments appear more enigmatic, but they also hinder hearing, vision and movement. Simply walking on the deck of a ship can become a life-or-death struggle in a gale-force storm.

Lighting

Careful consideration of the lighting of an environment is particularly effective, as it taps into one of humanity's oldest fears – fear of the dark. By pitching areas into darkness or building gloomy corners into a level, the designer can significantly raise the anxiety of a player. In the charged atmosphere of a game environment this is an extremely effective tool.

 Poor lighting
A good example of making the normal world eerie and sinister is seen in the Silent Hill games. An ordinary town is transformed into a sinister, frightening place simply through the use of mist and poor lighting.

 Environment checklist

Here are some questions to ask yourself when you are considering the environment concept:

- Is the game set in a high-adventure, glossy, comicbook world?
- Or is it a gritty, down-at-heel, on-the-skids type of game?
- Does the game need to represent the real world?
- Is it set in the present day, a period from history, or in the future?
- What kind of mood do you want to create – threatening, safe or exciting?

Remember – by getting the appearance of the game right, you aid the player in suspending their disbelief and entering the game more fully.

◀ Rendering

A game environment becomes atmospheric when it is fully textured and lit. These two student pieces show how simple and unremarkable, neutrally-rendered rooms become interesting gamespaces with the addition of lighting and texture. The environments begin to hint at the type of game action that may take place within them.

▲ ▶ Effects

Even with light and shadow, a scene can still appear a little 'flat'. With the addition of some atmospheric effects, directional lighting, and insignia, the space starts to display the potential for dramatic tension.

Form and scale

The form of an environment is an important factor to consider. On a subconscious level, humans accept a certain form of architecture and have a feeling for when a space is big or small. In the real world, people generally prefer their environments to be regular and neat. Even when buildings are unusual, monumental, or decorative, there are certain conventions of form that people expect. As an environment designer you have the luxury of subtly warping these forms; you can make spaces tight and claustrophobic or enlarge them until they are massive and dominating. Spaces do not have to be regular. They may use a certain decorative motif which is at odds with the usual ideal. Playing with these details can add an uncomfortable air to an environment that is difficult to pin down, but highly effective. Of course, the opposite is also true – if you want the player to relax you can take visual cues from pleasant and meditative spaces.

◀ ▼ Spaces

Take inspiration from the world around you. How do different interior spaces feel? Enclosed and claustrophobic? Or pleasant and meditative?

▼ Challenging

In *The Poseidon Adventure*, the mundane world becomes a challenge, as eveything is literally turned upside-down.

Tricks of perception

A useful trick is to make the familiar unfamiliar. This technique can be used to great effect in challenging the player's assumptions. By providing a space which at first glance seems natural and then introducing a change to that space you can provide the player with a surprise and a challenge. Cinematically this was used to great effect in the 1972 film *The Poseidon Adventure* (remade in 2006 as *Poseidon*). A passenger cruise-ship is turned upside down by a freak wave and a group of survivors have to make their way out of the inverted ship before it sinks. The fact that the ceiling becomes the floor, staircases are inverted, and doors are now high up the walls presents many challenges to the heroic band.

Set for action

The in-game environment is a stage-set for the action of the game to take place. Environments must provide the space and ambience to host the various challenges of opponents, puzzles and trials within the game. Once the look and feel of the environment have been designed, level design can begin (see page 108).

Take a fresh look at one of your favourite first- or third-person games and consider the environments where the action takes place. Now challenge yourself to describe in written words and pictures another environment, of your own choosing, for the game you chose. Consider how the environment should be to remain in keeping with the original game.

• What would the overall look be?
• What details would there be?
• What would the lighting and atmospheric effects be like?

Collect reference material to inform your idea (see page 88) and then begin to sketch out your proposed environment. A good way to test your ideas is to discuss with other gamers (who are familiar with the original game) whether or not they think your new environment would be suitable, and the reasons for their decision.

Observation

An observational exercise you can do to sharpen your environment design skills is to take note of the lighting and visual style of environments in films. This is made much easier with the judicious use of the pause button on a DVD player. Film-makers are experts at creating a visual setting very quickly and you could do much worse than borrow ideas from the masters. Similarly, if you ever visit a theme park or an amusement park, take note of the visual clues that the designers have used to set the mood of a ride. Ghost trains are an obvious example of a specific environment but there are many others.

1 Scary effects

Some of the most obvious scary effects are used in ghost trains, but still they make people jump!

2 Scale

Theme parks often have larger-than-life edifices designed to entertain and amuse. You can observe the visual tricks used by the designers in creating them.

Communication and writing

Selling your ideas

Developing the initial concepts of a game – the overall idea, the characters and environments – generates an enormous amount of important information. The clear and accurate recording of that information is therefore critical. Different stages of the process are associated with different kinds of documentation. Whatever purpose you are writing for, though, there are four simple rules to remember.

Be concise

There will be lots of information generated in the design and development of even the simplest game. Don't be verbose – you are writing a working document, not a novel. State the information in as short and precise a way as possible.

Be accurate

The document will relate to the endeavours of a team of people and will have serious financial implications. Inaccuracies and vagueness cause mistakes. If they are not spotted quickly mistakes can become compounded and grow into big problems. Check your accuracy and make sure what you write is right!

Provide easy access

In your documentation, make sure the text is well formatted and easy to read. Use page and section numbers logically. Put a contents page at the front of the document for easy access. Use clear headings and add footnotes for particularly complex parts of the document. Above all, use a clear font at a reasonable size. Do not set a document in a fancy font as it may be difficult to read. Likewise, making it any less than 10-point in size will only give people headaches – 12-point text is preferable.

Check spelling and grammar

Games documents must be read and understood by many people; often the document will be 'selling' your idea to somebody else. In this case, there is nothing worse than poor spelling and grammar. It looks unprofessional and clumsy, and will detract from your work. Word processors can spell-check and grammar-check with quite ruthless efficiency. Make sure you use this facility. However, even with this feature, word processors cannot proofread. Proofreading is the manual reading of a printed document, usually by somebody not directly involved with its creation. Proofreaders will spot mistakes such as the confusion between 'there' and 'their', 'where' and 'were' and so on. They will spot mistakes that computers can't pick up. Try always to get somebody to read your documents, especially if it is a sales pitch. If you have the services of a professional proofreader, treat them with respect as they can save you a lot of embarrassment.

Different games development companies will have different types of documentation so there is no industry standard as such. But there is one type of important document which is fairly universal – the pitch document.

▲ Cover

First impressions last. Make the cover of a pitch document atmospheric and exciting; make the reader want to open it and find out more. In this example, signs, symbols and terminology normally associated with danger were used to excite the reader's imagination and entice him in.

The pitch document

The pitch document is designed to sell or 'pitch' an idea to prospective game developers and producers. The pitch document is usually the first chance for people outside the original development team to see the game proposal, so it must make a very good impression. Pitch documents can vary in length between two and twelve sides of letter paper – their length is determined by the detail in the game. It is a matter of judgement as to the exact length – you should aim to be neither too brief nor too lengthy. Developers and producers get to see a large number of pitch documents in their working lives so if you are to be successful you need to make your pitch document stand out, grab attention and leave a lasting impression.

▼ ▶ Visuals

Make the pitch document look exciting. Make sure you use lots of the pre-production artwork and character models to give the reader an instant idea of the look and feel of the game and hopefully inspire him to find out more. Make sure the layout is clear and that all the facts contained within the document are accessible.

NOTICE

MASON

HIGHLY TRAINED SPECIAL FORCES OPERATIVE ABLE TO HANDLE A WIDE RANGE OF WEAPONS TRAINED IN HAND TO HAND COMBAT CAN BLEND INTO HIS ENVIRONMENT

Scrapbook style

The pitch document was designed as if it were a journal kept by one of the characters from the game, full of clippings and other information rapidly assembled in a scrapbook style. The terminology used is brusque and evocative.

Enemy concept

Concept artwork of an enemy has been presented as clippings and 'photos'. The clipped, punchy written description highlights the strengths, weaknesses, and abilities of the enemy.

Outline facts

At this early stage in the development process, it is unnecessary to burden the reader with precise statistics and game terminology; these details will probably change as the game is designed.

DANGER

ATOMIC LOOTER

WELL ARMED AND ORGANIZED ! WILL STOP AT NOTHING TO REMAIN UNDETECTED ! WORK IN GROUPS ! HEAVILY ARMOURED !

DANGER

FEELERS

HUNT USING THEIR HEIGHTENED SENSE OF ͓ CAN PICK UP ON THE SLIGHTEST VIBRAT͓ FOUND IN DAMP, WARM AREAS ! LONG AND POWERFUL FINGERS !

Detailed information

The pitch document is a chance to present your game's unique selling points. These are any factors that are not available in the current market. Is the game a completely different genre? Does it take advantage of new technologies? Highlight the unique aspects of your game that will make it a 'must-have' for gamers.

Identify the target audience for the game. Developers and producers are always interested in the size of the potential market for a game – the bigger the market, the bigger the sales. If a game will develop a new market or attract other players not normally associated with this market then it may develop a larger following.

Do not forget the technical aspects of the game such as platform, game engine or any potential developments. All of these factors can simultaneously incur cost (for example developing specific software) and indicate market size by popularity of platform.

▼ Game overview

The pitch document should provide an overview of the game dynamics. For example: are there any innovative mechanics? Does the game belong to a ground-breaking genre? Try to convey how the game will play and how exciting it is going to be.

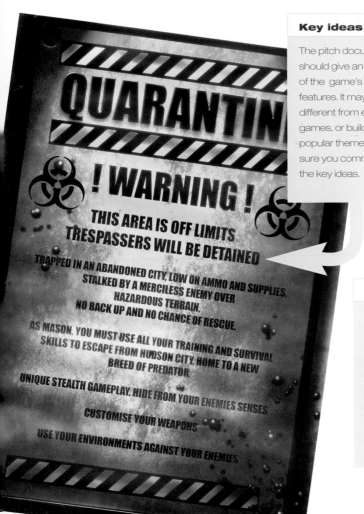

Key ideas

The pitch document should give an overview of the game's unique features. It may be entirely different from existing games, or build upon popular themes. Make sure you communicate the key ideas.

Storyline information

The game's storyline is developed in the pitch document, in this case taking the form of autopsy reports of creatures encountered within the game. As this is a concept for a single-player game, the storyline is extremely important. It is crucial to ensure that the pitch gives adequate coverage to the make-or-break themes of your game.

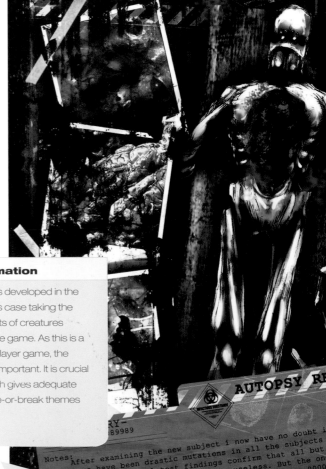

▶ Balanced tone

A pitch document should sell the idea without being overconfident; it should engage the reader without attempting to misguide them. When creating a pitch document be sure you are not promising concepts or ideas that you cannot hope to deliver. In the games industry you might get away with it once – but not twice.

Environment

The scrapbook feel of this pitch document is ideally suited to representing the physical characteristics and bleak mood of the gameworld, a shattered cityscape.

Pitch document checklist

- Make sure the overall integrated design (words and images together) of the pitch document supports the nature and intention of the game.

- Be as concise as possible. The pitch document has to catch the reader's imagination quickly and make him want more. If it becomes too verbose there is a danger the reader will lose interest.

- Make the design of the document reflect the excitement and flavour of the proposed game.

- Ensure that the game's USPs are made explicit and can be easily understood.

- Cover all the major aspects of gameplay and the gameworld so the reader will get an idea of what needs developing should the game be taken to the next stage.

- Don't promise what you can't deliver. The game concept should be exciting enough to carry the pitch without the need to make false promises and set unrealistic goals.

What next?

After the pitch document has been accepted, work can begin in earnest on developing the game. This activity goes hand in hand with the development of perhaps the most pivotal document – the Game Design Document (see page 104). The issues of imparting key information and clarity are as applicable to the GDD as they are to the pitch document.

Detailed design specifications
The Game Design Document

The detailed design specification is often referred to as a Game Design Document, or GDD for short. Each different games developer will have their own version of this document and its component parts. The example shown opposite is a generic summary to provide an overview of the elements that a GDD should contain. The GDD is a pivotal part of the design process. It becomes the main point of reference for the ongoing design and development of the game. Everybody in the design team will refer to it to guide their work. Clarity and an accessible format for this document is therefore paramount. It is a large document; but remember that size does not equal quality. You should always aim to be accurate and concise in your written work.

The sections of the GDD presented opposite may be combined in one document, or spread through several documents, based upon the decision of the team. The document should have one overriding editor who maintains consistency but, as you will see from the contents, the document is the result of differing contributions depending on the skill area.

Good practice

As the design process is a fluid one which will call for review and compromise during the development of a game, so too the GDD may change. It is important that the GDD logs change history in order to keep track of the decisions made during development. The sample GDD shown here acts as a general checklist; it cannot hope to be completely inclusive, as every game and design team will have different requirements. In the table, each section has subsections such as Technical Specification, Art Direction, Level Design Document, Technical Specification and Sound Specification. Designers should also remember the collaborative nature of developing a game; though this checklist is broken into areas of responsibility the reality is that every section of the development team will have an input of some sort into each area of the game. An obvious example is the shared responsibility for animation sets between the artists and the programmers.

 Sample GDD

This is an example of the sections of a GDD, with general indications of who is responsible for each section, and what the section contents are. Different games developers and designers have their own versions of this document, and it may also vary depending on the nature of the game. This example covers most of the main points that should be included in a GDD and is intended as a starting point for student designers.

Concept by: David Woodman
Date: 2007
Working title: The Lockup
Genre: View RPG; sandbox
Target age: 15 to 24
Platform: Sony PSP

▶ GDD opener

The front section of a GDD, comprising important details and a brief synopsis.

SYNOPSIS

Sentenced without trial or reason you play a character trapped in a maximum security prison in the Atlantic Ocean. Based on an old oil rig the prison contains some of the most violent men in the world, with your character thought to be no exception.

With no one believing your innocence and the odds stacked impossibly against you, escaping the fortress oil rig becomes your sole objective. With the ability to trade, steal, corrupt, and build, it's up to you to develop your mode of transport out of the prison in total secrecy.

STORY

Without trial or any visible reason, Robert Brennan is sent to one of the world's highest security prisons without a second thought that it might have been a case of mistaken identity or misplaced evidence. As Robert Brennan is taken away in a life-changing moment, thoughts run through his mind of how this could have happened – how could he have been mistaken for a world class criminal? Branded a convicted criminal, no-one believes a word he has to say, or cares whether he's innocent or not.

In the middle of the night Robert Brennan is removed from his cell and bundled into the back of a security van. Shortly after that he's hooded by the law enforcement officer and taken out of the van to what seems to be some sort of docks. A short conversation takes place and an exchange of papers before Robert is dragged onto a helicopter with several other people.

The Game Design Document (GDD)

	SECTION	CONTENTS
MARKETING	Cover page	Game name, company name, version number, chief editor.
	Game concept	A quick overview of the game concept. Some of this text can be lifted from the pitch document.
	Game synopsis	This is an overview of the actual game itself; an abbreviated version of the game narrative.
	Gameplay elements and features	A list of the major components and characteristics within the game.
	Market consideration	What market is this game aimed at? Size, popularity, competitors, opportunities, etc.
	Platform	Which platforms is the game aimed at?
GDD	Story synopsis	A short breakdown of the story to give the reader an idea of how the following sections about gameplay relate without having to read the full walkthrough.
ART	Look and feel	How the game appears visually, and its overall mood. Reference to colour palettes, lighting, other visual references such as films and so on. This gives the artists their direction when developing the visual character of the game.
GAMES	Game objective	What is the ultimate aim of the game in terms of the in-game activities as well as the player experience?
	Game mechanics	List and illustrate the mechanics that are used in the game.
	Menu systems	How does the player navigate through the game? *Introduction – game profiles – saved games – control settings – audio settings – graphic settings – difficulty level – multi-player options – special features.*
	Controls	Describe and illustrate how the player interacts through the gamepad or keyboard.
	In-game information	Does the game have a HUD? Are there health bars? What information is on screen during play?
	Character movement and interaction	Using the controls, how does the on-screen character move and interact with other characters? *Movement – combat – special actions – mapping – using items – inventory*
	Character health and power	How does the character's health work? What happens if they are damaged? How are they healed? How do they die? How do other measurable attributes work?

	SECTION	CONTENTS
TECHNICAL	Camera systems	Camera handling *Movement and boundaries – camera angle – uneven terrain – corners – walls – small spaces – player look, free look, defaults*
GAMES	Gameworld	What is the level-structure of the gameworld? Is it simply linear, hub and spoke, or sandbox with individual missions?
	Game physics	How do things work in the gameworld? How fast can the character run? How far can they jump? How do inanimate objects act and react?
	Non-player characters	A list of all non-player characters NPC stats – motivations – disposition – equipment – when they occur – place in the story
	Equipment and effects	What equipment is available in the game? What does it do? How does it affect the gameworld and/or NPCs?
TECH	Animation sets	List of all the animations that will be needed in the game.
ART	Animation sets	List of all the animations that will be needed in the game.
GAMES	Game script Game walkthrough	The story or narrative of the game. Level descriptions Level walkthrough – level maps (2D and/or block map) – NPC locations – encounter locations – game time elapsed
TECHNICAL	Program design	• Game engine • Collision systems • Physics • Lighting • Rendering • AI • Polygon counts • Draw distance • • Engine operations • Video streaming *Note: Despite the apparent shortness of this section, do not underestimate the significant amount of work it comprises.*
	Sound design	• Sound use • Dialogue • Spoken script • Music *Note: Despite the apparent shortness of this section, do not underestimate the significant amount of work it comprises.*
GDD	Appendices	Other information relevant to the game; particularly a list of revisions in order to track game development.

Level design

Games within games

The term 'level design' refers to individually designed sections of a game. The idea of levels comes from early shoot-'em-up and platform games, which would typically have sections of action, each increasing in difficulty. Level design happens after the main concept has been fleshed out and the game mechanics have been identified. This sequence is important as the level designers must have a sound understanding of the actions, locations and game mechanics appropriate to the game.

This original level format still exists in some simpler games such as 2D platform games and puzzle games, but the definite beginning and ending of a level as well as the order in which they can be tackled tends to vary in sophisticated modern games. Role-playing and sandbox games such as Grand Theft Auto and Elder Scrolls present the player with a variety of missions. These missions take the place of levels and allow the player to progress.

Subdividing the story

Computer games can be broken into smaller sections or levels just as books and films are broken into chapters or scenes. Action-packed scenes are often alternated with quieter sections. This helps to build the dramatic tension and provides respite between bouts of intense activity. Nonstop action would cause most players to become tired too quickly. Gentler play at the start of a game also gives the player a chance to become familiar with the game controls and mechanics.

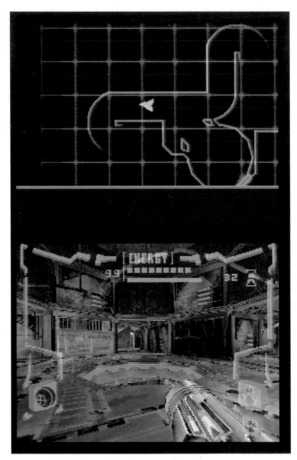

◀ Backwards and forwards

The levels in Metroid Prime offer some variety in how the player can tackle them. He may have to move backwards and forwards through a level to unlock secrets or obtain skills to access parts of the level he has passed through but been unable to reach. In general, each level must be completed in order to gain access to the next level.

▼ Linear progression

In Archer Maclean's Mercury, the player must guide a blob of mercury through tilting mazes. The levels in this game are somewhat linear but there is a small amount of variety in the order the player tackles them.

Key considerations for level design

When designing game levels there are factors to consider. If you are working on an established Intellectual Property there are likely to be additional guidelines.

Fun

People play games for fun. This can manifest itself in different ways – from being scared in a horror game to completing a pattern in a puzzle. A level that is too difficult or distracting should be revised or scrapped. When a game ceases to be fun, people stop playing.

Reward

When a player tackles an enterprise, subconsciously he expects a reward. This can take the form of an increased skill-level, an in-game item, a discovered secret, or simply the satisfaction of a challenging task completed successfully. The reward must be tangible in order for the player to feel a sense of achievement.

Risk

The reward should match the risk. If the player has found your secret chamber, battled past the extra-tough ninja zombies and made the pixel-perfect jump over a robo-piranha-infested lava lake, then reward him with something worthwhile or he may feel that the game is gratuitously challenging.

Likewise, if the challenge was simple then the reward should not be as valuable.

Challenge

Players have come to expect games to have varying difficulty levels. These levels of challenge are an important response to the types of player you may have. Some players will delight in being tested to the absolute limit; others simply want a distraction – mildly challenging but not requiring a huge time investment.

The pace of challenge is important – players appreciate the opportunity to start with an easy challenge in order to practise and learn. After this they can more readily accept an increased challenge.

Consistency

Be consistent in the types of challenges you include; things that look the same should act in the same manner. For example, if one red barrel explodes when shot at, then all other red barrels should do the same.

The game concept may explore the fact that similar objects do different things, but that would be an example of a consistent challenge within the game.

Be fair

Placing traps and challenges that a player has no chance of dealing with is unfair. This can lead to a player getting stuck within a game and progressing no further.

While a player will appreciate a difficult challenge they will expect it to be possible to overcome.

Interest

This concerns maintaining the player's engagement with the game. A game can only have so many game-mechanics and will only have a limited number of opponents or challenges. It is the job of the designer to keep mixing and matching these factors in order to present variety in the challenges to the player.

Missions

The Elder Scrolls IV: Oblivion is a good example of a game with missions to complete. They become increasingly challenging, requiring the player to improve skills and collect items. The player is also free to explore the gameworld, and to ignore or postpone the missions.

Levels make the game

After the designer has created a number of levels, these are brought together to make a whole game. During level design it is important to keep track of how the levels work together. They should be consistently engaging, present an even spread of action building up to a climax, and the game's narrative should 'flow'. Meeting these requirements should result in a successful game design.

► ## How to organise a game into levels

How you organise the game will partly depend on its genre, for example whether it is a narrative, puzzle or strategy game. When identifying sections, bear in mind that there needs to be an overall increase in drama and challenge throughout the game.

Narrative games have three main parts. First, the introduction in which the scene is set; then the action, with a crisis that needs resolving; and finally the climactic resolution. These simplified parts appear within parts of the story as well as the whole. For example, the whole story may be about a farmer who lives a peaceful life (scene is set); farm and family are destroyed by bad guys (crisis); the farmer extracts vengeance on the bad guys so they will not do it again (resolution). Within the story there may be smaller parts: the farmer has no experience of fighting (scene is set); he eventually persuades a martial arts master to act as a tutor (crisis); the farmer becomes expert at unarmed combat (resolution).

Narrative games:
• **Grand Theft Auto**
• **Metal Gear Solid (below)**
• **Half Life 1 & 2**

Puzzle games As players solve puzzles in a game, they learn to adopt the game designer's way of thinking, and so gain an advantage. To counter this, the designer must think laterally, with increasing obscurity, when setting challenges. The first set of puzzles should be based around familiar approaches to solving them. Later sets should begin to utilize abstract yet legitimate methods for their solution. By organising your puzzles into groups you can begin to arrange the levels according to difficulty.

Puzzle games:
• **Tetris**
• **Sokoban**
• **Pipe Mania**
• **Archer Maclean's Mercury**
• **Bejeweled**
• **Lemmings (below)**

Strategy games tend to have a definite learning curve, as the player is required to manage and react to a lot of information. There will come a point though, when the player has mastered the controls and the general scenario of the game. This is the time to put the player's ability to the test. For example: the player can now grow enough crops to feed his troops, in order to maintain a force to hold off the enemy troops. The level designer can test the player's abilities by providing enemies on two different fronts, or perhaps an unexpected (but reasonable) drought, which means that there are not enough crops for food. These problems will drive the player to use his knowledge of the game in different ways to resolve them. Challenges can be grouped and used as the basis for increasingly difficult sections of the game.

Strategy games:
• **Civilization**
• **Sim City**
• **Rome Total War**
• **Darwinia (below)**

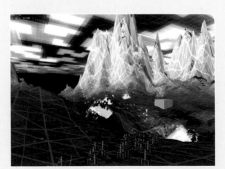

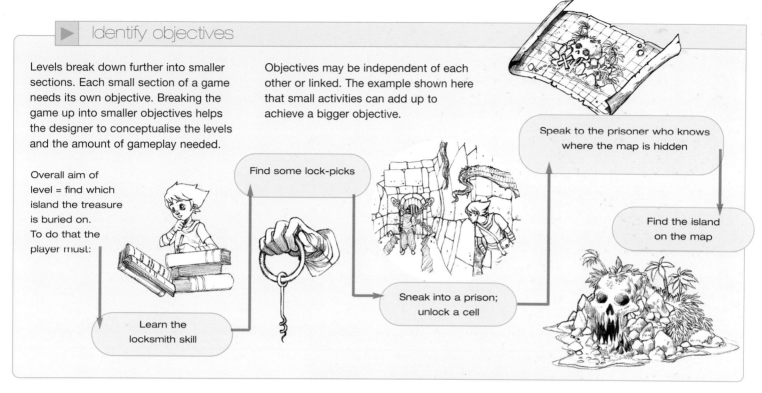

▶ Identify objectives

Levels break down further into smaller sections. Each small section of a game needs its own objective. Breaking the game up into smaller objectives helps the designer to conceptualise the levels and the amount of gameplay needed.

Objectives may be independent of each other or linked. The example shown here that small activities can add up to achieve a bigger objective.

Speak to the prisoner who knows where the map is hidden

Find the island on the map

Find some lock-picks

Overall aim of level = find which island the treasure is buried on. To do that the player must:

Sneak into a prison; unlock a cell

Learn the locksmith skill

Game mechanics

The game mechanics are the way that a player experiences the gameworld – the designer should use them as the building blocks of level design. The aim is to get the player to think about and exploit the game environment. A level designer should not make everything obvious. The player should always be encouraged to think of creative ways to use the game mechanics to achieve the goals of a level.

Training

When he begins, a player's knowledge of how to play the game will be limited. One way of familiarising him with the game is to include a training level. This appears at the beginning of a game and takes the player through every possible game mechanic step-by-step. A more subtle way of introducing the player to the controls is to simply start the game slowly – so that the first few 'challenges' involve very simple tasks.

◀ **Make a ramp**
Rather than a character climbing a ladder to get to a new level he may have to counterbalance a plank with heavy objects to act as a ramp, as in Half Life 2.

▶ **Create a distraction**
Instead of simply blasting away at guards a player may have to create a distraction to get them to move away, as seen in Splinter Cell.

Level Design Document

The whole creative process depends on thorough and concise documentation for it to be successfully implemented. Most written work will go into the Level Design Document (LDD) which is a sub-section of the Game Design Document (see page 106). This document is a clear description of the intended action and gameplay of a level. It explains how mechanics are used within the game and how the timing and pace of the level and game will work.

The LDD lists everything to be included in a level. This then needs to be drawn out as a simple plan with reference to the LDD. At this point you can begin to see how each 'encounter' relates to each other and how they may flow together. Remember this does not have to be linear (do A then B then C). Players might be able to accomplish several smaller tasks in any order before progressing onto the next stage, (do A and/or B and/or C before going onto D). In all of this you need to consider 'trigger points' – these are points the player reaches which trigger some reaction in the game. A simple trigger point is when a player character might become visible to the guards, or when he steps on the weak floorboard and falls into the cellar. They can also be used negatively so that a player may achieve his aim by not triggering a point, for example if the player does not pass over a trigger point then the guards will not see him and give chase. Trigger points are invisible to the player but give direction to the game's AI when occurrences should happen.

▼ Documentation

This is a section from a Level Design Document. The game concept is about a central character being chased by hordes of undead creatures. He stumbles across a mansion, home to a noble family, and the game revolves around his battle to survive and save the occupants using whatever comes to hand.

Timing

There is a need to account for the time it will take a player to achieve a level's goals. This is important in order to assess how long the game will last, in turn an important marketing factor which will affect players' feelings of value for money.

Timing also has an important role within the game. Games should not consist of continuous action – there must be lulls. Even within a level a player needs the opportunity to rest, heal wounds, take stock of the situation, or decide on his next move. Balance between action and rest must be considered.

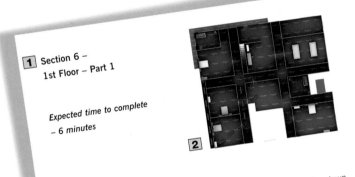

1 Section 6 –
1st Floor – Part 1

Expected time to complete – 6 minutes

2

This section will start with the Lord and Lady running from the landing down the hallway on the left. The Lord will now shout:

• *'Quick Jack, this way!'*

The player must now follow them and this will place another marker on the map for the player to make their way towards.

The player should now follow the Lord and his wife from the landing to the front bedroom. Upon reaching the bedroom the player will see the Lord and Lady over in the corner of the room, waiting. The Lord will say:

• *'Help me to move this wardrobe, Jack!'*

The player must now move the wardrobe by pressing the square button, revealing the secret passageway. Once the wardrobe is out of the way the Lord and his wife will make their way in and the player will be left to follow. When the player is in the secret passage the Lord will say:

3 • *'Move the wardrobe back across, Jack; we can't let them know where we are! With a bit of luck we can stay here until morning!'*

1 The level and part of the game is clearly indicated, with an expected completion time included.

2 A neutral block map of the level has been created to illustrate the level's layout and the path the player should take.

3 As the game is cinematic in nature some of the early script has been included to show how the action will develop.

Maps

Maps are very important tools for communicating how a level will flow to the people who build it. They show not only the physical environment but also the features, non-player characters, items and various other things the player will encounter on a level. Maps are also good for indicating the 'trigger points' in a particular level, which will not be visible to the player but are critical from a design point of view.

Sketches and flow charts

Ideas should be charted and mapped to support the written LDD. Remember that humans are visual beings – successful games rely a great deal on their visual layout. Sketching your ideas is invaluable to good level design. A flow chart is a good mechanism for visually representing relationships in sections of the game. These can represent game-flow as a series of activities that the player must complete.

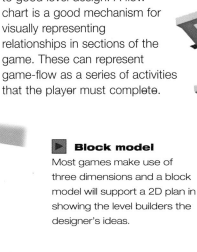

▶ **Block model**

Most games make use of three dimensions and a block model will support a 2D plan in showing the level builders the designer's ideas.

 Once again the player will need to use the square button to move the wardrobe along the wall. When the wardrobe has been moved and the three characters are in the secret passage, the entrance to the passage will start to rattle. The sounds of shuffling feet and groaning creatures can be heard, muffled through the walls. The wardrobe will now start to rattle and then with one loud crash fall away from the wall, revealing the entrance. The Lord will now shout:

• *'Quick Jack, there's another way out at the other end of the passage!'*

With this the creatures start to move into the passageway behind the Lord and his wife. A new objective appears on the screen:

• *Escape the passage!*

The player must now lead the way to the other end of the secret passage but just as they reach it a cut scene will begin.

Cut scene

The camera will follow Jack as he walks down the corridor, then with a sudden bang and scream turn around to focus on the Lord and his wife. The wall next to them will start to shake and dust and plaster fills the air. Then with a loud crash the wall caves in and creatures spill into the passage. They grab Lord and Lady Blacker and start to feast on them. With what appears to be his last breath the Lord says:

'Save yourself Jack!'

e player must now make their way to the end of the passage and
n, using the square button, slide aside the drawers to get into the
ter bedroom.

4 The necessary actions of the player have been described, including reference to the console control set.

5 Reference is made to the cut scene (a short animation) which further develops the story and enhances the drama in the game (see page 60).

▶ LDD checklist

• **Make it comprehensive.** Any person reading the documentation must be able to understand completely every aspect to be included in the level.

• **Make it concise.** These documents will be referred to by many people, time and again. Making them as short as possible can save a lot of time.

• **Reference it well.** It should be easy to find information without having to read unnecessary material. This helps with speed of access.

► Case study: **Level design for The Lockup**

This is a small section of an undergraduate student's game concept proposal. The game is called The Lockup and it is about a man imprisoned for a crime he did not commit. The twist in the tale is that the prison is an old oil-drilling platform in the ocean filled with an assortment of prisoners from around the world. The game is semi-sandbox type and is designed to play on the Sony PSP.

Even a relatively small aspect of a game merits a considerable amount of development – not only to create the concept, but to accurately record it for study by the design team.

1 Initial concept

Some of the initial sketches for the level design are set in the refinery amongst the rig's legs. These record the main features and the form of the levels.

2 Detailed map

This is a detailed map of part of the rig showing all the NPCs and game opportunities. Note the identification of the guards'

patrol routes; this is especially helpful for event-scripting such as encountering, or being seen by, a guard.

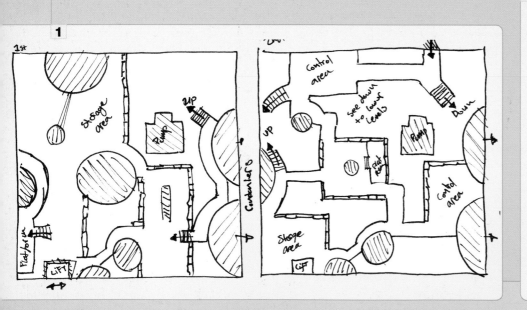

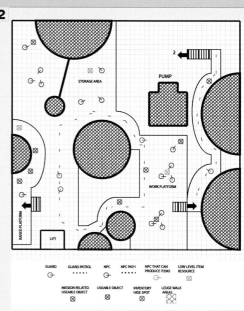

3

| Sentenced to a maximum security prison | ← | **Introduction** |

| Brought to the prison in the middle of nowhere, unsure what to expect | ← | **Start of game** |

| No one believes that you're falsely accused. Objective: to escape the prison | ← | **Tutorials** |

Set out to build a vehicle to escape the oil rig

uild alliances with angs of prisoners find parts | Corrupt prison guards to get hold of parts

Explore the environment to find places to build parts | ← | **Gameplay**

Hiding from guards to keep them from finding out

Build vehicle

Escape

Game ends

3 Flow chart

As this game allows the player to explore the environment freely as well as undertaking specific missions, there is an overview of the intended flow of the whole game.

4 Block map

The levels and rig are block-mapped to indicate the scale and 3D form of the area.

5 Fight mechanic

As part of the game centres around prison culture, certain game mechanics are dealt with in detail in terms of how they work in the game.

4

5

A fight is engaged by either the player or an NPC

Guard response countdown time started

Player is beaten by NPC(s)	Player beats the NPC; items drop	Guards intervene and both NPC and player get a beating
Player drops all items and is left to recover while NPC takes items, and guards take him away	Player has to collect items before guards take him away	Both NPC and player get locked into their cells
	Player gets locked into his cell	

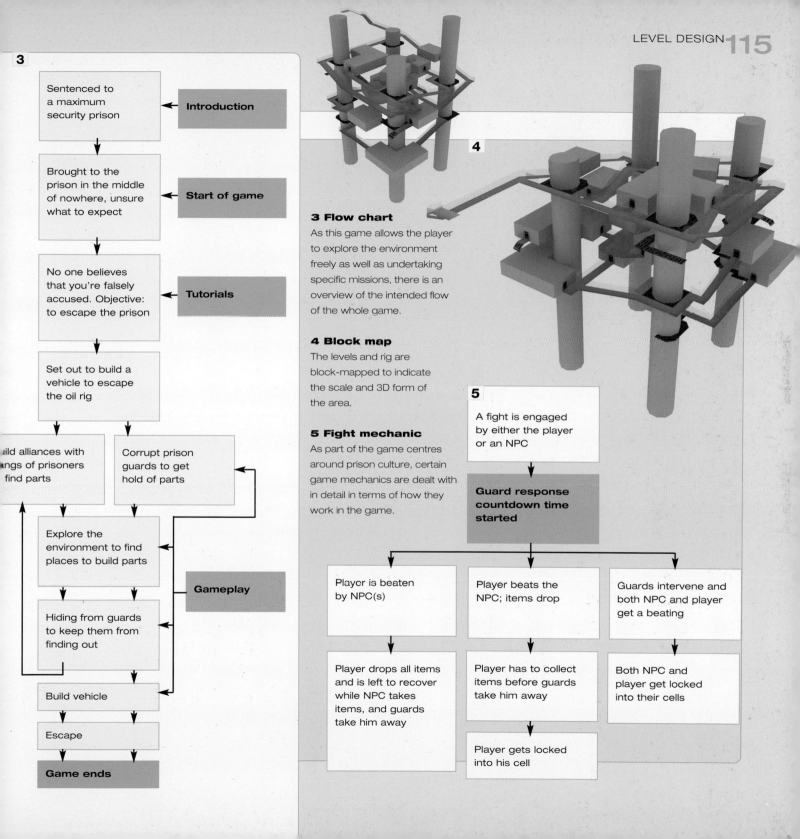

▶ Design exercise 1: **The Robot Problem**

The art of level design lies in getting the most use possible out of the smallest number of things, and making it fun. For example, in an FPS game, the level designer is given a fixed number of enemies of different strengths and weaknesses, and a number of weapons and ammunition types. The variety comes from the structure of the environment and from how the enemies are placed. In puzzle games, pieces must be arranged to complete the game, but there are rarely many piece types.

Coming up with a minimal set of objects that work well together, and that can be arranged in a range of ways to ensure variety and interest, is exceptionally difficult. As an exercise, it can be humbling to try to create even a single level for a simple, original, platform-based puzzle game. Although puzzle games aren't as high-profile as the bigger-budget FPS games, they are arguably even harder to design. Although the following exercise demonstrates failure to make a good set of objects, this failure is an important lesson in how simple ideas can quickly become over-complicated.

The puzzle is to get the Purple Robot to the Yellow Robot (see the picture, bottom left). If the Purple Robot touches the Red Robot, the player loses.

Even in this deliberately simple game there are many interactions to consider. The first is to figure out how the Red Robot should move:

- Left and right continuously?
- Toward the Purple Robot when the Purple Robot is on the ground?
- As close to the Purple Robot as possible at all times? In this case it will always be under the Purple Robot when it is on the top platform.
- Toward the Purple Robot when it is on the ground but return to guard the Yellow Robot when the Purple Robot is on the platform?
- And how fast does the Red Robot move? How quickly can it turn, if it can at all? There are many other options.

Also consider how the items interact with each other and the Red Robot. What happens if the Ice touches the Red Robot – perhaps they should both disappear in a cloud of steam? Or perhaps the Ice disables the Red Robot for a short time. Does it make a difference if the Ice is dropped onto the Red Robot or if the Red Robot just runs into it? Would the Red Robot avoid running into it? What should the Log do when it touches the Red Robot? Would it burn? Would it knock the Red Robot out? What happens if the Ice touches the Log? And so on.

You'll need to know how the Ice Log interacts with a normal Log, Ice, the Red Robot, the Purple Robot, another Ice Log and the Fire Log. AND you'll need to design what happens when the Fire Log interacts with a normal Log, Ice, the Red Robot, the Purple Robot and another Fire Log. You may have decided by now that the elements need simplifying.

The scenario
The Red Robot can't go up ladders. The Yellow Robot can't move. The player plays the Purple Robot which can climb ladders and push items. There are two items on the top platform: a block of ice and a log.

Design exercise 2: **Historical adventure FPS**

This is a more complex, 'real' brief which asks you to attempt to design a level for an FPS game (see page 20).

Brief

The game concerns smuggling during the 18th century. It is intended to be 'realistic' – there should be no magic or anything that might not be contemporary to that period. You must develop three levels.

The game is to be a first-person historical adventure game dealing with the adventures of a character from a port town, who gradually becomes involved in smuggling. It will incorporate some combat, but also elements of puzzle-solving, exploration, and challenging environments. It should be constructed using a first-person game engine of your choice (such as Half Life, Unreal, or Quake). In the main the design should follow the pre-scripted scenes provided below.

Scene 1

The smugglers' ship has run aground in the middle of the night. The revenue men are on their way, and the player and their NPC companions have only a small amount of time to grab some cargo. Starting outside the ship they are to find their way into the ship, locate valuable cargo, dash back across the rocks and beach, finally reaching the safehouse in the twisting streets of the harbour town. The players will not be sure when the revenue men will turn up, but it will definitely be sometime before they are in the town.

Scene 2

Having progressed within the smugglers' cadre, the player is now the captain of a small ship smuggling goods into the country. In sight of the shore they are stopped by a navy vessel in search of smuggled goods. It would be folly to fight or run from the ship so the player's only option is for an inspection. The player is to allow the customs men to search the ship whilst making sure the goods are hidden.

On completion of this section the ship docks at the end of the quay and the player must unload the goods discreetly and take them to the hidden store without arousing suspicion. At this point there may be guards to avoid or disable and some NPC interaction.

Scene 3

In order to clamp down on smugglers the Navy has sent the pressgang into town to round up as many menfolk for the Navy as possible. Taken by surprise, the player has to flee the chasing sailors. A hair-raising chase takes place throughout the twisted streets of the town (rooftops, sewers and gardens, in and out of buildings) with the occasional scuffle with sailors. Eventually the player should reach the open fields and make good their escape.

Requirements

You must produce a level design and walkthrough for each of the three scenes described above. You will need to complete the following for each scene.

- Typewritten walkthrough.

- Clear level plan showing level, potential player route and locations of encounters.

- Diagrams of special areas of action, for example, if the player had to counter-balance a hoist so that they could access a higher level.

- Each level will have a minimum of 12 'encounters' – these can entail NPC information or interaction, puzzle-solving, environmental challenges, hiding or stealth, flight from NPC and some combat.

User interaction design
Keeping the player informed

User interaction design is about how, when, and where to best present useful information to the player. With the very early games all the information in the game could be seen on the screen. Pac-Man and Space Invaders are good examples as they both showed the entire play area, all the enemies, score and lives remaining.

Games such as Defender and Elite only allowed the player to see the portion of the playspace in their immediate vicinity. A map or 'radar' gives the player vital information about the wider surroundings. This does take up some valuable screen-space but without it the player would have no idea of upcoming hazards. Elite also provided separate screens for different activities, such as trading and planning hyperspace jumps. The main views out of the ship were for tasks such as combat and docking. These views showed information that changed quickly, like shields and weapon temperature.

Many modern games have several layers of information, changing at different rates. The overall

▶ **Graphic display**
Elite Beat Agents has stylish, comic-style visuals. Information about the player's performance is designed to complement this strong graphic image.

Map

The action takes place within the white box, which represents the portion of the gameworld visible on-screen.

▼ **Divided display**

In Defender, the player can see only a portion of the play area but needs to know about objects outside this view. This is achieved using a map

which takes up some room on the screen but gives the player lots of information about the space around him.

Lives remaining

The player can see at a glance how many lives he has remaining, represented by the spaceship icons.

story tends to present itself slowly – through cut scenes, voiceover, and text – and health (or energy or resources) tend to change quite quickly – through simple graphics or counters. Because games have become more complex and multi-faceted, these different layers are forcing designers to think more and more about how to present them in a timely and clear manner.

Conventions

It has become fairly standard to put any text information at the bottom of the screen, similar to film subtitles. Images such as maps and health bars are usually found at the top or the corners of the screen. This has parallels with the findings of neuro-linguistic programming studies of eye-accessing cues, in which when a person looks up they tend to be recalling or constructing a visual image, and looking down indicates internal dialogue or kinaesthetic feelings.

Information design permeates all areas of design, including the general art and visuals. In most games, objects that are dangerous or harmful are angular, spiky and have highly contrasted colours. Useful and friendly objects are usually softer, rounder shapes and more muted pastel colours. In life, contrasted, pointy things are often dangerous (wasps, thorns) and soft, blobby things are generally good (water, fruit) so it makes sense to use these associations in a game. This is a design consideration which is put to use in many films and cartoons – it is often the dark, angular characters which are hostile and the soft, bright characters which are friendly. Darth Vader, Alien, Predator, the Wicked Witch of the West, Invader ∠im – these are all pointy, dark villains. Teletubbies, Mr Incredible, Wallace and Gromit, Mickey Mouse, Mario, Homer Simpson – these are all examples of curved, soft, friendly protagonists.

▲ **Communication devices**
Shown above are a variety of user information devices from games. Whether the design solution chosen is abstract and graphic, or more literal, success lies in marrying it to the overall design style of the game while maintaining clarity of communication.

▶ Universal responses

Wolfgang Köhler (1887–1967) was a German Gestalt psychologist. In a famous experiment in 1929 he asked a number of volunteers to label two drawings (right) with two words: 'Takete' and 'Maluma'. These words have no meaning in any language. He found that the majority named the angular, straight-line drawing 'Takete' and the curved line drawing 'Maluma'. This was tested across a broad range of cultures, and the results were the same each time. This suggests a universal human response. This is a simple example of a universal human reaction to visual stimuli. A more complex example is how people generally find babies cute, along with big eyes, small features and gentle curves. This is reflected in the appeal of teddy bears, as well as modern characters such as Elmo and Pokémon.

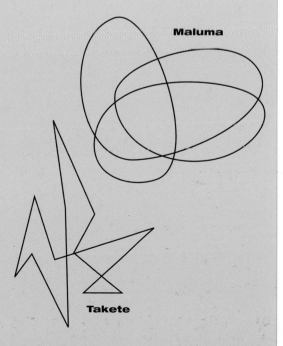

Maluma

Takete

Recent developments

More recent games are moving away from displaying information in an abstract way. In Peter Jackson's King Kong the player checks ammunition by examining the in-game gun. In Fight Night Round 3, the health of players is assessed visually, and should be immediately obvious. This move away from abstraction is possible as the technology is now able to give designers more natural ways of presenting the information. The difficulty then is that it isn't always obvious how to present information naturally. Visually and technologically it may present problems, but also the interface begins to become more important. The 'dual-shock' controller interface is really just an advance on the early controller. Some would argue it isn't even an improvement and that designers have

become sloppy with how they map actions to buttons. It is certainly true that hitting a button with an abstract symbol on it gives the player no idea of what that button will do until the action has happened. The Nintendo DS and Revolution interfaces are a welcome break from the standard controllers. For example, consider how much easier and natural it would be to simply tilt the controller to see how many bullets are in the gun, rather than press the 'B' button.

Streamlining information

It can be useful to think about what not to show to the player and when to hide information that isn't needed. In Frontier, Elite's sequel, the player had to raise and lower the undercarriage of the ship. This

▼ **King Kong**
Peter Jackson's King Kong lacks a traditional user interface; instead the player must gather information about his performance, health and ammunition for himself.

was an unnecessary detail as it could have been handled automatically and the game would be better for it. In Animal Crossing, the time is hidden from view until the player stops using the controls after which it pops up in the corner of the screen. In more and more games the health bar is hidden until it changes or when health is very low. Hiding unnecessary information generally makes the screen less cluttered and makes the information appear more important when it is displayed.

Sound design

Sound design is equally important and can be very effective in conveying information. Through sound design it is standard practice to inform the player about simple things such as mood of the environment or opponent, the material and mass of objects, and the proximity of attackers. Unfortunately it is rarely used to give finer detail, such as the health of an opponent or better distance cues. Wild Metal Country does however make good use of layered sounds to achieve this.

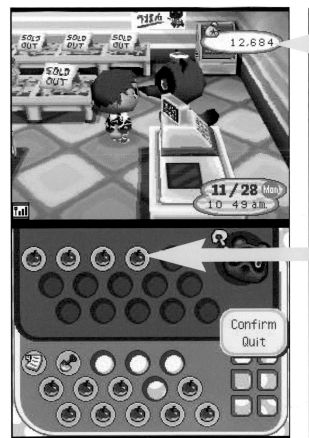

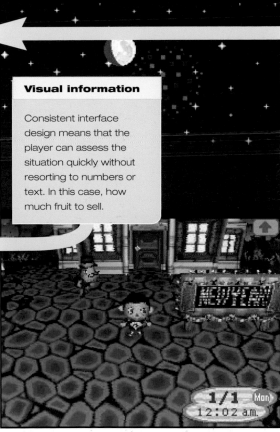

Visual information

Consistent interface design means that the player can assess the situation quickly without resorting to numbers or text. In this case, how much fruit to sell.

Relevant display

In Animal Crossing, information appears when necessary. For example, the amount of money the player has is displayed when he is about to buy something in a shop.

◀ **Elegant interface**

In Animal Crossing, the player requires a lot of information about the state of the game. Elegant interface design means that the information is clearly presented when needed, but concealed when it is unnecessary.

Games editors

The power to modify

Games editors are the tools originally created by the games companies to allow their designers and level designers to create levels for the games without having to resort to complicated programming. They are powerful programs in their own right with the specific purpose of creating a level and placing assets for that particular game. Though these editing tools were originally created for in-house use only, when id Software released the editor for Doom the players enjoyed creating maps and variants for the games as much as playing them. This was the beginning of the user-modification phenomenon, now commonly referred to as 'mapping' or 'modding'.

As newer games released their map editors, modification-tools companies discovered that some of the gamers actually made very good maps, and some went so far as to develop whole new games. One of the most famous is the Day of Defeat team who used Valve's Half Life editor – Hammer – to create a World War 2 combat game. This proved so popular and was so well made that the Day of Defeat team eventually joined Valve Software.

Level editor release

It is now almost the norm rather than the exception that a game is released with a level editor. Game development companies know that the players will create many more maps for the games they produce, and so prolong the market life of these games – this makes good business sense. Also these editors are ideal territory for the neophyte designer to begin to develop his game-creation skills.

User-friendly features

Games editors are becoming increasingly user-friendly, with sophisticated menu systems and WYSIWYG features, as in mainstream software. The editors are as open to beginners to create drag-and-drop basic maps and levels as they are to experts who can not only edit levels but import their own models and textures and even change some of the game's characters through software scripting. Maps and mods that are created in the editing program often have to be compiled in order to be played. There are usually several smaller utility programs to help players achieve this.

Valve's Hammer editor

Valve's Hammer editor has been around since the first Half Life game and was known as Worldcraft in its original form. It later became known as Hammer and now, with the introduction of Half Life 2 and Source, it is part of the System Developer Kit (SDK). The interface gives the user a plan, elevation, side, and perspective views in which to see his creations. Basic maps are built from 3D primitives such as cubes, wedges, and cones. These shapes can be textured using textures from the game, and user-modified maps can be developed. The simplest of maps are arenas for player-versus-player combat, but through the editor it is possible to develop very sophisticated single-player levels and games. Editing of levels and development of new mods and games has been embraced by Valve, and the Valve Web site and Steam portal offer user-developed material as well as licensed commercial material. Perhaps one of the oddest, yet most popular, mods using the SDK is Gary's Mod. This is a modification created by Gary Newman which allows players to access all of the physics and materials in the game and build all types of contraptions and generally play around in this sandbox environment.

▼ Upgrades

Valve's Hammer editor has benefited from extensive use and upgrading. It is used for many popular games, yet it is easy to learn the basics very quickly.

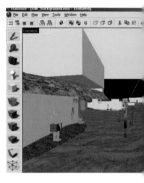

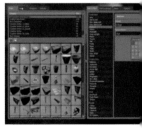

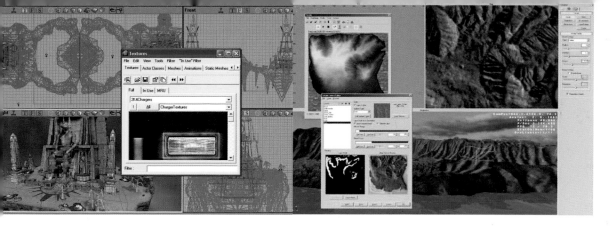

UnrealEditor

UnrealEditor comes with the series of highly successful Unreal games by Epic Games. It is usually referred to as UnrealEd. It is a highly sophisticated editing engine with a user-friendly interface. The scenery is modelled from primitive forms and some ready-made forms like staircases. These can be textured using inbuilt or user-generated textures. UnrealEd also has a built-in scripting language called UnrealScript which allows greater scope for modification for experienced users. In one incarnation – UnrealTournament – this particular level editor is used for generating multi-player maps.

Radiant

This editor is used for Doom, Quake, Call of Duty and various other games. Each game comes with its own version of Radiant which is tailored to the game. Like the other editors, Radiant has seen a lot of development and, like other editors, it is a powerful map-editing tool. Modelling occurs in a similar fashion to other editors with the nuances of the associated game included in the specific editor. As this editor is linked to so many different games it has a considerable variety of online communities dealing with all sorts of aspects of its use.

Far Cry editor

The game Far Cry by CryTek came with a built-in editor. As the game is set on a jungle-covered tropical island the editor responds to the need to create large-scale outdoor levels by working in real time. This bypassed the need to compile and run the game to see the effect of a change or an inclusion. Level designers could check the changes instantly.

This reportedly allowed designers to spend more time creating levels which could be approached in a variety of ways and gave the players more apparent freedom of choice.

These are just a few of the editors available with games today. Many RTS games include map-making tools, and some platform games like Worms include level editors. It would seem that players like making maps and levels for games just as much as playing them. Becoming familiar with a level editor is an ideal way to begin to get to grips with game design, and level design in particular. The benefit of this is that you can play the levels you have created, share them with your friends, and get some feedback on what works and what does not.

► Design exercise: **Edit a level**

Using a level editor, design and make a level or an arena for a game. Of course you will first need to gain some experience in using the editor but all of them have large online communities with plenty of tutorials for beginners. Once you have completed the basic tutorials then you can begin to work on your own level. Plan it out on paper first and make your first level straightforward but with one or two unique features like hidden areas or novel hiding spots. When you have made it you can try it out with your friends and get some feedback on it. This will help you design your next level.

Game physics

Properties of objects

The term 'game physics' refers to algorithms in the programming of a game which make the objects on-screen behave in a certain manner. For example, things fall if unsupported, a surface covered in ice is slippery, and wood and less dense items float on water.

A game's physics engine simulates Newtonian physics to a greater or lesser extent – it takes as a starting point the actions and reactions of objects in the real world. Objects will have an apparent weight to them; surfaces will display characteristics of friction; objects that are moving will have a velocity (this usually combines with a mass-value for collision effects); atmospheric effects like wind resistance can be simulated. All of these things are added together to give the illusion that the gamespace follows the same physical laws that the real world does. A typical method for enabling the interaction of objects is called collision detection. This is where the program detects the intersection of two objects and calculates their response in respect to each other's properties – so a rubber ball bounces off a hard floor; a hard stone will break a brittle window, and so on. The collision-detection mechanism renders the objects according to their physical properties. This gives the illusion of a physical reality within the game.

Rag doll physics

'Rag doll physics' is a particular type of object animation, and gets its name from the appearance of a character killed in a game who goes 'floppy', like a rag doll. This type of in-game physics means that adversaries will reel and recoil from blows with their limbs flailing, as you might expect of a real figure. It's not only characters which can be treated this way – inanimate objects can be given a 'skeletal rig' so that they fold and deform when a force is applied to them in a game. Rag doll physics is very computationally

Racing experience

The vehicle type and engine size can be modified by the players. Even the weight of the driver influences the physics of the racing experience.

▶ **Performance**
Mario Kart: Double Dash utilizes a specific set of physics in relation to the performance of different vehicles and their racing characteristics.

Defying reality

Physics engines do not always have to model reality accurately. In games such as Spiderman, there is an underlying physics engine which models the world in a fairly realistic manner, but also allows for the superhuman wall-walking and leaping abilities of the superhero character. In Mario Kart: Double Dash, the madcap racing antics of Mario and his colleagues mimic real life but also allows for cartoon-world variation to spice up the action.

The physics engine is an invisible aspect of a game, yet one of the most critical in the delivery of the overall game experience. While developing physics engines is purely the territory of programmers, designers should have an input in helping to conceive of the specification and style of physics required in a game.

expensive – that is, it requires the processor to make a lot of calculations in order to render an image to screen. But it is becoming more common in games, particularly FPS games, where the demise of opponents can now be accompanied by cinematic falls to their doom.

Procedural animation

Procedural animation is the term used for an animation that is automatically generated by the processor in reaction to a set of occurrences. An in-game animator cannot create every possible falling animation for a character; procedural animation undertakes this task when necessary. It will take into account what is happening to a character as a result of the in-game physics acting upon them, and then animate accordingly. For example, should an enemy fall with his body half-hanging over a ledge, then the weight of his torso will drag him off. This event cannot necessarily be foreseen in the randomness of a game, and so the action of the physics engine dictates that the body should fall; rag doll physics deals with the shape and movement of the limbs of the figure; and procedural animation generates the image of the character falling off the ledge.

 **Specialised physics engines**

The physics engine in God of War (top left) deviates from reality to enhance the gameplay experience. Project Gotham Racing 3 (above) has a highly specialised physics engine which models the handling of high-performance cars. In common with other FPS games, Half Life 2 (right), makes use of game physics by requiring the player to counter-balance objects to solve puzzles. Gordon Freeman's signature crowbar can also be used in inventive ways.

Digital modelling

Points in virtual space

The creation of three-dimensional digital models is the cornerstone of game development. These models build the virtual worlds the games take place in – every animal, person, building, and object is a three-dimensional model. Modern 3D modelling packages have extremely user-friendly interfaces to allow designers to build models without needing to know the highly complex mathematics in the underlying modelling processes.

The more polygons that go into building a model, the more life-like and smooth it will look. However, a greater number of polygons increases the number of calculations the modelling program (and later the game engine) must perform to create the 3D image. Even with contemporary high-end computers and consoles the number of polygons or the 'poly count' is still carefully budgeted for within the design to ensure that the game runs smoothly and does not slow down due to the calculation times required to present images on-screen.

Digital models are virtual entities – though they appear to have a depth, in reality they do not. The image on your monitor has only two dimensions. It is the performance of the 3D program which gives the illusion of depth. This requires the program to create a model of a three-dimensional space. To do this it generates three axes perpendicular to each other; reference to all three axes can set a point in space. The axes are typically termed x (breadth), y (height) and z (depth). The point where these coordinates meet is referred to as the 'origin'. A three-figure coordinate will place a point in space. Three of these coordinates will define a triangular polygon in space.

Polys

Three-dimensional models are formed from a mesh of interconnected points in a virtual 3D space. This mesh is made up of triangles, or 'polys' (short for polygon). The point at the corner of a poly is a 'vertex' and the line between vertices is an 'edge'. A poly may be referred to as a 'face', but this usually means many polys forming the side of an object.

The poly mesh forms a virtual surface onto which a colour or an image may be placed. A series of images that tessellate on each poly can be made to appear as a natural material – a 'texture'. (See page 138 for more on texturing.)

Mesh of points

This model of a room is formed from a mesh of points. The 3D program knows where each one of these points is in relation to the others. If the viewer's point of view moves, then the program calculates how the view should be changed to give the illusion that the object has three dimensions.

◀ **Lighting**

A common procedure for lighting a scene is 'raytracing'. The modelling program calculates the path of a ray of light, and how it interacts with all the surfaces it meets. This is done many thousands of times to build a finished lighting picture with appropriate highlights, shadows and contrasts.

Light

Digital modelling packages can simulate a whole range of light effects, from simple one-point sources, to multiple sources, and even realistic daylight effects. When a program is calculating how light will fall across a virtual object or surface it must consider how the light is being reflected, how it is affected by local colour, and how shadows are being cast. Calculating how light works in a scene, especially a daylit scene, is extremely complex. A procedure often used is known as 'raytracing', in which the software must calculate the paths of many thousands of rays of light.

Rendering

To view a 3D model the user has a viewpoint. When a finished model is built, textured, and lit, an image can be generated from this viewpoint – usually termed a 'render'. The modelling package has to work out how the model appears to the viewpoint, how the textures will appear, and how the lighting works. This requires a lot of complex calculations and a modelling program can take a noticeable amount of time to produce the image. This process is commonly referred to as 'rendering'.

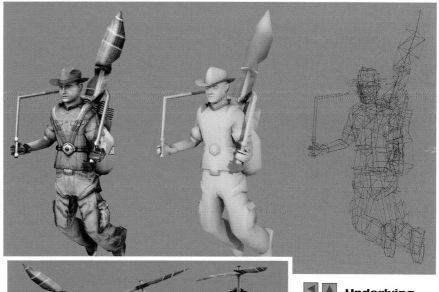

◀ ▲ **Underlying elements**

These illustrations reveal the underlying mesh of polygons which form a textured character model, and how it appears with a neutral surface.

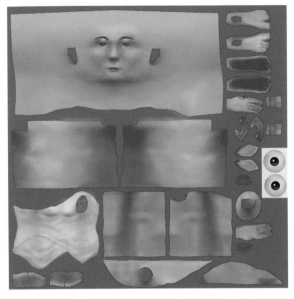

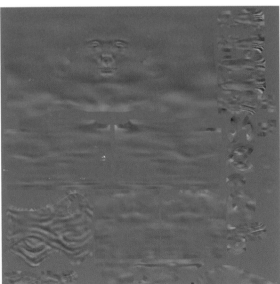

▲ **Texture map and normal map**

Shown here are a texture map (top) and a normal map (bottom) for the model on the right. The normal map adds shading for a more realistic effect without raising the poly count. (For more on texturing see page 138.)

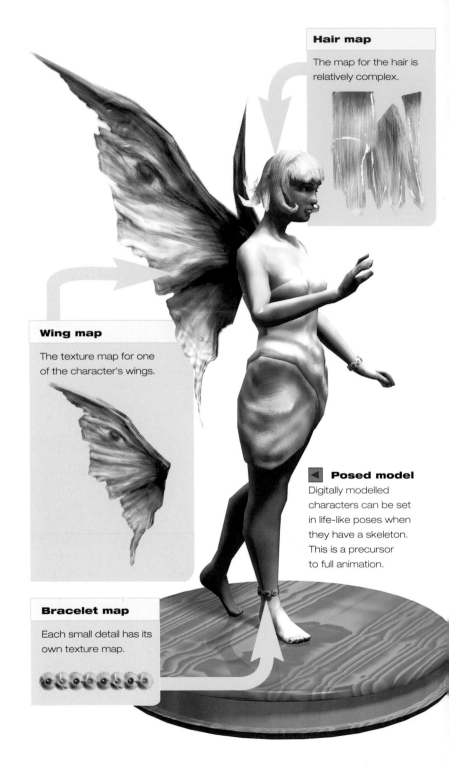

Hair map

The map for the hair is relatively complex.

Wing map

The texture map for one of the character's wings.

Bracelet map

Each small detail has its own texture map.

◄ **Posed model**

Digitally modelled characters can be set in life-like poses when they have a skeleton. This is a precursor to full animation.

Boning

To animate a character model, a 'skeleton' is placed inside it. This can then be moved and posed. Extending the skeleton metaphor, this process is referred to as 'boning' – giving your model bones and joints similar to a real person. The skeleton is not visible in the finished model, but in the modelling program appears in a different colour from the poly mesh; in this case it is shown in dark blue and green.

Mesh

The model mesh is shown here in light blue. In the finished model, texture maps will be applied to the mesh, hiding the boning and giving the character its realistic, three-dimensional appearance.

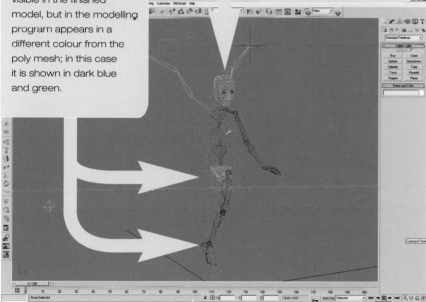

Animation

Digital models can be made to move and provide animations. When this work is being generated the user viewpoint is usually called a 'camera', and uses the notion of the viewpoint being a film camera. To animate a figure such as a person the program needs to know how each part will move in relation to the others. The program calculates this with reference to an invisible 'skeleton' placed within the character.

An animated sequence from a 3D program is really a series of still frames which are linked together to form an animation. Animating even a simple sequence takes time. A complex animation containing different textured objects moving in a correctly lit scene can take an hour to render a single frame, even with powerful computers. And an animation uses 24 frames per second!

Fitting into the design process

Digital modelling is certainly one of the most popular parts of game developing, perhaps because it generates the most obvious, visual, components of a game. It touches on all parts of the process, from the artists and modellers who create the digital models and the animators who make them move in a lifelike manner to the programmers who implement the models in the game engine. While not every person in a development team will be directly involved with digital modelling they all will be conversant with the issues and opportunities surrounding digital modelling for games.

Accessible interface

3D modelling packages provide the user with a series of different views of the object and a number of tools to manipulate the data and build a model. Behind this relatively accessible interface, the program works by performing extremely complex mathematical calculations in order to generate the image.

Digital modelling applications

Popular packages

There are many digital modelling applications available commercially, and quite a few that are available for free download. It is impossible to say which application is best, as they all perform similar tasks. While popular opinion might indicate that one package is better than another at a certain task, that doesn't mean the other programs can't do it. This section lists some of the most commonly used packages and their general strengths. Remember that learning how to model and texture properly is more important than learning to use a specific package. In general, each package works in a similar way and though the tools may differ, the modelling process is essentially the same.

3D Studio Max

3D Studio Max is a high-end package that is widely used throughout a variety of media industries. 3D Studio Max has all the features you would expect to find in such a program and is supported by a wide range of third-party developers who produce different plug-in applications to add functionality to Max. This is another high-cost package but one that is prevalent and is considered an industry standard. *www.autodesk.com*

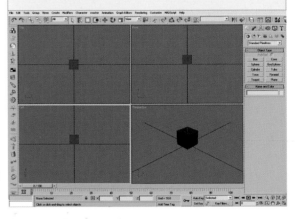

Maya

Maya is a high-end package that is widely used throughout the games, animation, film and television industries. It contains many features you would expect of a high-end package including advanced modelling, texturing, special effects and computer-generated effects like hair and cloth. It is expensive to purchase but is generally considered one of the industry standards. There is a Maya Personal Learning Edition available for free download from Autodesk. This offers an excellent opportunity to become familiar with the package. *www.autodesk.com*

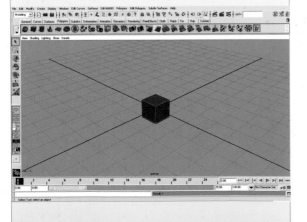

Softimage

Softimage has come to note partly due to the collaboration with Valve Software for the creation of Half Life 2. The release of a Mod Tool plug-in for this package aims it squarely at the games industry. However, this product also sees significant use in producing digital animation work for film and television. *www.softimage.com*

Lightwave

Lightwave has been around for years and is used in many sectors, from hobbyists to professionals. This package has many of the features necessary for game modelling and has a large user community. Lightwave has been used to generate CGI sequences for many blockbuster films. *www.newtek.com*

ZBrush

ZBrush is an interesting package, developing a big following due to the way it allows the modeller to 'paint' in three dimensions. The program interface allows the user to generate three-dimensional shapes with the aid of special tools which act like a natural paintbrush except in three dimensions. ZBrush sees a lot of use in creating highly detailed models quickly; these can then be exported as displacement/normal maps (used in rendering) onto lower-poly models to provide higher quality information for rendering. The digital modelling community as a whole is interested to see how the use of this program will develop. *www.pixologic.com/zbrush*

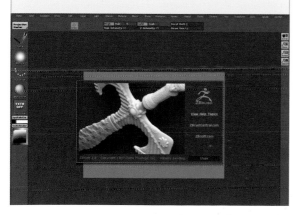

Choosing the right package

There are many commercial and free packages available for 3D modelling. They all display a range of features and the list presented on these pages is just a snapshot of what is available, without any implied preference or comment on suitability. A student modeller should perhaps begin with one of the free programs and begin to learn how to model with simple tools rather than being overawed by high-end packages.

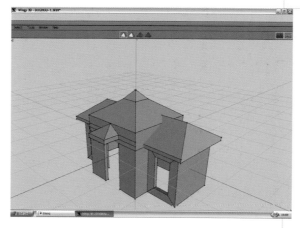

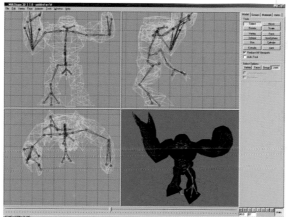

Free packages

◀ Wings 3D
Wings 3D is an open-source and free modelling package. It appears to be geared toward developing low polygon models suitable for in-game use. Wings 3D is very easy to learn and is supported by a large online community. *www.wings3d.com*

◀ Milkshape 3D
Milkshape 3D is a free program, primarily designed for creating content for game mods, particularly Half Life. This program is capable of generating characters for game mods and rigging them for animation. There is a strong support community and many online tutorials. *www.milkshape3d.com*

◀ Blender
Blender is an open-source free modelling package, with a large support community. Blender demonstrates many features present in high-end commercial products. It has a reputation for being hard to learn due to its user interface, but its active development may see some of these issues resolved. *www.blender3d.org*

3D modelling methods

Polygons, NURBS and subdivision of surfaces

The root of creating assets for 3D digital games is the three-dimensional digital model. This is the point where art and design meet mathematics and programming. Designers and artists create the vision for an object, while complex mathematical algorithms applied through the program define how this vision is constructed and presented. The best digital modellers have an artist's eye for visual harmony and a programmer's knowledge of how the modelling application can best be used to create the desired effects.

To the beginner, digital modelling can seem a little daunting. Modelling in a virtual three-dimensional space is not particularly intuitive. The human mind can easily grasp the concept of putting a pencil on a piece of paper, and moving it in a controlled manner to create an image. Creating a digital 3D model is not as simple and relies on a whole new set of skills; the user not only has to think in three dimensions to visualize the model, but must also use a series of complex program protocols in order to build it.

Learning the basics

It can be easy for the beginner at 3D modelling to become overwhelmed, so take small steps and learn the basics first. You do not have to understand the whole range of modelling techniques to get started. Remember that most modelling packages hide the complex mathematics behind their interface and allow the user to begin to model with simple hierarchical tools.

Using polygonal modelling

The advantage of polygonal modelling (see opposite page) is that it produces apparently complex forms simply, which allows the processor to animate them

easily. Polygonal modelling is ideal for games where there are many elements being rendered to the screen at a high frame-per-second rate. The models in a game must be made to appear on-screen in real time (minimum 24 frames per second to give the illusion of movement – and often much higher) and respond to the player's movements. As you can imagine, this involves a lot of calculating for the processor; cutting down how much work it has to do makes a game run more smoothly, with more appealing visuals.

As a polygonal model is constructed, the mesh becomes more complex and the form appears. The disadvantage of this type of modelling is that there are no curved lines – curved surfaces must be made up from many straight lines. When polygonal models are inspected closely, they can appear 'blocky'. The creation of simple, effective meshes is a key skill for a modeller. 'Low poly' refers to a model that uses as few polygons as possible to represent an image. Polygonal models are enhanced by the application of textures to their surface. (See page 138.)

Using NURB modelling

NURB models (see opposite page) have surfaces that are built up of complex curves formed from splines and control points. NURB modelling is not normally used in games as it creates mathematically complex models unsuitable for real-time rendering. Instead, NURB models are used for animations such as cut scenes (see page 60) where an action scene exists only as a recorded piece, with no interaction.

Where to start?

For the student modeller, the best place to start is with polygonal modelling. Getting to grips with the methods of modelling and developing your skill in producing effective low-poly models is a key proficiency if you wish to be a games modeller.

Highly detailed
NURB models are ideal for generating organic forms such as faces, people, and animals. These can then be animated to generate high-quality animated video sequences.

► Modelling concepts

It is helpful to understand the basic concepts that underlie digital modelling, and why and when they are used.

Polygonal modelling

Polygonal modelling is probably the simplest 3D modelling concept to understand, and one of the most common ways of modelling for games. Three vertices connected by three edges form a face or polygon. Link these polygons together at their edges and they will form three-dimensional shapes. The simplest of these shapes are known as primitives.

Three vertices and edges are considered because this is the minimum number of points and edges needed to form a 'face' (a triangle). This is the simplest form possible. By connecting many of these triangles together, polygonal shapes are formed.

Extruding

Modelling with polygons usually starts with a primitive, on which the modeller can perform simple operations to build and shape their model. The most basic action is 'extruding', in which the modeller selects a face and stretches it out from the original position to make a new shape.

▼ ▲ Primitives
Though simple in form, basic polygons, or primitives, such as the cylinder (above), or the cube being constructed in 3D Studio Max (below left), are the basis for all game models.

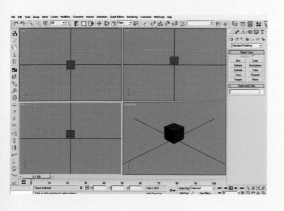

 Detailed model
By utilising a very fine 'mesh' of triangular polygons, incredibly detailed models of natural objects and people can be created.

Subdividing

Another common action in polygonal modelling is subdividing. This refers to the modeller cutting across a face with another edge. The result is two new faces which can be independently modelled.

NURB modelling

NURB stands for 'non-uniform, rational B-spline'. This is another method of defining vertices and edges in the modelling space. NURBs are a development of Bézier curves developed by a Renault engineer called Pierre Bézier. A Bézier curve provides a method of describing and forming complex curves by means of control points, which dictate how the curve will bend. Work in this area was also pursued by a Citroën engineer called Paul de Casteljau who developed an algorithm for computation of a Bézier curve. Following a great deal of development of these techniques, the work in these areas resulted in the use of NURBs for 3D modelling.

Subdivision of surfaces

Subdivision of surfaces is a refinement of NURB modelling. From a simple polygonal mesh, the surfaces are subdivided to create a more complex surface. This process can be carried on almost indefinitely until the mesh appears smooth and organic.

The subdivision of surfaces technique is used to produce highly detailed animated sequences.

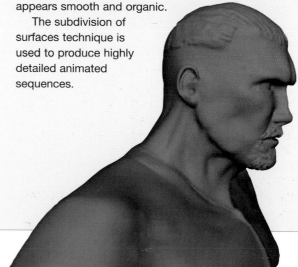

Props and set-dressing

Setting the scene

As games become more cinematic in nature, so too does the approach to 'setting the scene' within a game. Higher-powered consoles and PCs not only allow for larger and more compelling games, but they can also deliver vivid and highly detailed scenes as a backdrop to gameplay. Players' media-saturated senses tend to demand that these gamespaces are constructed to the same high standards as a Hollywood set.

Much of the time in the latter stages of game development is spent on setting the scene, adhering to the parameters laid out when the environment was first conceptualised (see page 96).

The example shown here demonstrates how designers flesh out the layout and surroundings of a playspace, from the basic block maps of a level right through to the finished article. Remember that this stage of the process is completed in conjunction with the level designers, who have their own responsibilities for making gamespaces exciting for players.

Concept and brief

For the example shown on these pages, the initial brief was to make a set based on a street scene in Cold-War East Berlin. The whole game concept was for a stealth-based game where the player character operated as a western spy behind the Iron Curtain. The game would require clever manoeuvring and sharp observation on the part of the player, and provide some conflict. This part of the game is a typical East German street at the height of the Cold War, with a military checkpoint.

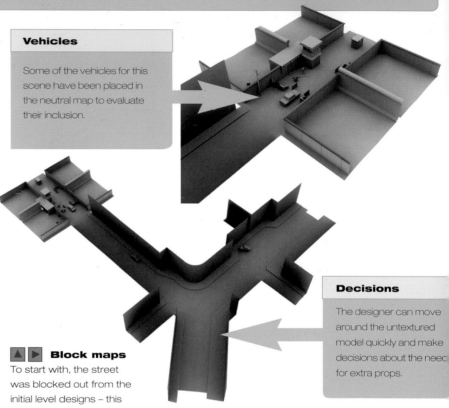

Vehicles

Some of the vehicles for this scene have been placed in the neutral map to evaluate their inclusion.

Decisions

The designer can move around the untextured model quickly and make decisions about the need for extra props.

▲ ▶ Block maps

To start with, the street was blocked out from the initial level designs – this would form the basic area of play. Though at this stage the block map looks simple with just a few stock props placed in it, it's important to get the size of the buildings and streets right, based on reference of the period. Even the Y-shaped layout of the streets reflects a more organic and medieval streetplan typical of European cities.

Once this stage was agreed, the model was detailed further and neutral texture maps applied (see page 140). The decision to use orange neutral maps was inspired by the designers at Valve and their work on Half Life 2. They used orange texture maps so that they could evaluate the form and gameplay of an environment without becoming distracted by unnecessary detail or half-finished texture work. If it works for the professionals, then the student designer could do worse than use a successful technique in his own work!

▲ Texture locales

These illustrations show the street form being developed and texture locales being identified. The white lines show the direction in which the texture will be applied.

Refining process

In these illustrations the sharp-eyed may spot a few mistakes. The benefit of going through this stage in this way is that mistakes (which inevitably creep into the process) can be spotted early before they become too embedded in the game. These images show the East Berlin street taking form and displaying the necessary characteristics.

After this stage, texturing, lighting, and all the other effect-work can take place. In this case, given the setting of the scene both physically and psychologically, the designers drew upon material from spy films of the period.

▼ ▶ Mood

It is night-time and the streets are in heavy shadow; there is a mist in the air which catches the light and obscures the view. It is a chill, cold, winter setting and therefore the trees have no leaves. The area has a slightly run-down and dilapidated feel about it with occasional piles of rubbish. All these items help to set the mood of the scene, and they tie in with the designer's ideas of places to hide and sneak, clues to be found, and guards to be avoided.

▼ Prop details

Alongside the street development, the vehicles which populated the street were developed too. References from Eastern European vehicles were used to build these props, and in these illustrations you can see the detail that went into the outside and inside of the vehicles. It's not difficult to imagine the player's point of view in the game as he hurries down a dark street, avoiding the ominous bulk of the armoured car and glancing into parked cars for clues and possible escapes. The detail presented in these models and textures all go to further develop the immersion in the game and the visual feast for the player's eyes.

▲ Texture map

Though the gamespace is a large street, the designer and artist create textures and models that include the small details of the vehicles to be placed within the street.

◄ Wire-frames

These illustrations show the wire-frame images from the modelling package. The cones of light and other areas of atmospheric effects are visible in the scene. This is the view the modeller sees and it is only when fully rendered on-screen that it finally takes on the appearance that would be seen in a game.

This example shows one approach to props and sets for a specific brief. Of course, game settings and stories change. It is important to remember that just as an exciting setting is nothing without considered gameplay, a good game lacks a certain something if the setting has not been carefully designed. Again games take cues from established media such as film, television, and illustration. The tools and processes available to designers are now so advanced that they have extraordinary power to create believable and unforgettable worlds.

▼ Scene is set

The vehicles are set in the street, the façades of the buildings are textured, and the cones of light catching the evening mist are there. This is an area for the player to explore and adventure in. The props are present and the set is dressed, the atmosphere is chill and foreboding. The action is up to the player.

Parked cars

Making the street appear as normal, a variety of cars are parked in the bay.

Real-life details

Taking cues from the real world, discarded newspapers and rubbish litter the street.

Texturing

Creating realism in models

Textures are placed onto the faces of a wire-frame polygon, to give a model its finished appearance. Models are rendered to screen in real time, so during a game they are kept as simple as possible to enable the game to run as quickly and smoothly as it can. The 'trick' that makes models look realistic lies in the application of texture. It is more efficient in processing terms to have richer textures and simpler model geometry. Our eyes can be tricked into thinking there is more depth and surface detail in a model than there actually is. Skilful texturing is the key to creating realism in game models.

What is a texture?
A texture, in game terms, is a small two-dimensional digital image which represents a surface. The view of the texture image is perpendicular to the texture; when it is used it will be wrapped around the model so that the model appears to be made out of the material the texture represents.

What format are textures?
Typically, a texture will be prepared in an imaging program such as Adobe Photoshop. While being worked on, the texture will usually contain lots of information and layers, and will subsequently be saved as a Photoshop file (.psd). When work on the texture is finished it is flattened into one layer and saved as a jpeg (.jpg) or a bitmap (.bmp). Quite often textures are saved as targa files (.tga) or tiff files (.tif). This is because these file formats can also include an alpha channel, which can be used for other texture effects.

Where do they come from?
Textures can be either manually painted in a digital image program or sourced from photographs of actual textures. The important aspect is that the texture either tessellates with itself or the other texture it will be placed against. The idea is that you should not be able to see the join between two textures. This can be very difficult with natural textures gained from photography. Often photographic textures need extensive work in an image-editing program (such as Photoshop) to make them tile seamlessly.

Manually generated textures
Textures can be created in most image-making programs. Once a texture size is set an artist can digitally paint a texture using a variety of paint tools. The difficulty in this approach is the need for a high level of skill on the artist's part, to create a texture that is as realistic as possible (assuming a realistic look is required). Painting textures in this way is generally used for inanimate objects, or fantastical creatures that are either easy to represent or have no basis in reality.

Photographic textures
With the easy availability of digital cameras it is very simple to record textures from real life. This is particularly useful for representing realistic buildings and people. When getting a photograph for a texture it is very important that the image is taken at a perpendicular angle to the viewer and that there is no distortion from the lens. Otherwise, when the image is being edited it will look as if it is skewed or bulging. Once a suitable image has been sourced, making it tessellate is the next task. The edges of any texture have to match seamlessly with the next portion of the texture, or the texture next to it. If not, an ugly seam in the texture will be noticed by the viewer and destroy any previous illusion of reality. Making a photographic image tessellate requires a great deal of careful work by the artist, using an image-editing program.

▲ Textures
Textures can come from anything – natural, man-made, or living. Game textures tessellate so that joins cannot be seen.

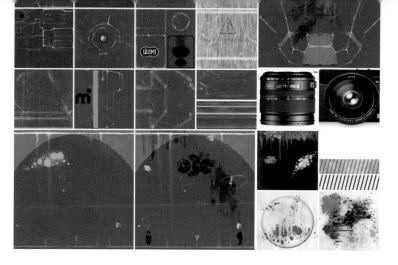

◀ ▼ **Character**

A model of a maintenance droid, paint-splattered and showing the knocks and scuffs of working life (below). To the left are the individual textures that make up this character – they have been laid out with white space between to help you spot where each comes from. This is a prominent character and therefore it has a high poly count and much texturing.

Procedural textures

Procedural textures are those which are generated by a programming algorithm. These textures appear natural but are completely computer generated by the use of fractal calculations to give the appearance of richly detailed, repetitive materials such as wood, metal, fur and so on. The reality of the appearance of these textures is a matter of some debate; often, though they seem real, our mind can tell us something is not quite right. No doubt as technology improves so will the realistic appearance of procedural textures.

Texture sizes

The image-size of a texture can vary depending on the machine it is working on. Generally, textures are made up of square or regular shapes to make the tiling process easier. Sizes of texture images are often square, and powers of 2, for example 32, 64, 128, 256, or 512 pixels square. Like polygon counts in a three-dimensional model, the size of a texture also demands processing time. The larger the texture, the more processing required. If you consider that in a typical game there may be several characters, buildings and items in the scene, you can appreciate that this information increases the demand for processing. Texture sizes vary depending upon the machine – typically a major character may have a 512x512 texture assigned to it with the possible addition of a 256 texture for the head or outstanding feature. The "next generation" consoles and PCs support higher graphics processing and are able to present High Definition Television images.

This means that not only a greater number of textures but also larger textures are possible and are used in the games on these consoles.

Mapping

Once the texture has been prepared it is then ready to be placed onto the mesh of the model – this is called 'mapping'. Placing the texture onto the surface of the model will give it the appearance of greater detail without increasing the complexity of the underlying mesh. If the object was simple in nature and only made out of one item then the task of texturing would be very simple. However, in reality designers are usually dealing with extremely complex shapes and might need a number of textures to be placed on the surface of the model in order to achieve the desired result. In order to do this they undertake a process called 'UV mapping'. The full term is 'UVW mapping' (usually shortened to 'UV map') where the letters UVW are the coordinates for the texture, just like XYZ (but these are already being used as a reference in the model space). A UVW map is a flat image, the points on which are related to points on the surface of the model. Once this image is created, the UV map can be applied to the model in order to give it its textured appearance.

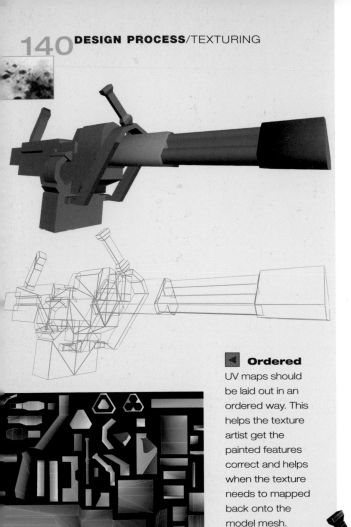

Most modelling programs will have a UV editor – this part of the program 'unwraps' the model's polygons and lays them out flat on a two-dimensional surface. These polygons can then be used as reference for the texture artist to create the texture relating to the part of the model in the area of the polygons as seen in the UV map. The texture artist needs to be very ordered with his laying out of the texture map in order to be efficient and allow ease of applying the UV map to the model mesh. As the examples show, a UV map can contain many disconnected parts of the whole texture. When the modeller places the texture on the model he has to tell the program which parts of the texture to place on what parts of the model.

Well laid-out UV maps help the texture artist get the painted features right first time, and make the process of mapping the texture back onto the model mesh much easier. The way the modelling program maps the texture back onto the surface of the mesh can also be varied, for example planar mapping – simply placing the texture flat onto the surface; spherical mapping – the texture is gathered around the object; face or automatic mapping – the texture is placed in relation to the surface it resides on. This latter method is most common and is used to give dynamic effects for complex meshes such as people and creatures.

◄ **Ordered**

UV maps should be laid out in an ordered way. This helps the texture artist get the painted features correct and helps when the texture needs to mapped back onto the model mesh.

▲ **Rendering**

In the example you can see a model of a futuristic mini-gun. The mesh is quite simple with no extra surface detail added. A UV map was generated from the wireframe and then the texture artist created the textures over this template. Finally the texture was re-applied to the gun to result in the final, finished render.

▶ Design exercise: **Wall texture**

In this exercise you will make a simple wall texture that will seamlessly tile when placed in an environment. First get an image of a standard brick wall (such as your own garden wall). Note that the image used must have been taken perpendicular to the wall.

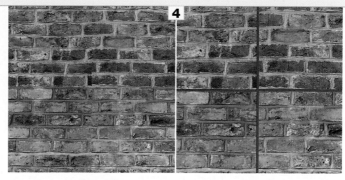

Step 1

Open the image up in your image-manipulation program (Adobe Photoshop in this example). Then choose an area roughly 512 pixels square (the size of the texture in this example). Be careful to pick a section that has no strong features in it. You will note in the original drawing there are some strong white patches and some chalk marks. These would stand out in the final texture and the repetition would ruin the effect for the viewer. Also check where your edges are, and try to guess ahead by selecting along mortar lines; try to avoid oversized bricks or over-thick mortar lines in the final piece. Also note that the section is from the middle of the image. Toward the edges of a photograph there may be some 'bulging' effect due to the nature of the camera lens.

Step 2

Size the image to exactly 512 pixels square, trimming and making sure the mortar lines are horizontal.

Joints

The joints in the texture can be seen. They need careful digital painting to remove them.

Step 3

Now comes the clever bit. In Photoshop there is a filter called 'offset'. This filter cuts the image into quarters and swaps them around as in the diagram.

Step 4

Set the filter to wrap around and the offset to half of the image size – 256 pixels. The result of this action is that the edges of the image will now match up to the corresponding edges of the adjacent images when tiled.

If your image-processing program does not have this filter you will need to manually cut the image into exact quarters and reposition it by hand.

Step 5

There are now visible seams in the middle of the image which must be removed. This is done manually by carefully working along the seam and painting over it with a selection from elsewhere in the image. In Adobe Photoshop, the clone tool allows you to select a piece of the image from another area and paint it in. This has the effect of hiding the seam. Other useful tools for hiding edges are the blur and smudge tools.

Step 6

Now you should have a brick wall with a seamless texture, 512 pixels square.

If you create a larger canvas and match up four examples of your texture side by side, they should tessellate seamlessly.

This short exercise was designed to show that part of the art of creating a texture is selecting a good image and carefully preparing it. There is no substitute for experience here and you should practise as much as possible.

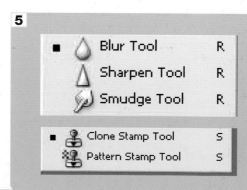

► Design exercise: **Textured crate**

The ubiquitous crate is a common sight in games. It can hold some helpful items, be useful to hide behind, climb on top of, or simply get in the way. This exercise takes you through the process of texturing a basic crate and gives you an idea of how textures are applied to meshes.

Before you start this exercise you will need to build yourself a crate texture like the one below. The one shown here used a 512-pixel square image, which was cut exactly into quarters and then painted as four sides of a wooden crate in Adobe Photoshop. Only four sides were needed as one or more can be used twice on the crate. The shading of the planks on the side of the crate was incorporated in the texture, to avoid modelling it and so keep the poly count as low as possible. Once your image is ready, save it as a .tga file and you are ready to begin.

This exercise uses Maya as the modeller due to its prominence in the games industry. If you do not have access to a full copy of Maya you can download the free Autodesk Maya Personal Learning Edition from the website www.autodesk.com. The tutorial assumes knowledge of the Maya interface via the built-in and online tutorials.

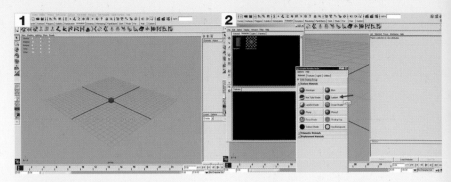

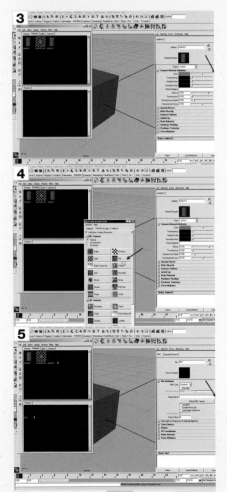

1 Open Maya and follow the instructions. Refer to the screenshots for reference. Some instructions are written as a series of **instructions** with a '>' to indicate steps. The first word is the initial menu command with the further instructions following in sequence.
Create > polygon primitives > cube.
Press '6' to see in textured mode.

2 Press 'f' to zoom extents –
this zooms in on the cube to fill the whole scene.
Window > rendering editors > Multilister.
In the **materials** tab select
Edit > create.
Choose Lambert.

3 Double-click on **new material** to get its properties.
Click on the **colour box** in the RH menu.

4 Then choose **file**.

5 Click folder icon next to **image name**.
Find your box texture file on your hard drive.

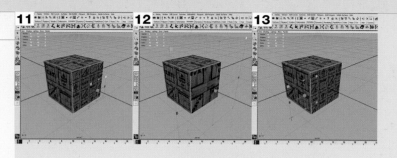

11, 12, and 13 Using the handles on the **planar projection tool** you can shift or scale the projection (This is optional.)

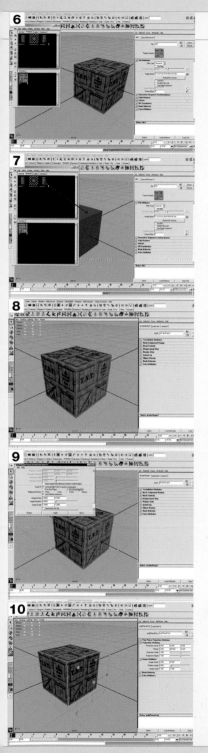

6 and 7 Drag and drop the material (not the texture) onto the cube.

8 Select the cube. Press **F11** to go into **face** mode and then select the face. It will highlight the face.

9 *Edit polygons > texture > planar mapping*. Select the options box icon at the right of the menu.
In the options select **Fit to bounding box** and check the **mapping direction**. In the example, look at xyz and see which way the selected face – in this case, x – faces.

10 Click **project** and the **planar projection tool** will appear.

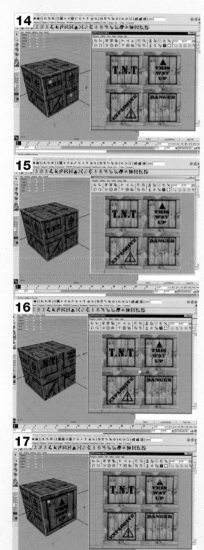

14 Select *Window > UV texture editor*, and the editor appears.

15 Right-click in the window and select **UV**. You will now be able to drag a window round the face (in the UV editor) and highlight the UVs in green.

16 You should be able to scale and move the UVs using the standard manipulation tools. You can manipulate them individually or as groups. (You don't have to do this as part of the exercise – it is here as a demonstration.)

17 Move, scale, or rotate the manipulator in the **UV editor window** until the projection just covers the one section of the texture you require. The scale goes into the negative – and then back out. Exploit this scale to 'flip' the projection, either creating reversed textures and text or fixing reversed textures.

► Design exercise: **Textured crate (cont.)**

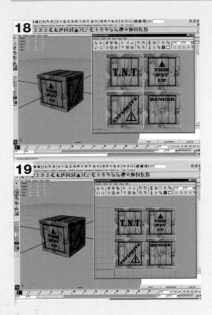

18 Click somewhere other than the cube in the main window to de-select the face, and select a new face. Repeat the action from before – *edit poly > texture > planar > options box* – on a new face and remember to choose the correct mapping direction for the new face.

Repeat this for every face. You should now have all of the faces mapped but there may be areas which appear a bit inaccurate.

19 You can now right-click in the **UV editor** and move the **vertices** around to make the exact vertices and edges of the geometry line up with the image.

20 You now have your finished mapped and textured crate.

This may be the the first step in your texturing career and there is a long way to go before you are modelling characters. This is a good beginner's exercise, but if you feel ready for another challenge, try thinking of other 'boxes' such as ammunition crates.

Alpha channels

Textures can also add other visual effects to a model beyond simple surface effects. The use of a fourth channel, other than red, blue and green – known as an alpha channel – can make certain parts of the model transparent to give the effect of a window or translucent material. Alpha channels can also add specular information – this indicates whether the item is shiny or not.

Alpha channels appear black and white in the texture editor with the black areas being a mask (opaque or no effect) and the white being the area of effect (transparent or shiny).

Bump mapping

Bump mapping refers to a grayscale texture image. When the image is rendered the data is used so that a lighter area is 'higher' and a darker area is 'lower'. This enhances the three-dimensional appearance of the object without building in more geometry.

Normal mapping

Normal mapping works in a similar way to bump mapping but it uses colour (red, green and blue, as used in monitors) to produce a textured effect. Normal mapping can be particularly effective because a normal map from a high-resolution (high poly count) model can be used on a low-resolution (low poly count) model. The effect is to give the appearance of a high-resolution model from a more efficient low-resolution model. Normal mapping is used extensively in current games as it gives excellent graphic quality with reduced processing demands.

Displacement mapping

Displacement mapping uses a greyscale image as an information channel but this time the data from the tones in the image are used to actually move the model vertices in order to create a textured effect.

Vertex and pixel shaders

These aspects of texturing and modelling are at the forefront of technology in games. Shaders can affect the final appearance of a model's surface such as the amount of light reflection, how the light is diffused, and further effects on texture, refraction, shadows and other aspects. Vertex shaders work on moving the vertices of the model mesh while pixel shaders work on the colour of individual pixels in the image.

Future developments

With the increase in speed and processing power of PCs and consoles there are sure to be many new developments in modelling and texturing. Vertex and pixel shading are finding their way into many games engines and many special visual effects are delivered via texturing techniques. One such development is the mega texture. Developed by id Software, mega textures have been developed to represent large-scale environments (such as outdoors) without the drawbacks of repeating textures forming visible patterns in the landscape. A mega texture can be 32,000x32,000 pixels square (1 giga pixel), which can cover the polygonal mesh of a landscape with a single texture. This gives a unique and highly detailed non-repeating terrain over a large play area. The code behind the mega texture can also hold information about the terrain such as ambient sound and physical properties in an efficient manner. It is thought that this approach will give better, more detailed scenes as opposed to current technologies using tiled textures.

The raw power in the newest machines means that they can utilise larger tiling textures and output them at HDTV resolutions. The increase in power can also support higher polygon models and present more surface detail and texture, giving a richer, finer image. The job of the texture artist will be to continually develop techniques to deliver ever more visually believable worlds.

▼ Sophisticated texture effects

Enemy Territory: Quake Wars uses "mega textures" to create sophisticated light and shadow effects across a large, outdoor environment. As well as creating complex effects such as foliage, mega textures can also contain information about sound and game physics.

Texture over geometry

The modellers' and texture artists' continual struggle is to keep the processing requirements of models and textures low in order for games to run smoothly. It requires more processing power to represent a model mesh on the screen rather than a texture. It is therefore better and more efficient to have a simple model with a complex texture than a more detailed 3D model.

Lo-res textures

On-screen textures are lo-res – 72 DPI, the same as a monitor or TV screen. They can look extremely simple when reproduced in print. But when they are used together in a game they can create a very convincing effect.

Cargo

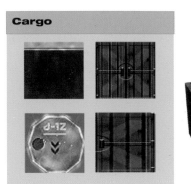

Girders and roof

Walls

Floor

Details

▲ Ready for texturing

An untextured interior surrounded by some of the textures prepared for the surface of the model.

Illusion of complexity

The illustrations below and right show a grim and gritty, complex-seeming warehouse interior, with striking light effects. This is a perfect scene for a game to take place, with a wealth of detail and atmosphere, each surface bearing the marks of industrial use.

But compare this with the flat, shaded model of the same interior on the left, and the construction begins to look rather plain and simple. You can see that all the walls, barrels and containers are nothing more than simple, smooth polygons.

If you then look at the flat texture samples, you should begin to spot the individual images which have given the impression of complex surfaces in the fully rendered scene. You will notice that some are used many times within the scene.

▲ **Textured mesh**
Cargo textures have been used to make simple meshes appear as cargo-type objects in the scene.

◄ ▲ **Finished rendered scene**
This rendered scene demonstrates how very simple textures work together to create an atmospheric, seemingly complex interior.

Building a character

From concept to virtual being

Building an in-game character is one of the most complex jobs facing a designer. Not only is representing a human form a demanding task but the creation of textures and rigging for animation are equally challenging. The character in question might not even be human – it might be an animal, cartoon character, or an alien, with its own type and number of limbs, body shape, and ways of moving. If you refer to the section on character concept (see page 94) you should have a mental picture of what your character is like, and this is an excellent point from which to start the building phase.

Concept art

The starting point for any character is the artists' concept illustrations. The artists will generate many sketches of the character in different styles and with varying attitudes, until the design team decides that they have the right one.

◀ ▼ **Armoured trooper sketches**

These illustrations show a design for a futuristic armoured trooper. Using a mixture of traditional and digital media the artist has developed visuals which show a variety of troopers. Though these will be the main playable characters in the game it was decided that they should look menacing to tie in with the dangerous tasks they will be executing within the game.

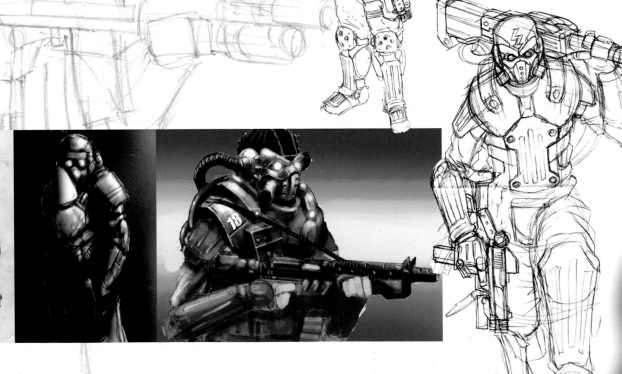

Design exercise: **Sketches**

Select a character concept to illustrate; you may wish to use the character concept you created for the exercise on Character concepts (see page 94). Whatever character you choose, make sure your first one is not too outlandish and has visual characteristics you can reference well.

The designer's role

Execute a number of sketches to design and develop your character. While you are drawing, continually ask yourself if your illustration fits the concept. Can you make any part of the character look better or more interesting?

Use lots of references from the Internet, magazines, or even photographs you have taken yourself. Try to avoid existing fictional creations as you run the risk of simply imitating an existing character style – the aim is to create your own.

Produce as many sketches as you are comfortable with, and draw the character at rest as well as in action. What does he/she/it look like from the back, the side and at odd angles? By the end of this exercise you should be familiar with the visual style and appearance of your character.

▶ **Internet research**
The Internet can be an excellent source of reference material to inform your character design sketches, as these examples show.

▲ **Trooper design**
The preferred design was arrived at, with the trooper having a dark jumpsuit over which plates of armour are attached for defence. There is a slight echo of modern SWAT teams with the right amount of unique 'equipment' to make the characters look futuristic. The design team also decided on face protection for the character to enhance the threatening look.

09

Modelling

With the design settled, the artist now prepares a clean and accurate working illustration of the front and side of the character. Sometimes a plan and a rear view are used as well. These drawings will form the base from which the model will be built.

Bulk of body

First, the body is built from individual polygons; the bulk of the body is defined.

Details added

The body begins to take shape, and more details are added.

▲ Two planes

This example uses Alias 3D Studio Max but the process is similar for other modelling packages too. In the modelling program two planes are created at right angles and the images are placed onto these as textures. They are correctly proportioned to the character. Using these references the modeller can now begin to build the model over the images. By looking directly from the front or the side the modeller can see the profile straight on and begin to create geometry to match. In this case the modeller used flat planes within the model and extruded edges and moved vertices in order to create the geometry.

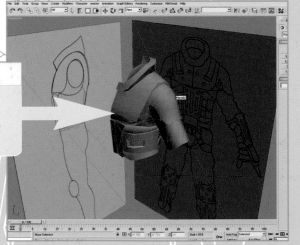

◄ Moving vertices

In the illustrations you can see how the modeller first looks at the front of the model and then the side in order to develop form. This method begins with flat planes to build the model. Other methods start with a cube or cylinder and extrude faces from those. The principle in both methods is the same, which is moving vertices to align with the illustration reference. This part of building the model is quite painstaking and the modeller will have to continue to switch views back and forth and keep checking if the model he is building is accurate. The modeller continues in this manner until he is satisfied.

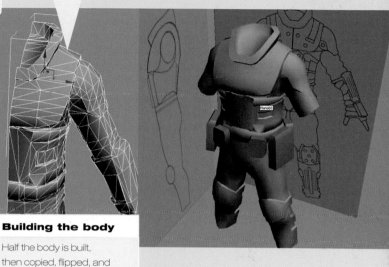
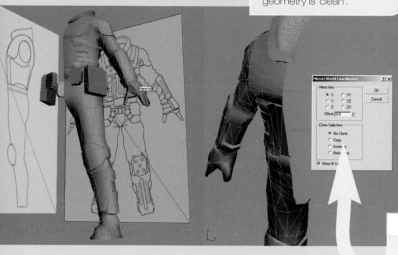

Polygon check
Viewing the edges of the polygons allows the modeller to check the geometry is 'clean'.

Building the body
Half the body is built, then copied, flipped, and attached to the other half to build a complete body.

▲ Building half a model

It is interesting to note that only half the model is built in this fashion; this is because if the character is human it is also symmetrical. When half of the character is built the modeller can simply mirror it within the modelling program and the other half will appear. Working in this way also makes sure that no discrepancies sneak into either side of the model to make it look lopsided.

▶ Body model

The model of the body is built. Because this is a central character in the game, and will be seen a lot by the player, it has a relatively high polygon budget (see page 126) and that means it can be a more complex model. This gives the modeller the opportunity to model the head separately and pay particular attention to getting the form of the mesh right.

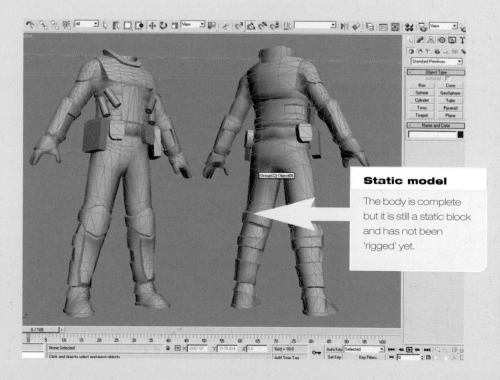

Static model
The body is complete but it is still a static block and has not been 'rigged' yet.

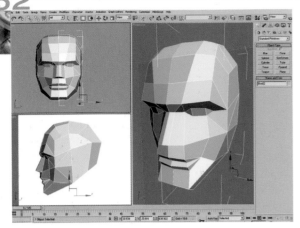

◀ Building a head

Using a different technique from that used to construct the body, the modeller first builds a dummy head to the correct scale (this will be deleted later). This is used for reference for the helmet. The modeller builds half the helmet and spends time making sure that the artist's original vision is maintained.

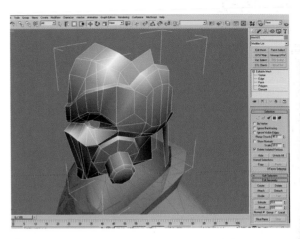

▶ Mirroring

As with the body, the head is constructed as one half, copied, and mirrored to make it complete. Careful inspection of the quality of the model mesh is required to make sure it is well ordered.

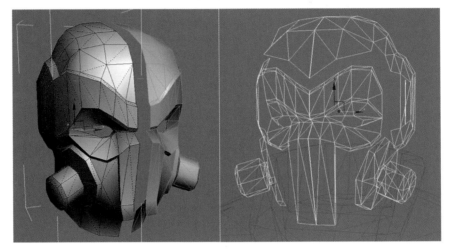

▲ Neck check

The head is continually referenced with the body during the build to ensure the polygons in the neck can be attached easily to those of the torso.

▼ Poly count

The head has a higher density mesh than the body; the form of the character's face is very important.

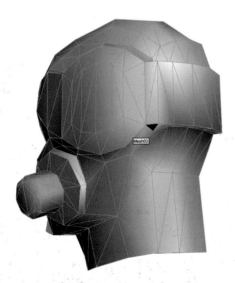

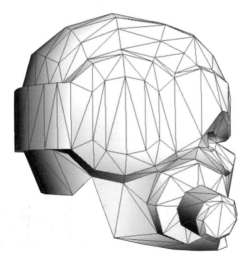

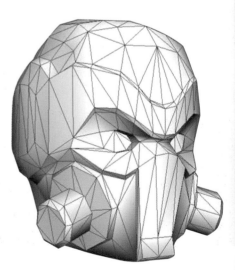

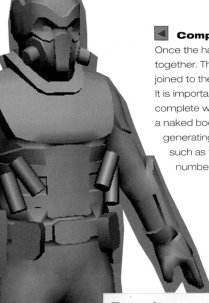

◀ Completing the model

Once the half-head is made, it is mirrored and joined together. The vertices at the neck of the head are then joined to the neck of the body. The model is complete. It is important to note that the model is constructed complete with the character's clothes. You don't model a naked body and then add clothes. This is to avoid generating unnecessary polygons that will not be seen, such as the inside of a jacket, leaving the maximum number of polygons available for outside detail.

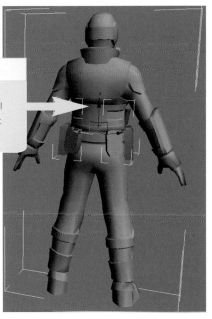

Rear view

The finished model has as much attention to detail from the rear as there is at the front.

▶ Design exercise: Working drawings

Using the sketches from the previous exercise (see page 149), produce working drawings of your character from the front, side and top. The drawings must all be to the same scale. They should be line drawings, describing the major shape of your character. Drawings of this type would be used as model reference drawings, as shown on these two pages.

◀ Modelling clothes

Modelling clothes and making extra adornments that are not part of the character is only done for high-end animation purposes where effects such as the folds of cloth or hair are required. In some instances, in-game clothes may be modelled separately, for example to allow a cape to move naturally, or other items that move independently of the character, but this is usually reserved for the main character.

▼ Props

This character has a prop – his gun – and this too requires modelling, with the same attention to detail, poly count and reference to the artist's designs as for the character.

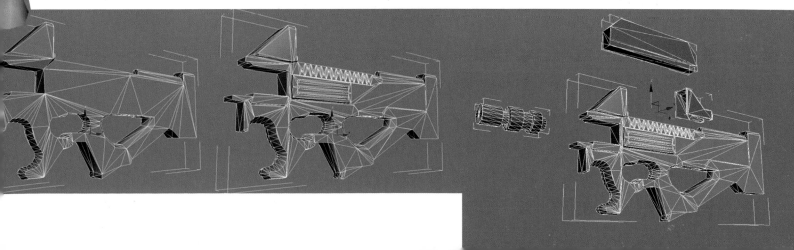

Rigging

The finished character model is simply a solid block like a statue; it cannot move or be moved as required for the game. In order for it to become animated, it requires a skeleton to be placed inside it which can be moved in a similar way to a human skeleton. This process is often referred to as 'rigging'. A humanoid skeleton, or rig, is usually included in a modelling package and this can be adjusted to suit the tastes of the modeller. It is also possible to adapt and create your own skeletons and rigs within modelling packages.

◄ Joints

A rig is made from bones and joints (to use the skeleton analogy). Each bone will be connected by a joint and there will be a hierarchy of movement. The program controlling the movement of these will also have limits to how they all move in relation to each other – this is called 'inverse kinematics'. To understand this you only need to look at the joints in your body, as these are what the rig is representing.

Movement

Visualise your arm – your wrist (joint), your forearm (bone), your elbow (joint), your upper arm (bone) and your shoulder (joint). There are two bones and three joints. Your arm joints can only move in certain ways – they cannot twist in every direction, and there are limits to your movement. If you want to put your hand above your head all the other bones and joints have to move as well. This is a demonstration of inverse kinematics – how elements move in relation to each other.

To rig a model you first need to insert the rig, either supplied by the modelling program or custom-built. This sits inside the model and is only visible in the modelling program. The next stage is to relate parts of the model mesh to the rig – this tells the program that when a certain bone or joint moves, the model should move in the same manner. So if you take the hand bone of your character model and move it above its head, the rest of the arm should move with it, as a human arm would.

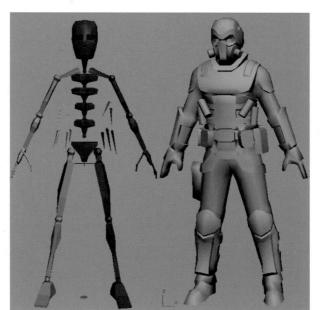

◄ Attaching a rig

The rig (left) must be placed within the finished character model (right) before the character can be animated.

Handles

The skeleton, or rig, is attached to corresponding joints in the main model. This provides 'handles' for the animator to grab in order to pose the model.

Joints

If you look at your arm again you will notice that when you bend it at the elbow your skin on the outside and inside of your arm flexes to accommodate the movement. When building an in-game character, special care is taken over the places in the model where joints will be and they are modelled in a manner that will make them appear natural when they bend. Again there are no hard and fast directions here and knowing how to effectively build realistic joints comes with practice and experience.

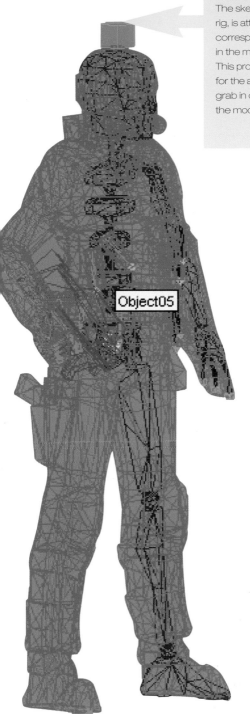

Object05

Rigging details

The rig of the belt pouches corresponds to the main model.

◀ Rigs for objects

Rigs in models need to not only be applied to the figure, but to anything that might move with the character. You may note in the initial trooper rig illustration that there are several pieces of skeleton around the waist area. These are applied to the pouches and equipment linked to the trooper's vest to give them the ability to move as the trooper moves, and make them bounce realistically as the character moves.

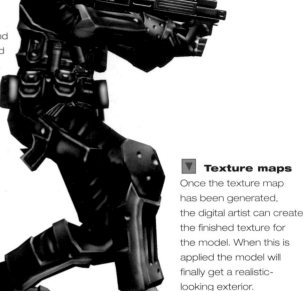

Texturing

Texturing can be quite complex (see Texturing, page 138), particularly on a character. A character will have to be unwrapped and the unwrapped areas laid out in a texture map (see page 140). This texture map will then be created by an artist in a 2D program such as Adobe Photoshop, and skin and clothes will be created for the character. The texture map can be a combination of photographic references as well as digitally painted work.

▶ Inspection

The completed rigged and textured character should be posed and inspected. Even at this late stage there may be some problems where textures do not fit properly, or limbs do not bend naturally. A last-minute check is always recommended.

▼ Texture maps

Once the texture map has been generated, the digital artist can create the finished texture for the model. When this is applied the model will finally get a realistic-looking exterior.

Checkered map

A checkered texture map guides the UV unwrapping process. The modeller can see where the chequered pattern distorts around the body, and make adjustments accordingly.

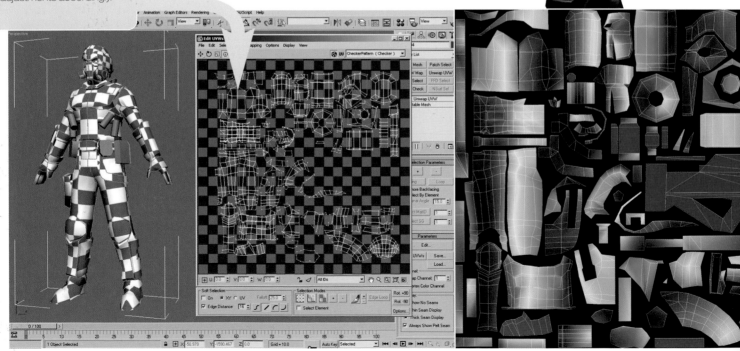

Animation

Now the character is rigged and built it is ready to be animated. Yet again this requires a different set of skills and more often than not it is carried out by specialist animators. A rigged character can be posed just like a real model, and the animation process is not dissimilar to stop-frame animation techniques where the pose is altered minutely, recorded, and then moved again. However with games it all takes place within the modelling program. A character will be seen doing many different things in a game – walking, climbing, falling, etc. Each of these actions will have a short animation of the character moving in the relevant manner; these are generally called animation sets. So for each action your character will do, there will be an animation set and the game engine will play that animation whenever the character is engaged in that action within the game. These sets are usually cyclic so that when they run they return to a neutral position. These are called cycles. The simplest form is the walk cycle. Rather than a long animation of somebody walking, the animator will simply animate

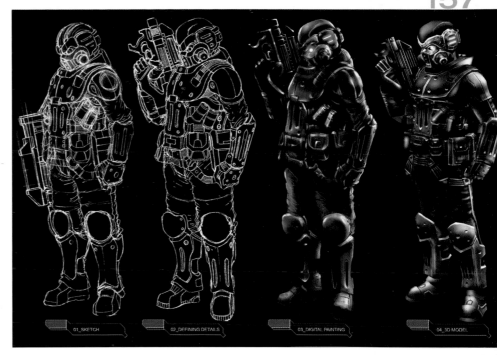

01_SKETCH   02_DEFINING DETAILS   03_DIGITAL PAINTING   04_3D MODEL

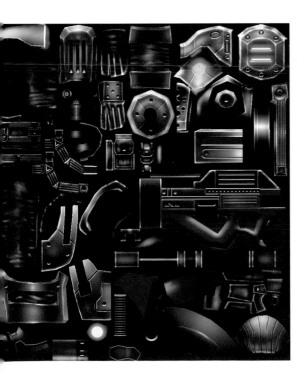

the character taking one step. The animator will make sure that when the character has taken its step it will be in the same position as the start. If you continually play this cycle you get the appearance of the character walking. To give you some idea how much animation that is, on the following page is a list of animation sets for a concept proposal concerning a game set in an international prison.

▶ Finished model

The trooper is now complete with skeleton and texture and a polygon count suitable for inclusion in a game engine. A piece of work like this represents a considerable amount of experience and expertise on the part of the artist and modeller. A single character like this may represent several weeks' worth of work to build from scratch and it might be one of many within a game.

▼ **Animation sets**

An example list of animation sets for a game that takes place in an international prison.

Base Animation Set

Walk_01	Character basic walk
Run_01	Character basic run
Use_01	Character uses a object in front of them at table height
Use_02	Character uses a object in front of them at head height
Idle_01	Character stands idle, hands in pocket, looking around
Idle_02	Character kicks dust on the floor, looks around behind him
Idle_03	Character looks down at watch and scratches head
Watch_01	Character crosses arms and watches / listens to NPC or fight
Talk_01	Character talks to another NPC
Talk_02	Character talks to NPC suggestively by moving arms around
Sit_Idle_01	Character sits idle waiting
Sit_Idle_02	Character sits idle more forward reading
Sit_Eat_01	Character sits and eats
Sit_Watch_01	Character sits forward resting arms on knees watching NPCs
Sit_Watch_02	Character sits upright watching NPCs
Punch_01	Character throws a basic punch
Hit_01	Character gets hit by a punch
Hit_02	Character gets hit by a two-combo punch
Hit_03	Character gets hit by a three-combo punch
Hit_04	Character gets hit by a four-combo punch
Hit_05	Character gets hit and goes down on one knee
Hit_06	Character gets hit and goes down
Block_01	Character basic block from a punch
Fight_01	Character takes up a fighting stance

Neutral NPC's Specific Animations & Cullen

Work_01	Character operates machinery (construction yard)
Work_02	Character operates tool (construction yard)
Work_03	Character operates machinery (oil refinery)
Work_04	Character operates tool (oil refinery)
Combo_01	Character throws a two-punch combo
Combo_02	Character throws a three-punch combo
Combo_03	Character throws a four-punch combo
Carry_01	Character carries light object
Carry_02	Character carries heavy object
Idle_03	Character stands idle leaning over railing
Cheer_01	Character stands cheering (fight / sport)
Cheer_02	Character stands cheering fight with bet object in one hand

British NPC's Specific Animations

Play_07	Character stands idle with soccer ball
Play_08	Character runs dribbling soccer ball
Play_09	Character kicks soccer ball to another NPC
Play_10	Character tackles another NPC
Play_11	Character kicks soccer ball into goal
Play_12	Character receives a pass from another NPC
Fight_03	Character squares up to a NPC (gang-specific)
Taunt_04	Gang specific taunt
Taunt_05	Gang specific taunt
Taunt_06	Gang specific taunt
Work_09	Character operates machinery (construction yard)
Work_10	Character operates tool (construction yard)
Work_11	Character operates machinery (oil refinery)
Work_12	Character operates tool (oil refinery)
Combo_01	Character throws a two-punch combo
Combo_02	Character throws a three-punch combo

Combo_03	Character throws a four-punch combo
Carry_01	Character carries light object
Carry_02	Character carries heavy object
Idle_03	Character stands idle leaning over railing
Cheer_01	Character stands cheering (fight / sport)
Cheer_02	Character stands cheering fight with bet object in one hand

Mexican NPC's Specific Animations

Play_01	Character stands idle bouncing basketball
Play_02	Character runs whilst bouncing basketball
Play_03	Character throws basketball
Play_04	Character blocks move to stop a NPC throwing basketball
Play_05	Character throws basketball into hoop
Play_06	Character catches basketball
Fight_02	Character squares up to a NPC (gang-specific)
Taunt_01	Gang specific taunt
Taunt_02	Gang specific taunt
Taunt_03	Gang specific taunt
Work_05	Character operates machinery (construction yard)
Work_06	Character operates tool (construction yard)
Work_07	Character operates machinery (oil refinery)
Work_08	Character operates tool (oil refinery)
Combo_01	Character throws a two-punch combo
Combo_02	Character throws a three-punch combo
Combo_03	Character throws a four-punch combo
Carry_01	Character carries light object
Carry_02	Character carries heavy object
Idle_03	Character stands idle leaning over railing
Cheer_01	Character stands cheering (fight / sport)
Cheer_02	Character stands cheering fight with bet object in one hand

Prison Cook Specific Animations

Combo_01	Character throws a two-punch combo
Combo_02	Character throws a three-punch combo
Combo_03	Character throws a four-punch combo
Work_13	Character working in kitchen
Work_14	Character working in kitchen
Work_15	Character serving food
Carry_01	Character carries light object
Carry_02	Character carries heavy object

Italian Mafia Specific Animations

Play_13	Character deals cards
Play_14	Character plays cards
Play_15	Character throws betting object
Play_16	Character collects betting object
Fight_03	Character squares up to a NPC (gang-specific)
Taunt_04	Gang specific taunt
Taunt_05	Gang specific taunt
Taunt_06	Gang specific taunt
Work_09	Character operates machinery (construction yard)
Work_10	Character operates tool (construction yard)
Work_11	Character operates machinery (oil refinery)
Work_12	Character operates tool (oil refinery)
Combo_01	Character throws a two-punch combo
Combo_02	Character throws a three-punch combo
Combo_03	Character throws a four-punch combo
Carry_01	Character carries light object
Carry_02	Character carries heavy object
Idle_03	Character stands idle leaning over railing
Cheer_01	Character stands cheering (fight / sport)
Cheer_02	Character stands cheering fight with bet object

Italian Bookie Specific Animations

Bet_01	Character collects bet objects
Bet_02	Character gives out bet objects
Bet_03	Character points to fight area
Bet_04	Character counts bet objects

Guard Dog Specific Animations

Idle_04	Character sits idle
Idle_05	Character stands idle
Alert_01	Character is alerted gives light pull on leash
Alert_02	Character is alerted and gives a medium pull on leash
Alert_03	Character is alerted and gives a heavy pull on leash
Alert_04	Character is alerted at maximum level and ba
Attack_01	Character attacks NPC / Player

Light Guard Specific Animations

Call_01	Character calls to another guard for help
Idle_06	Character stands idle playing with weapon
Guard_01	Character on guard
Patrol_01	Character on guard patrolling area
Guard_02	Character on guard with dog
Patrol_02	Character on guard patrolling with guard
Fight_01	Character uses weapon and hits NPC / player
Block_02	Character blocks with weapon
Pickup_01	Two characters pick up player
Item_01	Character discovers player item hiding area
Altert_05	Character discovers player in restricted area
Search_01	Character searches NPC or player

Heavy Guard Specific Animations

Call_01	Character calls to another guard for help
Idle_06	Character stands idle playing with weapon
Guard_01	Character on guard
Patrol_01	Character on guard patrolling area
Fight_01	Character uses weapon and hits NPC / player
Block_02	Character blocks with weapon
Item_01	Character discovers player item hiding area
Altert_05	Character discovers player in restricted area
Search_01	Character searches NPC or Player
Taunt_07	Character taunts player after fight and hits hi
Taunt_08	Character taunts player after fight and hits hi
Taunt_09	Character taunts player after fight and hits hi

Player Character Specific Animations

Combo_01	Character throws a two-punch combo
Combo_02	Character throws a three-punch combo
Combo_03	Character throws a four-punch combo
Carry_01	Character carries light object
Carry_02	Character carries heavy object
Sneak_01	Character crouches slightly to sneak around at night
Ledge_01	Character walks onto ledge, back facing
Plant_01	Character plants object on a NPC
Distraction_01	Character in sneak mode bangs a wall to distract guards
Bribe_01	Character bribes guard

Motion capture

Motion capture is the technique by which the action of live actors is captured on special video systems and then applied to a rigged model in order to animate it. This can give some very realistic results as the small movements and nuances of expression can be caught by the camera. This can give the model a very lifelike set of movements. However, motion capture remains an expensive and inconsistent technology. The cost of actors and the specialist equipment usually puts motion capture out of the reach of small studios, though it would seem reasonable to expect that as technology improves the cost of motion capture will fall. The main problem with motion capture is that the systems do not always work as expected and the data needs extensive 'cleaning' to be made to work, or even scrapping and re-recording. With the danger of this hidden expense it is often felt better to give the time and support to traditional animators to create the animation sets for games.

▲ Motion capture shoot

The two actors shown here are performing a fight sequence for the game Metal Gear Solid 3: Snake Eater. Sensors have been placed on the actors and the cameras are set to record their motion. These points are related to joints within the model mesh of the game characters, and are used to drive their movements on-screen.

▶ Design exercise: **Character model**

There are no half-measures with this exercise; you need to be fairly familiar with a modelling program. Set up the drawings from the previous exercises (see pages 149 and 153) on reference planes and attempt to model your character. It will be difficult the first time and you will make mistakes. Patience is the key here, and if this is an area of the games industry that interests you then you must keep trying until you get it right. At first do not attempt to put too much detail into your character – concentrate on getting the basic form correct and looking humanoid. You can always be more elaborate in your next creation. When you feel you have accomplished this to your satisfaction, you could always try texture-mapping your model!

Music and audio design

From bleep/bloop to sophisticated soundtracks

Music and audio design in computer games had an inauspicious start. Early arcade machines, computers and consoles were known more for their flashing lights than their pinging noises, and 'computer game music' was a term of abuse. Fortunately, those days have gone, and modern games consoles and PCs have very sophisticated sound hardware, freeing up the imagination of audio engineers and composers.

Despite huge advances, audio technology, music and sound rarely take the lead in games development. When RAM budgets get tight, audio is the first thing to be scaled back. This is because audio files can be huge. Uncompressed, high-quality sound effects and music quickly eat into your overall system RAM. Creating a convincing soundtrack to complement the game requires many individual sound files. So while an artist and coder may have spent a lot of time and effort creating a world-destroying explosion, using a frugal partial system, for the game's ultimate weapon, without a similarly huge and speaker-shattering explosion, the effect of the weapon will be lost. The problem is that the longer the sample, the more system memory it eats up. There are, however, many techniques possible using hardware and software to help the sound designer create the most impressive soundtrack in as small a space as possible.

History of audio

Here's a quick history lesson in computer game audio. The first games device for the home to be blessed with anything like good sound playback was the Commodore 64. A whole host of clever programmer musicians (you really needed to be a programmer and a musician back then) created some impressive and memorable game soundtracks

for the C64, despite the severe limitations of the hardware. Toward the end of the C64's lifespan programmers had even got their rudimentary sample playback working, even though there was nothing in the hardware to play samples back.

Playback of compressed samples

The next big jump in audio for computer games came from Nintendo. The Super Nintendo was the first console to have a sound chip that allowed compressed samples to be played back. This was a pretty basic system that allowed a straight 4:1 compression of sound. This means that each sample will be a quarter of its RAW size. Often, the sound designer and musician were only allowed 64k to do all the game's sound effects and music. Also, because the Super Nintendo was a cartridge-based system, there was no cheating to be done with CD playback or streamed audio.

Music on the Super Nintendo (and most early consoles) was MIDI or 'sequence' based. That means that the game had code for a music player that read a data file that contained the notes that needed to be played to create the musical soundtrack. The bulk of the sound storage on the cartridge was used as a 'sound bank'. This is a set of data that contained all the instruments and sound effects for the game.

▲ **Synthesized sound at home**

The Commodore 64, a popular home computer, had a specific sound chip called SID that had all the basic elements needed to create synthesised sound. It had three channels of sound that had to be used for both the music and the sound effects.

◀ Compressed sample playback

The Super Nintendo had a sound chip that could play back compressed samples. The compression was necessary as the games came on expensive cartridges with limited data storage.

▲ Increased storage capacity

The PlayStation enabled sound streaming from CD, and offered massively increased compression, giving sound designers more scope than before.

Doubling up

A lot of impressive game soundtracks were created in the limited amount of memory space available. Sound designers were forced to become very creative, for example pitching or changing the envelope of snare drums so they could double up as gunshots or explosions. This practice still goes on today for games on mobile phones. Just as with a Super Nintendo console, RAM on a mobile phone is limited for sound, so clever use of software compression on playback and reuse of sound effects is essential. Super Nintendo and C64 soundtracks are easily downloaded from the Internet for playback in software like WinAmp. Try downloading some and have a listen to what was possible with such limited sound hardware.

CD sound

The next big leap in game audio was made by a company known primarily for portable audio. The Sony PlayStation helped lift computer game audio out of the stereotype of 'bleep and bloop'. For the first time a games console enabled the creation of complex musical scores to be streamed from CD, while allowing the sound designer 512K of sound RAM. Sample playback also had 4:1 compression, effectively allowing the sound designer to use 2mb of RAW sample data at any one time. Because of the increased storage capacity of the CD, each game level could have its own sound bank, allowing for a true variety of audio throughout the game.

Increasing capabilities

When Microsoft introduced the Xbox it promoted 'Direct Music', part of the core 'Direct X' libraries used to control the hardware. 'Direct Music' was basically a way of controlling sound and music playback based on events that happen in the game. The game can talk to the music system, telling it, for example, how many enemies are attacking the player so the music can adjust accordingly. If nothing is attacking the player, a suspenseful piece of music is heard. If the player is suddenly attacked by a hundred ninjas, hyperenergetic fight music begins to play.

New prominence

The sound hardware on the Xbox shares the same system RAM as everything else, allowing the age-old arguments over the space required for audio to rage throughout the entire project's lifespan. Most modern games consoles and PCs now follow this unified architecture with sound and music taking their share of RAM and CPU for storage and processing.

As the technical capabilities of sound hardware increased, so has the professionalism of the people creating music and sound effects for games. Once the domain of bedroom hackers, modern game soundtracks are produced in expensive studios using exactly the same kind of equipment as Hollywood blockbusters.

▲ Unified RAM architecture

The Xbox sound hardware shares the same RAM as other game components, but memory space is still at a premium.

Pro Tools

The workhorse at the centre of all music studios is Pro Tools. A Pro Tools rig can range from something incredibly expensive, with lots of outboard processing feeding directly into the latest digital mixing desks, to a small blue box that sits neatly next to your laptop. Regardless of scale, the software essentially does the same thing – multi-track audio. Pro Tools allows the sound designer and musician to layer multiple audio tracks together to create a complete soundtrack. This could be anything from arranging a live orchestra for a full musical score to a few individual sounds played together to produce a new explosion sound.

Sound editors

Pro Tools is great for creating final soundtracks. However, it is often necessary to edit individual sounds with extreme accuracy before dropping them into the final mix. This is where a sound editor comes into play. There are three main sample-editing packages available: Sound Forge and Audition on the PC and Bias Peak on the Mac. Often that explosion sound you created will end up in one of these packages, to be trimmed when you reach the RAM limit. Sound editors allow you to quickly and easily chop away at sound files and reduce their resolution by changing the bit and sample rates. There are demo versions of these sound editors on the internet, as well as a number of free programs with more limited features if you're developing on a budget.

Useful websites

Pro Tools: www.digidesign.com
Sound Forge: www.sonymediasoftware.com/products/soundforgefamily.asp
Audition: www.adobe.com/products/audition
Bias: www.bias-inc.com

◄ ▼ Editing and mixing
Adobe Audition allows sounds to be manipulated, corrected, cleaned up and mixed. Parts of the interface resemble a physical mixing desk, providing the user with a quick visual point of reference. Sound recordings can be edited in a 'non-destructive' or 'destructive' way; trimming the sound-wave down to remove flaws.

Sequencers

Unless you are recording only live instruments, such as an orchestra, you will probably compose the music for the game using a sequencing package. Again, there are three main packages in use: Cubase, Logic, and Live. Logic is now exclusive to the Mac while Live and Cubase are available on both PC and Mac. Sequencers are compositional aids for musicians. They allow the musician to record both MIDI and audio performances to build up whole music tracks. Sequencers can control external music equipment such as synthesisers, samplers, and effects units. However these external hardware boxes are increasingly being replaced by software versions known as 'virtual instruments'. The introduction of virtual instruments has allowed many musicians to simplify their studio down to a laptop, a high-spec audio card, and a small musical keyboard to enter notes. There are demo versions of sequencers on the internet, as well as many different alternatives that range from being free to very expensive.

Sound effects

A musician and sound designer need to have sounds. For sound effects there are a number of (expensive) sound-effects libraries, often produced by movie companies such as Warner and 20th Century Fox. These libraries are, in effect, huge 'box-sets' of CDs, full of sounds designed for movies. The sound designer can browse the libraries for a suitable sound for anything used in the game. Similarly, musicians now have access to huge libraries of instrument sounds. Musicians who want to create an authentic-sounding orchestra soundtrack will turn to something like the 'Miroslav Vitous Symphonic Orchestra'. These are extremely high-quality recordings of the individual instruments of the orchestra that can be played back in your sequencer of choice.

Useful websites

Cubase: www.steinberg.net/24_1.html
Logic: www.apple.com/logicpro
Live: www.ableton.com

Visuals

Logic Pro 7 is supported by QuickTime, providing the user with a visual point of reference for sound editing.

Score transcript

The audio is transcribed into a score in real time.

▲ **Processing**

Logic Pro 7 is a powerful composing, recording, editing and mixing tool. Its processing power can be massively enlarged by linking computers across a network.

▶ **Software**

As well as enabling basic sound manipulation, Logic Pro 7 contains software that can simulate real-life sounds, create rhythms and construct infinite sound-loops.

Licensing

One other aspect of audio and music is music licensing. Since the original WipeOut game on the PlayStation, publishers have been using more and more licensed music. A game like Need For Speed: Most Wanted, for example, uses licensed music almost exclusively. However, licensed music only really works for specific genres. A street-racing game with a gritty hip-hop soundtrack is one thing; Sim City with a gritty hip-hop soundtrack is quite another. Music and audio must always suit the nature of the game.

03: Design Production

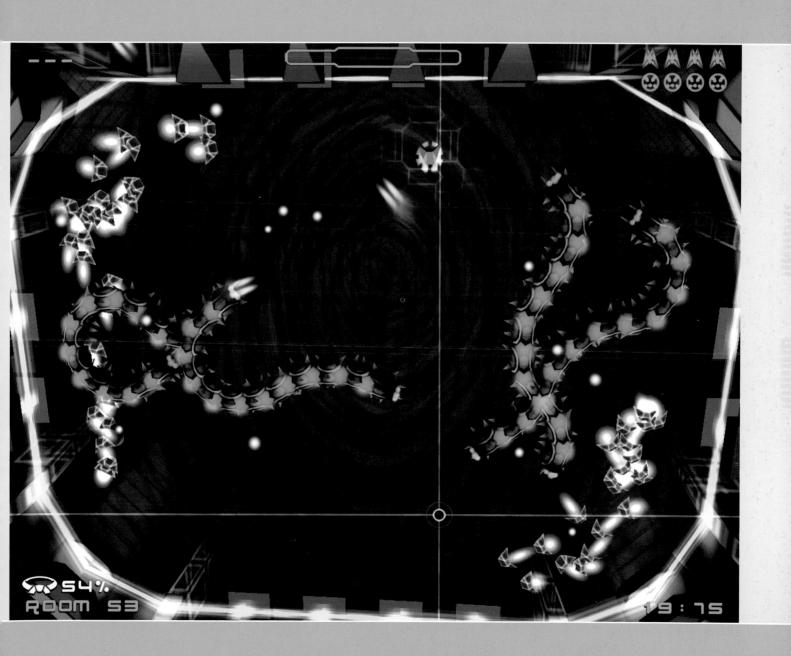

The production process

Project management and planning

The production process encompasses every stage of developing a marketable game, from initial idea to eventual distribution. The whole process demands a great deal of organisation and coordination to get right. With many modern games costing millions to make, deadlines are often absolute, frequently with punitive financial penalties attached to them if they are not met. Skills in personnel and project management come into play – in this way game development is no different from the manufacture of other consumer goods such as automobiles. Even with foresight and skilled management, there are usually unforeseen problems. The management of this type of mishap – to reduce its likelihood of occurrence and minimize its detrimental effects – is key.

Planning factors to consider

- Asset list
- Task breakdown
- 'Milestones'
- Human resources
- Equipment
- Contingency

Breakdown of elements

One of the earliest tasks in a project is to perform a breakdown of the assets required in the game. This is an element-by-element list of the actual art content required for the game design – characters, objects, game mechanics, levels, interface elements and so on. It forms an essential part of the Game Design Document (see page 106) and part of the production strategy. The asset list is a catalogue of goals that must be achieved.

Alongside this is a task breakdown – the tasks that need to be undertaken in order to create the required assets. The order in which the tasks are to be carried out is important too; some will need to happen before others, some can happen simultaneously. In this way, the game creation is broken down into manageable parts that individuals or teams can work on.

Production schedule

The production schedule timetables when tasks need to be completed and assets made ready. Usually, the schedule identifies minor and major deadlines for completion of work, often referred to as 'milestones'. Even a proposed schedule that might last two or three years will be detailed down to the week and day, to allow for the myriad of assets. Contingency should be built in to accommodate the inevitable glitches that occur in development.

The person responsible for planning must know how long jobs generally take and be honest in the evaluation of the time they require. Attempting to do things too quickly will put too much pressure on the team and burn them out. If the plan is too generous, the cost of developing the game might exceed the potential earnings and therefore make a loss.

Human resources

An important factor is human resources – how many workers are available and what skills they have. If there are too few workers, things will take longer since people can only do so much in a day. Another consideration is equipment – usually computers and software. If your equipment is inadequate the performance of your employees may be compromised. On the other hand, too many people and too much equipment adds cost and threatens the profitability of your game and company.

Roles and delegation

It is very rare on a sizeable development project that an individual will be working on one aspect on their own. It is more likely that he will be working in a team with a delegated and clearly identified job. In charge of that team there will be a senior member of the team, usually termed lead artist, lead programmer, or lead designer. These leads will either report to another overall manager or directly to the producer(s).

The producer

The producer is responsible for liaising between the publisher and the developer and the development staff. This is a senior role and the producer will most likely have a lot of experience at different levels of the games industry. They will be responsible for the licensing arrangements and the attendant contracts and will have a large input into maintaining development budgets. Managing a budget usually goes in tandem with overseeing the development schedule. Senior team leaders will report to the producer and they will liaise over all aspects of the development process. One of the critical roles for a producer is to make sure that the development schedule meets all of its milestones and is completed on time.

Teamworking

As the whole production process is broken into tasks and goals, so are the groups of people broken into groups to deal with specific parts of the project. These groups are usually fluid and break up and come together depending upon the skill requirements of the project. They might stay together for a whole game or the group might change depending upon the stage and emphasis of the project. Sometimes groups may be moved between differing projects. Early on in the development process there may be opportunities for the groups to be of mixed disciplines such as designers, artists and programmers as the early stages of a game are created and the requirements of each specialism are accounted for. As the production schedule gets underway the teams might be more skill-focused as groups of artists or programmers or designers work on a particular aspect relevant to their aptitudes.

Responsive to needs

It is difficult if not impossible to give a definitive organisation for games development as the involvement in a creative process demands a lot of flexibility. The best organisations are very responsive to the demands of development, and support their personnel and teams as they rise to meet these challenges.

Project structure

Each department has a lead who steers it and is the main contact for the other departments. All projects have a lead designer, lead artist and lead coder and each is responsible for the output of their department. On most projects they all report to the producer.

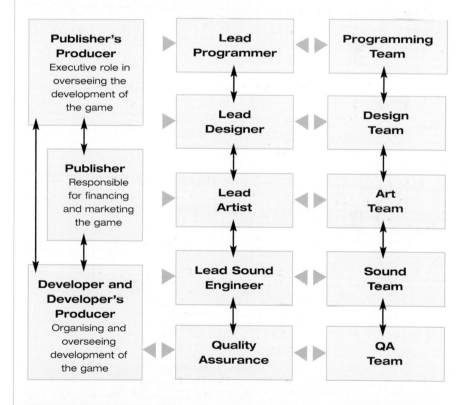

This is a simplified version of the organisation of teams in the production process. Note that the lines of communication are in both directions.

Project management tools

Once planning decisions have been made they are usually recorded in a chart.

▶ Gantt chart

| | Month 1 Milestone | Month 2 Milestone | Month 3 Milestone | Month 4 Milestone | Month 5 Milestone | Month 6 Milestone | Month 7 Milestone | Month 8 Milestone | Month 9 Milestone | Month 10 Milestone | Month 11 Milestone | Month 12 |

Design
- Develop game concept
- Develop game story
- Develop game levels
- Design game mechanics

Art
- Produce concept art
- Develop visual identity of the game
- Asset generation
- Digital modelling

Programming
- Develop game engine
- Prototype game
- Implement mechanics

Animation
- Digital modelling
- Rigging
- In-game animation
- Cut scenes

Sound
- Sound effects
- Music

Testing
- Play prototype games to spot faults

The most common type of planning chart is a Gantt chart. It breaks a task down into goals, the order these need to be tackled in, and when they need to start and finish. Milestones can be highlighted. These may occur at the same time as each other, and some may require others to be completed before they start.

▶ PERT chart

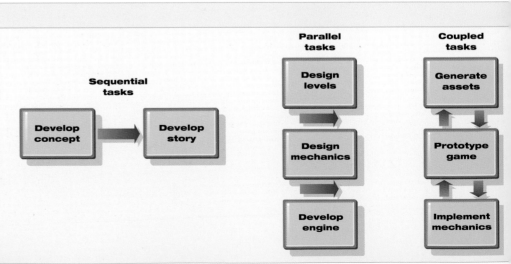

Another common project-management tool is the Program Evaluation and Review Technique (PERT) chart. PERT charts list the tasks and the time they are allotted as nodes which are then linked by lines. A PERT chart can clearly show a critical path through a project—a connected series of events that has to happen in order for the whole project to be a success.

Sequential tasks

Develop concept → Develop story

Parallel tasks

Design levels → Design mechanics → Develop engine

Coupled tasks

Generate assets → Prototype game → Implement mechanics

Pre-production

Pre-production is the first stage of development proper. Most often, pre-production will start once a GDD or pitch has been written that is promising enough to warrant developing further. There is no absolute definition of where pre-production ends and production starts. In an ideal situation, pre-production would finish once all the design is finished, the art style locked down, the tools and production pipeline tested and the technical challenges worked out. Development could then begin with full confidence in the design, artistic direction, workflow and technical solutions. This almost never happens, but pre-production is gaining importance and developers are becoming more insistent on getting more time and money spent on this critical phase.

Pre-production is useful to management as they can use information gained during pre-production to estimate team sizes, costs and timelines. With a suitable GDD and/or prototype it also easier to track progress as the project enters production.

Risk reduction

A long pre-production stage can reduce risk, identify problems, establish methods, increase scheduling accuracy, and reduce time spent coding, designing and producing art and audio for elements of the game that won't make it in for whatever reason. It really is invaluable and can even be quite inexpensive, requiring only a few key people. If done thoroughly it makes for a much easier project to manage and a much more focused goal for the team. Because pre-production can work with small teams it also means that the team and the project can be much more flexible and incorporate ideas quickly and effectively, as well as remove ideas that are unnecessary.

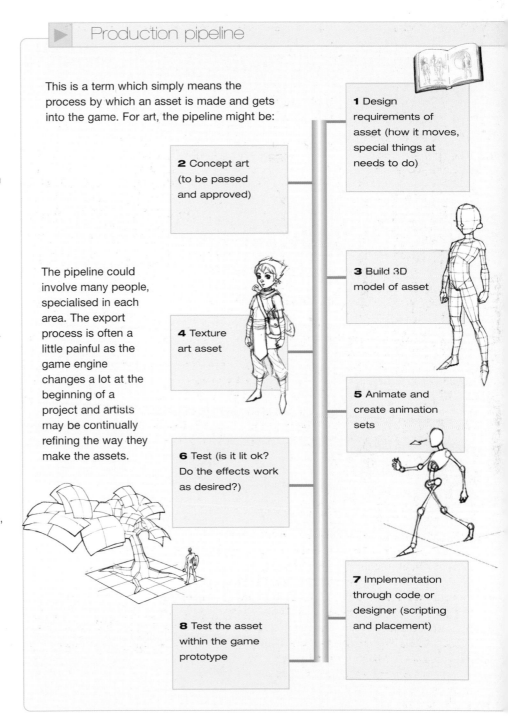

Production pipeline

This is a term which simply means the process by which an asset is made and gets into the game. For art, the pipeline might be:

The pipeline could involve many people, specialised in each area. The export process is often a little painful as the game engine changes a lot at the beginning of a project and artists may be continually refining the way they make the assets.

1 Design requirements of asset (how it moves, special things at needs to do)

2 Concept art (to be passed and approved)

3 Build 3D model of asset

4 Texture art asset

5 Animate and create animation sets

6 Test (is it lit ok? Do the effects work as desired?)

7 Implementation through code or designer (scripting and placement)

8 Test the asset within the game prototype

Production realities

Practicalities to consider

Despite the seemingly straightforward theoretical approach to the production of a game, there are many other considerations that can make the process more complex and potentially different every time. Each new project will be unique, but following are some common factors and considerations to think about in advance to make the process potentially less awkward.

Cross-platform engineering

If you intend your game to be available on a number of platforms, such as consoles and PCs, then you will find that for each of them you will need to develop new code, and probably new game assets. There is little commonality between platforms, and each has its own peculiar requirements. Games released across all platforms are usually those by large development houses, or come with big budgets attached, such as film franchises.

With consoles you will also need a developer kit for that particular console, and probably more than one. Console developer kits are special pieces of hardware that can assemble code into a format readable by the console. These machines and their operation are unique to each platform, so as well as carrying out a separate set of tasks for each platform, you will also need personnel experienced in working with and using the developer kits.

Project tracking

Having developed your production schedule, you then need to delegate staff to oversee it and make sure things are happening when they should. Overseeing such a large, complex project can be an extremely demanding job. Failure to complete a task is not a palatable option, due to the potential costs involved, and the knock-on effect. It is the role of the manager overseeing the process to make sure that

he knows how projects are going and to be aware of problems before they happen.

Having identified a potential problem, the manager must deploy resources, manpower, or extra support in order to eradicate or minimize it. With many separate development tasks occurring at the same time this can be an almost impossible job. In networked offices there are usually project management programs, such as Alienbrain (http://www.alienbrain.com), which are designed to keep track of a number of different people working on files for the same project over a PC network. This type of software eases the communication issues and gives the manager an overview of the activities within the project, but it still requires a person to monitor progress and help as required.

Quality assurance

Games that go to market with mistakes and bugs in their code have potentially disastrous consequences for a development company. In every aspect of the game, making sure there are mistakes or errors, through testing, is a key issue. The best companies have a pervading culture of quality assurance and each individual plays his part to make sure that no errors go unchecked.

Quality Assurance is also where the game testers earn their keep. Testers will play and replay levels, usually with the aim of getting the machine to crash or something to happen out of place. If this does happen it means there is a fault that needs to be fixed.

It is rare for a game to go to market with a major mistake or bug in it, but rectifying that bug after it has gone to market is much more costly for the developer than spotting it beforehand. The damage may be more than financial – the company image risks being tarnished, meaning that subsequent games will not sell as well, whatever their quality.

Production checklist

- Which platform? If more than one, consider cross-platform engineering issues.

- Do you have a manager and systems in place to track the production process?

- How will you assure quality? Set up systems and have testing staff in place.

- Where will your game engine come from? A new development or reuse of existing?

- Do you plan to license an existing IP or copyrighted material?

Game engines

What is the underlying engine that will drive your game? Do you license an existing one or do you develop your own? Each choice has benefits and problems.

Developing your own game engine

If you choose to develop your own game engine then you are free to do with it what you will. You do not have to pay royalties or licensing fees; in fact, if it is good enough then other companies may want to license it from your company. But building the engine from scratch is hard work for your programmers – it can take a long time and be problematic to remove all the bugs in the code. If aspects of the project take too long then costs can start to rise and threaten the financial viability of the project.

License an existing game engine

You may choose to use an existing game engine and license it from another developer. The code will have been written and proved in the production of at least one game. The programming work may be reduced if the game has a good level and scripting editor. However, this will cost you money; if you are going to sell your game commercially the owner of the original engine will want a share of the profits to recoup their cost of development. Finding the right engine might be problematic too. One that meets your needs might not exist in its whole form and you may need to modify the code. This too can be a tricky job, and depends on the owner of the code granting permission to modify it.

Middleware

You might choose to develop part of the engine yourself, and use middleware to supply some of the other components of the code. Middleware is a piece of software that performs a task and connects other pieces of software. A well known piece of middleware is the physics engine Havok (http://www.havok.com/), which has been used successfully in many games. This approach minimizes the risk in developing your own code from scratch, but reduces the amount of royalty payments you will have to make.

 Modders
Minh 'Gooseman' Le (left) and Jess Cliffe (right), developers of the independently successful mod, Counter Strike.

Modding

You might consider creating a modification of an existing game, using the level editors and script facilities provided. 'Modding' has started many smaller companies off by allowing them to focus their attention more on the gameplay and visual content, rather than developing a whole game engine. One of the most successful and well known full modifications is Counter Strike by Minh 'Gooseman' Le and Jess Cliffe. Counter Strike is now an acknowledged staple in the tactical first-person shooter line-up.

Movie to game
Batman is an example of a very successful movie that was later licensed for development as computer games. Various games were produced for a range of platforms. Licensing issues resulted in the individual games being very different.

The pitfalls of licensing

Licensing existing copyrighted material such as a film or a book can seem like a sure-fire winner, especially if the original is popular. Licences like this are, however, extremely expensive. In developing the game you must ensure that you meet existing fans' expectations, while also attracting gamers. The owner of a licence may retain the right to be involved within the development of the game and dictate what can and cannot be included. They may not agree with your ideas and proposals for a great game. This can be very awkward and not always conducive to the development of a successful game.

Tools of the trade

Accessible software packages

Widely-available and relatively inexpensive software gives one-man or small development teams the capability to create exciting games from their own homes. Some of these software packages are freeware or shareware; others do cost but are within the price-range of the keen amateur. Many accomplished designers started out with this type of software, and developed their ideas independently. Even in this age of highly-produced games, easily accessible software packages such as these continue to provide designers with the means to create innovative and interesting independent games.

The types of programs you are likely to use depends on where your specialism lies (if you are thinking about going it alone you will need to develop all-round skills). Applications you are most likely to encounter are: Word, or other text editors or word-processors; 3D modelling packages such as Maya, 3D Studio Max, Milkshape, or SketchUp; image creation software including Photoshop and Paint Shop Pro; applications for adding music and sound effects; and programming engines designed to create 2D and 3D games very quickly.

Depth of knowledge
Which of these you end up using and how deeply you need to understand them can vary enormously. Some companies have proprietary tools that work entirely inside a package such as Maya and if you are a level designer, this might be all you use all day. Other jobs may require you to make GDDs, illustrate them, edit in-game art assets, or make and edit sound effects and script levels, in which case you'll need a working knowledge of most key programs to do it all.

Word processors
Word is a word-processor made by Microsoft, which almost everyone in the industry uses to make pitch documents, GDDs and LDDs. It is also a standard word-processor in many other industries, and is

▼ **Powerful tool**
3D Studio Max's menu interface can look daunting, but it is useful to be familiar with it.

routinely installed on most new computers.

Text can be edited in a word processor, and pictures can be added to create simple layouts. Edited text can also be exported to other applications to create more complex illustrated documents.

Text editors
Text editors are light, simple applications which allow you to edit text files at a basic level. Some are free, and the ones that support tabbed browsing of files are particularly useful. These programs are great for keeping notes and editing scripts and are less complicated than Word. However, they do have limitations and are not suitable for making attractive documents.

3D modelling
Maya is an expensive 3D modelling, animation and rendering package. It can look a bit daunting if you've never used anything like it before, but as a games designer, you'll only need to use a tiny fraction of what it can do. Typically, you'll only be using this package to move items around a level, set up cameras, and create paths for enemies and trigger-areas for events. None of these tasks require more than a basic knowledge of the package which can be learnt in a few hours. However, a good working knowledge of it can be very advantageous.

3D Studio Max is a similar application to Maya but has a different interface. Some companies use Maya and some use Max; both have their advantages and disadvantages but for design work they do pretty much the same thing. Maya and Max are now both owned by the same company so some merging of technology is expected in the future.

For bedroom coders (see page 178), Milkshape is an excellent low-polygon modeller, originally designed for Half Life. It is extremely suitable for all types of low-poly modelling for games.

User Created Screen Shot

This screen shot was taken by a member of our FPS Creator forum. They designed and built the level themselves, feel that showing you what others are making with FPS Creator is the best way to demonstrate what it's capable of

◄ **Drag-and-drop interface**

FPS Creator is similar to a level editor, but it has a drag-and-drop interface, and all the difficult implementation of a design is undertaken by the inbuilt engine.

Model Pack 4

FPS Creator Model Pack #4 is now available! This pack contains 21 new characters for your FPS Creator games.

21 New Characters ready for FPS Creator with extra features and brand new animation sequences

Wings 3D is another good modelling package for low-polygon models, and is available across all computing platforms. Like Milkshape, it has a good online community for tutorials and support.

Sketching in 3D

SketchUp is a wonderful package which allows you to create non-organic 3D geometry quickly and easily. It is particularly good for blocking out shapes and arrangements for levels, as well as providing useful conceptual images for GDDs. Blocking out 3D levels was a particularly tricky thing to do before SketchUp came along, unless you had a good knowledge of Maya or Max. Now, designers everywhere can quickly try out ideas without needing an artist to do all the legwork. It is free, and so anyone can download it and learn to use it at no expense.

2D art packages

Photoshop is the most common package used for 2D art in the games industry. As a designer you may not need to use it often but if you have any artistic ability it can be useful for illustrating ideas or even making placeholder graphics. Quite often it is used for annotating maps and levels to be used in GDDs, in-game, or simply to assist the QA team.

Paint Shop Pro is less popular than Photoshop, but much cheaper. It is quite powerful, but the interface does not seem as intuitive as Photoshop's.

For 2D sprites and textures, Gimp is a free and powerful 2D image editing package.

Music and audio effects

Live and Reason are both reasonably priced and versatile packages designed to provide music and audio effects. Reason is sometimes considered easier to get to grips with, but Live may have the edge on production and versatility.

Programming

Games Factory 2 and Game Maker are two very simple programs that enable you to make simple games very quickly. They provide ideal starting points for trying out ideas about design and playability.

FPS Creator is a stand-alone program that allows the user to create a full 3D first-person game extremely easily and quickly, due to its easy-to-use drag-and-drop interface.

Bedroom coders aren't usually as well funded as larger companies, but budget restraints needn't exclude them from choice. For programming, BlitzBASIC (also BlitzMax), DarkBASIC and GarageGames' Torque Game Builder are all good, low-cost packages.

Useful websites

3D modelling
Milkshape
www.milkshape3d.com
Wings 3D
www.wings3d.com
FPS Creator
www.fpscreator.com
SketchUp
www.sketchup.com

2D art
Gimp
www.gimp.org

Programming
Games Factory 2
www.clickteam.com/eng/index.php
Game Maker
www.gamemaker.nl/index.html
FPS Creator
www.fpscreator.com
BlitzBasic
www.blitzbasic.com
Dark BASIC
http://darkbasic.thegamecreators.com
Torque Game Builder
www.garagegames.com/products/torque/tgb/

Prototyping

Putting the concept to the test

Prototyping is the process of creating a portion of a game to test new ideas. It is most often used to test core mechanics such as the main features and actions of the player character. This can be an exceptionally exciting time in the development process, as everything is new and changing very quickly. It's all too easy to get carried away and end up with lots of good ideas thrown in which don't work well together, so it's important to subtract as well as add at this stage.

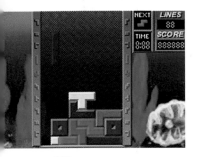

▲ Practical demo

It's difficult to imagine that Tetris would ever have sounded like a multi-million-selling, mass-appeal game on paper. Abstract game concepts such as this can sometimes only be effectively communicated in the form of a prototype.

Timing

Prototypes are most often made after a GDD or games design pitch has been approved and the resources are granted to make one. This is because prototypes are usually the work of many people, and so cost more than a GDD to produce. This is changing, though, as tools become available which allow very small teams to prototype ideas to a high degree of detail in a short space of time.

On the other hand, a few great games grew 'organically' out of prototypes, and the GDDs were written later. One advantage (of many) of this approach is that ideas which are difficult to articulate on paper may be easy to understand when played.

▶ The prototype team

Because the prototype is all about how the mechanics balance and interact, the prototype team defines the whole development process and final game experience. Ideally the team should comprise an experienced designer and game programmer. But the most technically-able programmer may not always be the best person for the job, and often finding the best team to make a prototype can be revealing.

Keeping it simple

To save time and money, some prototypes use art assets (such as pictures, 3D models, or animations) only where they are needed to test the new ideas. Even if resources are available it's often best not to add art as it can easily draw attention away from the important issues that need to be addressed with the underlying mechanics.

Prototypes are extremely useful as they show up problems in a design very early on and provide an excellent focus and reference for development. They can be used later on in production to try variations and settle arguments that might otherwise sidetrack the main development. It often requires a leap of imagination to understand how an early prototype could ever become a great game when it lacks all the frills of artwork, sound and polish. It's certain some great games have been cancelled because they were shown to the wrong person at the wrong time. Unfortunately many publishers are still frightened off by basic prototypes and so they are used internally until it is possible to flesh them out for presentation.

Vertical slices

Another sort of prototype is the 'vertical slice' prototype. This is when an entire section of the game, usually a smallish level, is made to a very high production standard complete with features. This is often very expensive, but the advantage is that it is much easier to sell the idea to a publisher because it looks like a finished game. The design team will have a very high understanding of the game and so extending production to more levels is relatively easy. It is very risky though, as these sorts of prototypes are often partially or fully funded by the development team, so if a publisher does not pick the game up it can break the development company.

When a prototype works and production of the game begins it is considered good practice to archive the prototype and start again from scratch. This ensures that the code is clean and properly designed using lessons learned from the prototype.

Create simple game level with placeholder characters and objects.

Refine game in response to findings.

There is no standard way to program a prototype. Each new idea will have different requirements which will suit some programming languages better than others. Examples of languages are C++, C, ActionScript (Flash), Blitz BASIC and Dark BASIC.

One simple and cheap way of testing an idea at a very basic level is to make a 'paper prototype', using paper and card, sketches, and tokens and pieces from real board games to represent game assets.

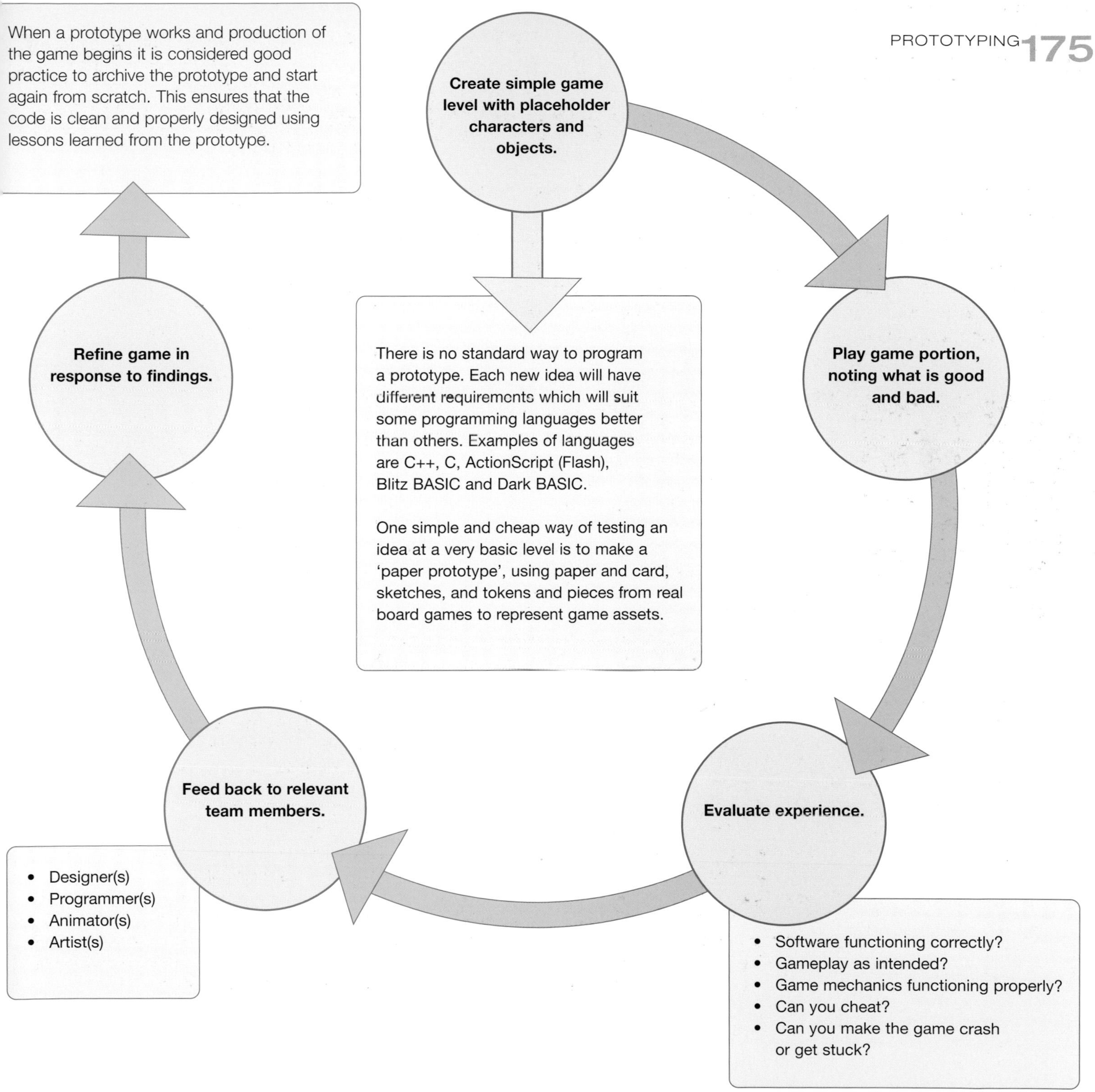

Play game portion, noting what is good and bad.

Feed back to relevant team members.

- Designer(s)
- Programmer(s)
- Animator(s)
- Artist(s)

Evaluate experience.

- Software functioning correctly?
- Gameplay as intended?
- Game mechanics functioning properly?
- Can you cheat?
- Can you make the game crash or get stuck?

Pitching ideas

Getting your game published

As a designer, your work is always going to come under a critical eye. Everyone has an opinion and people are unlikely to trust your judgement until you've proved your worth. However, your team are much more friendly than the potential publishers, and rightly so. Publishers are the people controlling the money to make your game. They have different concerns to you. For example: does your game stand a chance of standing out in a crowded marketplace? Can the team get it finished on time and within budget? How will it be marketed? Throughout the project's lifespan your judgement is going to be questioned by your publisher—but first you have to get a publisher. To get a publisher you have to pitch.

▼ Conventions
Pitch meetings may happen at conferences or conventions, such as the Tokyo Game Show.

When you're pitching your project you have to remember that the publisher will need to be convinced that they actually want your game. They are much more likely than you to see the multi-million dollar risks involved in taking on your project.

Initial meetings
The pitching process starts with a simple 'getting to know you' meeting. Initial meetings often happen at conventions such the Tokyo Game Show. During these conventions the publisher is going to be pitched lots of ideas and presented with new business propositions. Key to these early meetings is to be punctual and polite. Of course it helps to have an idea or demo ready to give purpose to the meeting, but it's more than likely you'll be forgotten by the end of the day.

Following up on initial meetings is essential. They won't call you. Once you're back in touch you'll have some idea of how the meeting actually went. If your calls are returned, the pitching process can begin in earnest. Often this will mean visiting the publisher's headquarters for what is really the first meeting.

▶ ## The pitching experience

Pitching can be terrifying, but as long as you stick to some essential principles, you'll get through it.

1 Have conviction in your project

If you don't think your project is going to work, a publisher will notice this quicker than you can imagine, and your hard-won opportunity will be lost.

2 Defend your project to the hilt

Publishers ask hard questions. After giving a detailed project presentation, you may simply be asked: 'Why?' This is possibly the most difficult question you will ever be asked – make sure you have an answer ready for it.

3 Don't be too precious with your idea

When you pitch you have to remember that your publisher has a different agenda to you. They are thinking about how your game is going to fit into their development line-up. If you're planning a soccer game and your publisher throws you a wild idea like 'How about if we put Tom Cruise in it?' it means that they have an exclusive deal with Tom Cruise to do a game and have no idea how to use it. Your immediate reaction may be 'no', but bear in mind that the suggestion of Tom Cruise is positive. It means they are seriously considering your project for their line-up. Be diplomatic – say something like 'Tom Cruise! Wow! We'd have to think how best to use him in the game. Is he a soccer fan?'

It's more than likely this Tom Cruise connection will never happen and they will go with your original plan, but don't dismiss the idea. It shows the publisher that you are flexible and willing to listen to their suggestions.

4 Think big; know your publisher

If you're simply meeting with a new publisher to throw around new ideas then it pays to think big. If you're going to see Eidos, for example, pitch your take on Tomb Raider. Do your research – know everything that's worked in Tomb Raider, everything that hasn't, give it your own unique spin, and pitch it enthusiastically. You're highly unlikely to end up doing a Tomb Raider game but your sheer ambition will give the publisher confidence.

5 Practise pitching before the meeting

You're going to be nervous – everyone is. The only way to gain confidence in pitching is to practise. Practise on your team and on anyone who will listen. Get used to talking about your project. The more you do it the better you will become.

Some people are naturally better at pitching than others. If there's someone on your team who oozes confidence and fully understands the project, let them lead the pitch. You can always jump in when there's an area you can help communicate better—but never talk over each other.

6 Have fun!

Pitching can be fun once you get over the fear factor. Remember, a great idea, meticulous preparation, and a healthy dose of luck can bring great rewards.

▼ **Engineering your pitch opportunity**
Increasingly, computer game shows are becoming industry-only, such as the E3 show (pictured here). However, pitching need not be restricted to these events; many meetings happen as a result of contacting specific companies.

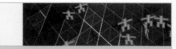

Bedroom coders

Taking on the big boys

The chances are that if you are reading this, you aren't in the games industry yet. You may be wondering how to get in and might even be on a college course that specialises in games. It may seem like a long way from testing to designing games, but there are shortcuts, and even alternatives to working for a games company.

Bedroom coding is a safe and extremely rewarding way to get into the games industry and find an alternative to the normal corporate games development system. With careful planning it is much easier to get an original design made independently than through the normal route of joining a games company. These companies are usually risk-averse, unadventurous and at the mercy of publishers' wishes.

The trick to making a game on your own or with a group of friends is: finish it. There is so much to learn from properly finishing a game and, more importantly, you can't sell an unfinished game. If it's only moderately good, but finished, it will be much easier to get a job in the industry, if you choose to, using your game as proof of your determination and dedication. A game idea of unsurpassed genius which never gets finished won't impress anyone.

The term 'bedroom coding' might seem frightening to a designer with no programming experience, but there is little reason to be alarmed. There are great packages out there, such as Blitz BASIC and Dark BASIC (see page 173), with large online communities to help you get started. It may look daunting at first but by taking one thing at a time you'll soon learn to enjoy programming. That might sound like madness to a non-programmer, but it really can be rewarding. More importantly, a designer who can prototype his own ideas has the power to try anything he likes and can learn a great deal about design itself from programming. Another benefit is that a designer who can work well with a

 Small developer
Mutant Storm – an addictive, psychedelic shmup – was created by a small UK developer called PomPom. Mutant Storm Reloaded is now available on Xbox 360's Xbox Live Arcade Service.

Pros and cons of bedroom coding

Pros:
- You reap all the rewards if your game's successful
- Take all the risks you want, and be as off-the-wall as you like
- No compromises, long meetings or interference
- No 'fixed' working hours – work when you like for as long as you like.

Cons:
- No fixed income
- Lots and lots of competition
- It's difficult to make people aware of your game, even if it's good and original
- It's hard to do any game requiring a large budget or team.

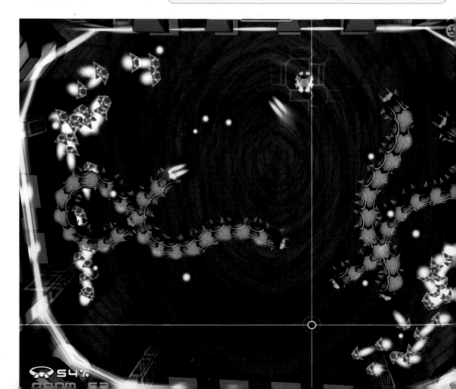

darwinia

EVERYONE E | PC CD-ROM SOFTWARE | CINEMAWARE MARQUEE

Virus

The red virus spreads out-of-control in the gameworld. The player can fight it with Squads, the main weapons.

Souls

When a virus is killed, it leaves behind souls. These can be converted back into the Darwinians they once were.

Darwinians

The Darwinians cannot be directly controlled by the player, but they can be influenced.

programming team can be very attractive to a games company if he decides he does want to sign up. Either way, the ability to program is a skill you'll never regret learning, and with many designers now having to write scripts for levels and enemies it is becoming more and more important to be multi-skilled. However, if you are dead-set against programming, team up with someone who can do it.

Some extremely interesting and successful games (critically and commercially) have come from teams who are effectively bedroom coders. Probably the most notable of late are Introversion (Uplink, Darwinia, Defcon), Chronic Logic (Bridge Builder, Gish), the Behemoth (Alien Hominid), PomPom (Mutant Storm) and Stephen 'Cakey' Cakebread (Geometry Wars). Even more encouragingly, distribution systems such as Steam (the Valve distribution system for Half Life) and Xbox Live Arcade are embracing games made by independent companies in an attempt to capture wider markets. Nintendo and Sony are sure to follow with similarly attractive propositions to independent developers after the huge success of games like Geometry Wars.

Labour of love

The action in Darwinia happens in a virtual theme park that has been overrun by an evil computer virus. The player must eradicate the virus to save the Darwinians from extinction. Darwinia was Introversion's second game, released after nearly 3 years' work.

Where to from here?

Career paths and possibilities

So what next? As you will have seen there are many different aspects to and roles within the games industry. This book has given you a taster of the skills and knowledge you need to develop to get a job. So what are the next steps to take and what are the options open to you?

One piece of advice for every aspiring game designer, artist, programmer and modeller, is to strive to be the best in your chosen subject. Nothing less will do. The evidence for this is simple to see – pick up any modern game and look at it hard. See the quality of the artwork and modelling that has gone into the game. Appreciate the intelligence behind the challenges and the gameplay. Understand the complexity and skill that has gone into developing the program for the game. This is the industry you seek to be part of and, as you can see, the standards of quality are extremely high. Don't be disheartened by this – dedication and hard work will develop your skills. You can be part of this varied and exciting industry if you are prepared to give it the dedication it requires.

Study

As the games industry has matured, courses have developed to educate and prepare people to work in it. There are a variety of games-related courses across the spectrum – art, design, modelling, theory, and animation to name but a few. They exist from school or college level, through degree level, to postgraduate level. Many institutions in the United States and the UK now offer these courses. Many games industry workers have also come from more traditional illustration, computer programming, or design courses, developing the same set of skills that are necessary for working in games development.

▶ The portfolio

A portfolio is a visual record of your skills. For artists it is fairly straightforward as their folio will contain samples of their artwork. But designers and programmers can develop folios too, and they are invaluable in landing you that job.

Here are some loose guidelines for portfolios:

- Always make sure that the folio is neat and well-ordered. It is worth that small investment for a nice binder or folio from an art or office supplier. Not only does it protect your work but it also makes it easier to display.
- Make sure that the folio is in a logical order; use neat and discreet labels if necessary. It should 'read' interestingly and show off your skills.
- Don't try to stuff every piece of work you have done in a folio – be selective. Choose your best and most recent work and keep it to an amount that you might talk an interviewer through in 5–10 minutes.
- Remember that people will be interested in what you can do today, not what you did five years ago.
- Tailor your folder to the company. If the company mainly makes racing games and your folio only shows work of giant robots and spaceships, they may not feel that you can work in a manner sympathetic with the company's core activity.

Before you enrol on a course think about where you want to go in games and what skills the jobs you are seeking require. Many companies post the skills they require of applicants on their Web sites. Look at the syllabus of the courses and see if they match your aspirations. It's worth doing the research to find a course with the right emphasis on the skills you need. Having a qualification does not automatically ensure you will get a job – a potential employer will want to see that you have the skills that they're looking for.

▶ Tailoring your portfolio

Different careers demand differing approaches to compiling portfolios, to appeal to particular employers.

Artist

As an artist, a portfolio is the most familiar way of presenting your work.

- Demonstrate a wide range of techniques and media relevant to visualising for games.
- You may have an individual style but try to demonstrate flexibility too; if you only draw in one style and it is not the one the company is after then you won't get the job.
- While sketching from existing games demonstrates that you can work in that style, make sure there is plenty of your own work otherwise you can seem too derivative.
- Don't forget to include some traditional art such as life drawing and landscape drawing to demonstrate you have the basic skills.

Modeller

A 3D modeller's portfolio shares similarities with an artist's.

- Prints and renders of models work in a similar fashion to drawn artwork. It's also good to include wireframe models and details of polygon counts to show your skill at modelling.

- Include original sketch-work, even if it is fairly rough. It is important to show how you can develop ideas and work from artwork provided.
- Include examples of textures, bump maps, and so on, to show the whole process.
- As well as the more fantastic models you may have, it does not hurt to have a few mundane models of existing vehicles, buildings, or simple people, to show that you have the necessary basic skills.

Animator

An animator's portfolio will be similar in nature to a modeller's portfolio.

- Print out stills from your work to show how it looks.
- Include sketches, and preparatory work such as storyboarding, to show your familiarity with the whole process.
- Part of an animator's portfolio will be a showreel of work, but a well thought-out portfolio can complement a showreel.

Designer

A designer's portfolio helps get around the fact that a lot of work tends to be written – there may not be time for the interviewer to read your work. Your folio should offer a glimpse into your concepts and the ideas behind them.

- Elements of the design work can be presented in storyboard format.
- Clear diagrams can show flow of play and game mechanics.
- Level designs can be presented in plan format with a clear key to critical elements in the design as well as flow of play.
- If you have used a level editor then get some screengrabs of your levels to include in your folio.

Programmer

A portfolio for a programmer might initially seem the weirdest of ideas, yet it can be useful.

- If you have worked on any games, even simple ones, a screengrab of the game can give you a focus to talk about what was achieved, and you can explain how you did it.
- If you had to break down any problems into logical chunks you can explain your process with a neat flow chart or similar diagram.
- No doubt you will have some demonstration work on disk, and as with the animator, the folio may be a physical accompaniment to this digital work.

Digital alternatives

Work can of course also go on a DVD or be presented on a laptop or a website. Remember though, that printed work never crashes out, does not need specialist software to load, or access to the internet. You cannot always count on these things being present in an interview, and a small folio will always be useful and always work. A folio also gives your interviewer something interesting to look at while you are setting up a laptop or a DVD.

The folio, be it digital or physical, is the evidence that you can do what you say you can do. Hopefully it will showcase your talent and commitment to the job. Folios are not the preserve of students and graduates. There are many self-taught individuals out there with the right level of skill, but all need to demonstrate it to a potential employer.

Website

As well as the folio you should also get yourself a website to market your work. Developing webpages is relatively straightforward and there are many template-based services that allow you to create your site with ease. Not only will a website be a platform for your skills but it is also another sign of your professionalism and commitment to your career path. If you bump into somebody at a conference or contact somebody on the internet you can always direct them to your site if they are interested.

Finding a games job

There are many games developers around the world and they are continually hiring people. Like all industries the games industry will have its ups and downs but it is reasonable to assume it is here to stay for some time. If you feel you possess the skills to work in the industry and are invited for interview then you might just be lucky. Do your research about the companies you are applying to and may be interviewed for. A common interview question is: 'What do you know about us as a company?' Show that you have had the sense to do some basic

preview images

Introduction

As with any written information, keep the text on your website concise and to the point. Make it relevant to the audience.

CV links

Link to your CV in a variety of formats, to help the user.

Bullet points

Use bulleted lists to pick out key information. Use brief, punchy phrases rather than long, complicated sentences. Make everything easy to read.

Samples of work

Include samples of your best work at a suitable size. Protect your work by adding your own credit line in a prominent position.

Sell yourself

A website is a great opportunity to show off your work and advertise essential information about yourself to interested people. Make it easy to use and don't overload it with images that take ages to open, or you risk losing interest. You should check any links you include to make sure they work properly, and keep information such as contact details updated.

research about a potential employer. Remember that all the applicants love games and will have played them since they were small children. This is not a good enough reason to get a job in the industry! Rather, employers might be interested in why you chose this career, what your plans are, and what skills you have that will be useful to the company. While it is laudable to aspire to become the CEO of a company, be prepared to start at the bottom or at least at a level commensurate with your current experience. It will be sufficient at interview to demonstrate your willingness to get on in the industry rather than display over-ambitious aspirations.

Entry-level ways in

Not so long ago getting a job as a tester was relatively easy and it was a good entry-level way into the industry. The pay was the lowest but the rewards were to play games before they were marketed. Currently this is not the case as the job of Quality Assurance and game testing becomes an important factor in games development. Those jobs do still exist but there is a lot of competition for them. Keep an eye out for companies who specialise in testing and subcontract for development houses. This traditional first rung on the ladder has not completely disappeared yet.

Pitching an idea

It is fair to say that most development companies get a lot of mail, email and phone calls from people with a 'killer games idea'. It is also fair to say that most companies are either unable to entertain the idea no matter its merit or are just not interested as they have plenty of ideas themselves. That is not to say that you shouldn't attempt to pitch your idea to a company – just be prepared for a lot of knock-backs. If you do get to pitching an idea then do not forget the guidance given earlier in this book and try and make your pitch as succinct and concise as possible while conveying its exciting potential. See Pitching ideas on page 176.

Going it alone

In this day and age of the mega-developer and the millions required to develop a game, it may be easy to think that it is just not worth doing it yourself. But do not be disheartened. Introversion Software (www.introversion.co.uk), creators of cult hits such as Uplink and Darwinia, are still a small team and bill themselves as 'the last of the bedroom coders'. You and a small band of friends might have what it takes to develop a game that will be popular. It may not make you millionaires but the reward of a well received game could be enough. See Bedroom coders, on page 178.

The Internet is an ideal shopfront for your idea and a well-designed website can attract a lot of attention. Your first game may be a mod or a level map. You might work in Flash or Java to deliver a web browser-based game. The web can offer support and critique through a larger network of like-minded individuals. Also note that Xbox Live Arcade has shown there is still great interest in simple, short games even today.

These are just a few of the options open to people wanting to get into the games industry. Hard work and dedication always pay off and in that respect, the desire to work in the games industry is no different than wanting to work in any other field.

You have started your journey now and it is time to get on developing the skills described in this book and broadening your knowledge. Start to develop your portfolio and maintain a professional attitude in your work. Good luck!

Resources

Websites

General research and inspiration

Wikipedia
http://en.wikipedia.org
Online encyclopedia which covers all subjects, including a huge amount of information on computer games past and present. Also useful for general research and inspiration, and full of hyperlinks to other, related subjects.

Reuters
http://today.reuters.com
A useful general resource for the latest world news.

National Geographic
www.nationalgeographic.com
Inspirational stories from the natural world, with stunning photography.

Wired
www.wired.com
News stories and features with a technological slant.

New Scientist
www.newscientist.com
The latest news stories from the scientific world.

Entertainment Software Rating Board
http://www.esrb.org/

Spacewar!
http://spacewar.oversigma.com/
A Java version of the first-ever computer game.

Dedicated gaming sites

Gamasutra
www.gamasutra.com
News from the computer game industry.

Steam
www.steampowered.com
An online portal for gamers.

Games editors and modding

Hammer
http://collective.valve-erc.com

Radiant
www.qeradiant.com

Far Cry
http://farcry.ubi.com/mods.php

Digital modelling applications

Autodesk Maya & 3D Studio Max
www.autodesk.com

Softimage
www.softimage.com

Lightwave
www.newtek.com

ZBrush
www.pixologic.com/zbrush

Free digital modelling applications

Wings 3D
www.wings3d.com

Milkshape 3D
http://milkshape3d.com

Blender
www.blender3d.org

Music and audio design sites

Sound Forge
www.sonymediasoftware.com//products/soundforgefamily.asp

Audition
www.adobe.com/products/audition

Bias Peak
www.bias-inc.com

Cubase
www.steinberg.net/24_1.html

Logic
www.apple.com/logicpro

Computer Game Design Courses

University of Central Lancashire
www.uclan.ac.uk
BSc (Hons) Computer Games Development
BA (Hons) Games Design

University of Abertay Dundee
www.abertay.ac.uk
MSc/PGDip Computer Games Technology

Staffordshire University
www.staffs.ac.uk
BSc (Hons) Computer Games Design

University of Wales, Newport
www3.newport.ac.uk
BA (Hons) Computer Games Design

University of Lincoln
www.lincoln.ac.uk
BA (Hons) Games Design

University of Teeside
www.tees.ac.uk
BA (Hons) Computer Games Design

University of Paisley
www.paisley.ac.uk
Computer Games Technology course

Coventry University
www.coventry.ac.uk
Computer Games Design and Development short course

Norwich School of Art and Design
www.nsad.ac.uk
Foundation Degree in Games Art and Design

University of Derby
www.derby.ac.uk
BSc (Hons) Computer Games Programming

University of Bradford
www.brad.ac.uk
BSc Interactive Systems and Video Games Design

University of Salford
www.salford.ac.uk
MSc Creative Games
BSc (Hons) Computer and Video Games

University of Bolton
www.bolton.ac.uk
BSc (Hons)/HND Computer Games Software Development

Southampton Solent University
www.solent.ac.uk
BA (Hons) Computer and Video Games

University of Westminster
www.wmin.ac.uk
MSc Computer Games Graphics

London South Bank University
www.lsbu.ac.uk
BA (Hons) Games Culture

University of Bedfordshire (Luton)
www.luton.ac.uk
BSc (Hons) Computer Games Development

**City University London
(Centre for Human Computer Interaction Design)**
www.city.ac.uk
MSc Human Centred Systems

Glossary

2D game
A game with actions, activities and mechanics that work in two dimensions. (A 2D game may have 3D graphics).

3D game
A game with actions, activities, and mechanics that work in three dimensions.

abstract game
A game that does not aim to replicate reality or real-life situations.

adaptive play
When a game's AI monitors the player's performance and changes difficulty levels in response, for example making the game harder when the player is performing well.

animation
Making models or images that move.

anti-hero
A game protagonist with questionable morals, methods or motivation.

arcade game
A game designed to be played on a gaming machine, usually in a public place, for a small amount of money or a token.

artificial intelligence (AI)
A branch of computer science and engineering, referring to programs that appear to 'learn' and can display 'intelligent' reactions.

asset
A component of a game, such as a character or object; or even a texture, sound effect or script.

bedroom coding
When developers produce games from a small-scale, probably home-based, set-up.

block map
A simple 3D map built up from a 2D plan, for example showing the layout of a level.

boss
The stage in a game when a player takes on a major character in combat – in a kill-or-be-killed situation.

camera-relative controls
When control of an on-screen toy happens from the point of view of the camera. For example, a character facing towards the player will move to the right of the screen when the left control is activated.

career mode
A narrative device for plotting a course through a game. For example, in a tennis game, selecting 'career mode' would result in a series of matches with rival players, as in a real-life tennis tournament.

character-relative controls
When control of an on-screen toy happens from the point of view of the character. For example, a character facing towards the player will move to the right of the screen when the left control is activated.

code
The written program for a game or game engine.

console
A personal, dedicated gaming machine, designed for playing games at home.

cut scenes
Scenes between gameplay that are used to fill in sections of narrative or provide information. These can be long and cinematic in style, or quite minimal. They may be video scenes, providing high-quality visuals, or rendered using the game

engine, resulting in a more seamless (but relatively primitive) effect.

deathmatch
A fight between several players, across a computer network, in a special level of a first-person shooter game known as an arena.

dual-shock controller
A two-handled controller designed for use with PlayStation and PS2, with multiple buttons and the ability to vibrate in response to in-game action, powered by the console.

environment
The setting of a game – the physical landscape and general ambience.

first-person perspective
A view of the gameworld through the eyes of the main character.

first-person shooter (FPS)
A game in which the player experiences the gameworld – and confronts their enemies – through the eyes of their character.

game design document (GDD)
A lengthy document that records every aspect of a game in written and visual form, from overall outline to details of the game mechanics.

game engine
The programming code which controls the structure and mechanics of a game.

game mechanics
The rules of a game; the systems that govern the way it is played, for example, how a character moves and attacks.

game physics
Programming that controls how objects move and interact with each other within the game – governing everything from a water droplet splashing to a truck crashing through a barricade.

gameplay
The total experience provided by a game's structure and mechanics.

game structure
The way the narrative and action of a game unfolds – for example, a game could be linear (objective-based) or sandbox-style (open-ended).

games editor
Software which allows players to make modifications to a game, resulting in a new version, often entirely different from the original.

Gantt chart
A project-management tool, used on some major game projects, that breaks a project into individual tasks, and plots the time these will take and when they need to be finished by.

god game
A game which allows the player an overview of the whole gameworld, and allows him to control elements of that gameworld.

graphical user interface (GUI)
On-screen information that lets the player know his status, for example how much ammunition he has left, or his health level.

head-up display (HUD)
An on-screen display which presents vital information to the player, such as health status or amount of remaining ammunition.

health
This concept refers to the strength of a character, dependent on the amount of damage that has been inflicted. It can be represented graphically, or with numbers.

hero
The main protagonist of a game; the player's character.

independent games developers
Small-scale games developers, often producing experimental games for web browsers, PCs or mobile phones.

intellectual property (IP)
Creativity or ideas that belong to a person or team in the same way that physical property does.

level design
The specialist design process of a discrete section, or level, of a game.

level design document (LDD)
A lengthy document that records every aspect of a level in a game in written and visual form, from overall outline to details of the mechanics and smaller objectives within the level.

level editor
Software which allows players to make modifications to a level of a game, resulting in a new variation of a level, often entirely different from the original.

level
A discrete section within a game. Sometimes levels must be completed in a set sequence in order to succeed in a game.

linear game
A game with a set path, or narrative, to follow in order to successfully complete it.

MMORPG
An acronym for Massively-Multiplayer Online Role-Playing Game. Thousands or millions of players interact in a virtual, online world.

modding
Producing modifications to a game using a game or level editor.

motion-capture
A technique in which a person wears electronic markers which detect movement. This movement can then be accurately plotted using software, to provide a digital representation of the movement to use in the context of an animation.

multi-player game
A game in which the player plays with or against other human players.

non-player character (NPC)
A character or object controlled by the computer.

NURB
An acronym for Non-Uniform Rational B-spline – a method for modelling curves.

open-ended game
A game in which the player can approach challenges in any order and still achieve success. It also allows for exploration of the gameworld.

PERT (Program Evaluation and Review Technique) chart
A project-management tool that breaks a project into individual tasks, and makes links between related and interdependent tasks.

pitch document
An illustrated document designed to sell a game idea to potential publishers or developers.

platform
The type of hardware a game is designed to be played on, for example console or PC.

platform game
A game in which the player must navigate a hazardous environment, in a quest to achieve a particular aim and so restore order – traditionally the action was played out on two-dimensional 'platforms' allowing a view of an entire level, but this has since evolved.

playfield
The area in which game action
can happen.

poly count
The number of polygons used to build a
3D object, for example a character. An
in-game object with a high poly count uses
more valuable memory and takes longer to
render than one with a lower poly count.

polygons (polys)
In computer game design, polygons are the
small shapes that make up the virtual
surface of a digital model, for example of
a character.

portal
A web site that provides links or access to
software and other material.

power-ups
Opportunities for a player to improve or
recharge abilities, health or ammunition, for
example by collecting particular objects.

production process
The sequence of events involved in making
a computer game, from initial concept to
distribution.

prototype
A portion of a game that has been created
to test how it works in practice. A 'vertical
slice' prototype creates an entire level to
a high standard, with the dual intention
of testing the game and providing a
marketing tool.

puzzle game
An abstract game that requires a solution –
it could take the form of a shape
association, maze, or building game, or
may be a computerised version of a
traditional puzzle such as solitaire.

Quality Assurance (QA)
The team of people who test a game
for bugs, inconsistencies, and how well
it plays.

rag doll physics
A branch of game physics that refers to the
way characters' bodies behave when they
are injured or killed – going floppy and
flailing. The game physics control how solid
objects (such as limbs) behave when they
are linked together.

real-time strategy (RTS) game
A strategy game in which the opponent –
human or computer AI – is competing
for control of the game at the same time
as the player (as opposed to a turn-
based system).

rendering
Generating a finished view of a 3D object
on screen.

respawning
When a character returns to a game after
being killed.

rigging
The 'skeleton' inside a 3D character model
which can be moved in order to animate
the character.

sandbox game
A game in which the player can approach
challenges in any order and explore the
gameworld as he chooses.

shoot-'em-up (shmup)
A game in which the player must destroy
as many opponents as possible, as quickly
as possible.

simulation game
A game that aims to replicate a realistic
situation or experience.

single-player game
A game in which the player competes or
cooperates with characters and objects
controlled by the computer.

sound editor
Software for manipulating sounds.

spawning
When a character is introduced to a game.

strategy game
A game in which a player commands a
large number of characters and resources,
and attempts to maintain a state of
equilibrium and develop the gameworld.

technology (tech) tree
The set order in which a player must
complete stages of a strategy game to
increase the level of skills and equipment
available to his people.

texturing
Adding a graphic representation of a
surface to a digital model.

third-person perspective
A view of the gameworld from an objective
point of view.

toy
An in-game character or object that can be
interacted with or controlled in some way.

training level
A level before the main action of the game,
in which the player has the chance to get
used to the controls and experience all
the possible game mechanics.

UV mapping
Placing a texture onto the mesh of a
3D model. UV is short for UVW, the
coordinates for the texture (XYZ are the
coordinates for the 3D model).

wire-frame
A 3D mesh model.

Index

Credits

Quarto Publishing plc would like to thank the following individuals and agencies for supplying images reproduced in this book (key: a above, b below, l left, r right, c centre):

2–3, 72–73, 91, 113, 114–115, 127, 134–137, 158 (list), 184–185 (list) David Woodman; 12al Michael Freeman/CORBIS; 12ac Gianni Dagli Orti/CORBIS; 12br Ryuhei Shindo/Photonica/GETTY; 14a RISK® & © Hasbro, Inc. Used with permission; 15b Hans im Glück (Germany) and Rio Grande Games (USA); 16 Wizards of the Coast, Inc., a subsidiary of Hasbro, Inc.; 54ar iStockphoto.com/ Daniel Brunner; 59a A BAND APART/MIRAMAX/THE KOBAL COLLECTION; 62–63, 80–81, 90 (art), 111a, 169 Corlen Kruger; 74bl MIRISCH-7 ARTS/UNITED ARTISTS/THE KOBAL COLLECTION; 75br MGM/THE KOBAL COLLECTION; 75al, 75bl, 86l LUCASFILM/20TH CENTURY FOX/THE KOBAL COLLECTION; 89a Patrick Bennett/CORBIS; 90 (butterfly) iStockphoto.com/Madeleine Abrahamsson; 90 (brown grasshopper) iStockphoto.com/Pavel Lebedinsky; 90 (green grasshopper) iStockphoto.com/Roy Steele; 92 Tim Hill; 99a Shanedi Matnarudin; 99b, 102–105, 140, 146–147, 148–157 Shaun Mooney; 100c Craig Lovell/CORBIS; 100b, 171b WARNER BROS/THE KOBAL COLLECTION/BARIUS, CLAUDETTE; 101l Trevor Smithers ARPS/Alamy; 101r James Braund/Lonely Planet Images/GETTY; 112 Adam Harland; 116 Barnaby Berbank-Green; 126 Adam Vickerstaff; 128–129 Vincent Dale-Smith; 132–133 Andrew Gilwhalley; 139 Simon Harrison; 141 (wall) Jim Thompson; 142–144 Josh Taylor.

Quarto Publishing plc would also like to thank the following publishers and developers for the use of their images reproduced in this book:

1, 24a, 24l, 25b, 30a, 31br, 33, 34, 35l, 35r, 37, 55a, 64r, 71, 79, 84, 86r, 89br, 108a, 118a, 121, 124 © Nintendo; 6–7, 11, 19a, 19r © Treasure Co., Ltd; 17, 29 Warhammer 40,000: Dawn of War illustrations and images © Games Workshop Ltd 2000–2006. Used with permission. All Rights Reserved.; 18l, 38l © Taito Corp 1978; 18c Courtesy of the Computer History Museum; 18r, 118b © THQ Wireless; 19l Defender © 1980 Midway Amusement Games, LLC. Defender © 2002 Midway Amusement Games, LLC. All rights reserved.; 20a © BAM! Entertainment; 20bl, 20br, 21a, 39al, 145 © Id Software, Inc. All Rights Reserved; 21b © Bungie Studios; 22a, 35cr, 46, 65b, 125a, 125c © Microsoft Corporation. All rights reserved.; 22b, 95b, 125b © Vivendi Games; 23, 51a, 64l Courtesy of Rockstar Games; 24r, 25al, 58l © SEGA; 25ar, 36a © Sony Computer Entertainment America; 26 Sid Meier's Civilization III developed by Firaxis Games © 2005 Take-Two Interactive Software. All rights reserved. Sid Meier's Civilization III is a trademark of Take-Two Interactive Software Inc.; 27a, 27b © 2007 Electronic Arts Inc. The Sims is a trademark or registered trademark of Electronic Arts Inc. in the U.S. and/or other countries. All Rights Reserved. Used with permission; 27r, 65a © 2007 Electronic Arts Inc. SimCity is a trademark or registered trademark of Electronic Arts Inc. in the U.S. and/or other countries. All Rights Reserved. Used with permission; 28 © The Creative Assembly; 30c © PopCap Games, Inc.; 70r, 94b © Oddworld Inhabitants; 31al © Thinking Rabbit Co., Ltd; 31ar, 108b © Ignition Entertainment Ltd; 32, 36bl, 36br, 48l, 53b, 60 Resident Evil, Devil May Cry and Viewtiful Joe are trademarks of Capcom Co., Ltd., which may be registered in certain jurisdictions. © CAPCOM CO., LTD. All Rights Reserved; 35cl All Myst, Riven, Uru and D'ni images and text © Cyan, Inc. All rights reserved Myst ®, Riven ®, Uru ® and D'ni © Cyan, Inc.; 35c, 57, 58r, 61a, 98, 110l, 159 © Konami Digital Entertainment, All Rights Reserved; 38r, 40r, 49al, 49ar, 53a, 85c, 171a © Valve Corporation, all rights reserved; 39ar, 39br, 40l World of Warcraft® images provided courtesy of Blizzard Entertainment Inc.; 39bl © NCsoft Europe Ltd. All Rights Reserved. City of Heroes, City of Villains and all associated logos and designs are trademarks or registered trademarks of Cryptic Studios and NCsoft Corporation; 41, 47b, 67, 70l © Sony Computer Entertainment Inc.; 47a, 83b © Namco Bandai Games Inc.; 48r, 178 © PomPom Games; 49ar, 49b © DreamCatcher Interactive; 50, 51b © Team17 Software Ltd; 52b, 78, 96 © Eidos Interactive Ltd.; 54l, 54b © Activision Publishing, Inc. Licensed by Tony Hawk Enterprises; 56, 120 Peter Jackson's King Kong The Official Game of The Movie © 2005 Ubisoft Entertainment. All Rights Reserved. Ubisoft and the Ubisoft logo are trademarks of Ubisoft Entertainment in the U.S. and/or other countries. Universal Studios' King Kong movie © Universal Studios. Licensed by Universal Studios Licensing LLLP. All Rights Reserved.; 58c, 95ar, 111b Tom Clancy's Splinter Cell © 2002 Ubisoft Entertainment. All Rights Reserved. Splinter Cell, Sam Fisher, Ubisoft and the Ubisoft logo are trademarks of Ubisoft Entertainment in the U.S. and/or other countries.; 59b FINAL FANTASY XII ©2006–2007 SQUARE ENIX CO., LTD. All rights reserved. Character Design: Akihiko Yoshida; 61b DRAGON QUEST: The Journey of the Cursed King © 2004–2006 ARMOR PROJECT/BIRD STUDIO/LEVEL-5/SQUARE ENIX. All Rights Reserved. © KOICHI SUGIYAMA.; 69 © 2007 Electronic Arts Inc. Burnout is a trademark of Electronic Arts Inc. in the U.S. and/or other countries. All Rights Reserved. Used with permission; 70r, 94b © Oddworld Inhabitants; 82 © 2005 Activision Publishing, Inc. Activision and Call of Duty are registered trademarks of Activision Publishing Inc. All rights reserved. Images reproduced with permission.; 83a, 85b © ZOO Digital Publishing; 83c, 110r, 179 © Introversion; 94al, 94ar, 95al Call of Cthulhu: Dark Corners of the Earth™ © 2005 Bethesda Softworks LLC, a ZeniMax Media company. Bethesda Softworks and ZeniMax are registered trademarks of ZeniMax Media Inc. Developed under license from Headfirst Productions Ltd. (UK). Call of Cthulhu is a registered trademark of Chaosium, Inc. All Rights Reserved.; 109 The Elder Scrolls® IV: Oblivion™ © 2006 Bethesda Softworks LLC, a ZeniMax Media company. The Elder Scrolls, Oblivion, Bethesda Softworks, Bethesda Game Studios and ZeniMax are trademarks or registered trademarks of ZeniMax Media Inc. All Rights Reserved.

The following is a list of the pages on which each author's articles start:

Jim Thompson: 'For all my students and what they have taught me.'
12, 14, 20, 26, 30, 32, 46, 54, 70 (with BB-G), 74, 78, 84, 88, 92, 94, 98, 102, 106, 108, 118 (with BB-G), 122, 124, 126, 130, 132, 134, 138, 148, 166, 170, 180

Barnaby Berbank-Green: 18, 36, 38, 40, 48, 50, 66, 70 (with JT), 118 (with JT), 172, 174, 178

Nic Cusworth: 24, 42, 52, 58, 60, 62, 64, 160, 176

All other images are the copyright of Quarto Publishing plc.

Quarto Publishing plc has made every effort to contact contributors and credit them appropriately. We apologise in advance for any omissions or errors in the above list; we will gladly correct this information in future editions of the book. The publishers and copyright holders acknowledge all trademarks used in this book as the property of their owners.